To the
Revd George Duffield, D.D.
with the Compliments of
his friend
Lieut Robt B. Riell,
U.S. Navy,
Decr 25th 1858,

Pope, or President?

STARTLING DISCLOSURES

OF

ROMANISM

AS REVEALED

BY ITS OWN WRITERS.

Facts for Americans.

"It has always been the subtlety of grand deceivers to graft their greatest errors on some material truths, thus to make them pass unnoticed by those who look more at the root, than at the fruits. Their most destructive principles have ever been founded on some necessary and important truths."

STILLINGFLEET.

NEW YORK:

R. L. DELISSER,

(LATE STANFORD & DELISSER,)

No. 508 BROADWAY.

1859.

TO THE PEOPLE

OF THE UNITED STATES.

"THE keen vibration of bright truth is, hell."—YOUNG.

THE extreme incredulity of the American people to believe, that their civil and religious freedom is eminently perilled by the Roman Hierarchy, has induced the publication of this volume. Its principles, practices and aims as revealed in the authorities quoted are, for the first time, presented to the American public.

It is not because the Roman Catholic Hierarchy is founded upon superstition; but because it involves a conspiracy against human freedom, that we now address this volume to you, people of the United States.

The works of Romish theologians are all printed in a language foreign to our country, and consequently *sealed* books; except to scholars, who from culpable blindness on the subject, have never undertaken a thorough exposition of their principles. For this reason the people are incredulous, and cannot comprehend the danger which impends over them.

The Papal Church has now become a destined and formidable power in this republic. It therefore becomes vitally important, that some one should *dare* assume the responsibility of revealing the astounding mysteries of the Vatican. We have allowed *its own writers* to untangle the fearful meshes of their crafty and corrupt system, and to prove to the American people by their own authorities, that the Romish priesthood are here to subjugate the liberties of this country; and should these truths be impugned by the adherents of Rome, we are prepared to make still further disclosures of their principles and practices.

CONTENTS.

CHAPTER I.

CHAPTER II.

CHAPTER III.

CHAPTER IV.

CHAPTER V.

CHAPTER VI.

CHAPTER VII.

CHAPTER VIII.

CHAPTER IX.

CHAPTER X.

CHAPTER XI.

CHAPTER XII.

CHAPTER XIII.

CHAPTER XIV.

ROMANISM AS REVEALED
BY ITS OWN WRITERS.

CHAPTER I.

POPERY PROVED A HUMAN INVENTION.

No such Person as Pope in Christianity—No Successor of Peter appointed—When the first Pope arose—First Forgery, and Proofs—Second Forgery, and Proofs—Third Forgery, and Proofs—Who made Peter a "Pope," and put him among the Papal Imposters—When the Bishop of Rome was first called Universal—When first a Temporal Bishop—Hildebrand, the Tyrant and Poisoner—Archbishop Kenrick—Stupendous Fraud—The Master-piece of Satan—Quotations—The Main Dogmas all proved to be Novelties in Religion—Dates—Proofs—The Voice of Scripture.

The hierarchy of Rome which has occupied so large a portion of history; which has so forced itself upon communities and nations by priestly ambition and thirst for dominion; which arrogates to itself divine supremacy, and blasphemously usurps the prerogative, titles, and sovereignty of God—to absolve from sin, to dispense pardon and eternal blessedness or eternal damnation to the souls of men—and which has so bound the conscience and frightened it into submission to itself, we now proceed to show is a mere human invention.

Under the garb of religious claims, this human device has deluged the world with its floods of crimes,—incest, perjuries, murders, extortions, concubinage, avarice, assassinations, tyranny, immoralities, and bloody persecutions.

We give the dates and the proofs when this hierarchy arose and its dogmas were enacted.

We exhibit it as based on forgeries and fiction. Our proofs will be clear and incontrovertible, deduced from history and from Romish authorities.

As this chapter is designed to be but an epitome of the argument, we shall condense the whole subject into as brief a compass as possible. We shall assert nothing —we shall assume nothing on doubtful authority. We shall fortify our facts as we proceed from step to step, by the highest and most incontestible proofs.

Our proposition is this:—

That Popery is a mere human invention for the advancement of prelatical ambition, wealth, and power; and that it is founded on forgeries and fiction.

First Proof.—No such person as Pope existed or was known in the Christian church in the days of the Apostles or for five hundred years afterwards. The Apostles were all on an equality.*

Second Proof.—There is no chronology or history which certifies that Peter was ever at Rome, or that any bishop became his successor as head of the church. Let the reader bear in mind, that in the New Testament, inspired by the Spirit of God, minister and bishop mean precisely the same thing—they are convertible terms. We mention this fact as of importance, for, in the present day, persons not acquainted with the original Greek in which the New Testament was written, and as superiority is fancifully ascribed to a bishop, may suppose that a distinction exists between these terms. But it is not so;

* History of the New Testament. Coleman's Chris. Antiqui. Mosheim's Eccle. Hist. Gibbon's Rise and Fall of R. E. Haweis' Church History.

minister and bishop mean one and the same thing in the New Testament.

The first bishop who was called "Pope," was Sommachus in 501. But he was only one bishop among all the others, having no superiority over them.*

The bishops of the principal cities of Constantinople, Jerusalem, Antioch, Rome, and Alexandria were all independent of each other during the first seven centuries, and were sometimes called "patriarchs," which name the bishops of Constantinople and the Eastern Grecian churches retain to the present day.†

Boniface III., a bishop of Rome, was, in the seventh century, or 606, *first* called *Universal* by the emperor Phocas of Constantinople, a murderer and a tyrant. And in 588, John, bishop of Constantinople, assumed the same title of *Universal.* Both were usurpations.‡

In this sixth century, and during the three preceding, the bishops began gradually to usurp prelatical powers, and Eunodius in his Apology for the obsequious acts of the Fourth Council, held by order of Theoderic, 503, said that the bishop of Rome was subject to no earthly tribunal, and styled him judge in the place of God, and the vicegerent of the Most High. This was the first time that such a blasphemous title was given to the bishop or Pope of Rome. And thus we see Paul's prediction fulfilled. "So that he as God sitteth in the temple of God, showing himself that he is God."§

Now, reader, observe how during the fourth, fifth and

* Wilkes' History. Bower on the Popes.

† Coleman's Chris. Antiquities, Sec. p. 56. Gieseler's and Mosheim's Eccle. Hist.

‡ Waddington's Church Hist. of the Sixth Century.

§ 2 Thess. xi. 4. Gieseler, Vol. I, p. 339.

sixth centuries, the bishops dispensed with the plain simplicity of the ministers of the gospel, and gratified their thirst for wealth and splendor as well as power, by the following testimonies: "When the Emperor Maximus, surrounded by his illustrious guests, sat in his banqueting chamber, Martin the Bishop of Tours, and one of his presbyters, sat next to him in all the pride and pomp which attended on a stimulated ambition. According to the usual custom, an attendant 'presents a chalice of wine to the emperor, who commands it to be offered first to the bishop, that he may receive it from the prelate's hands; but no sooner has Martin drunk, than he passes the wine to his presbyter, as next in importance to himself, while the empress bathes his feet with her tears, wipes them with the hair of her head, attends as a slave to every mean indulgence, and regards the crumbs of his meal as the richest delicacy. Thus early had the nominal followers of Christ departed from Christian simplicity."*

No wonder, then, that in the third century history thus describes the existing state of the Christian church: "Long peace had corrupted the discipline divinely revealed to us. Each was intent on improving his patrimony, and had forgotten what believers had done under the apostles, and what they always ought to do. They were brooding over the arts of amassing wealth; works of mercy were neglected, and discipline was at its lowest ebb; luxury and effeminacy prevailed; meretricious arts were practised. Many bishops, neglecting the peculiar duties of their stations, gave themselves up to secular pursuits; they deserted their places of residence and their flocks; they traveled through distant provinces in quest of pleasure and gain, and they gave no assistance

* Sulp. Severus, chap. 20.

to their needy brethren, but were insatiable in their thirst of money. They possessed estates by fraud and multiplied usury.*

Thus, by reference to the New Testament, we have shown that there was no such person or title as Pope. We never read there of Pope Paul or Pope John. We do not find one particle of authority given to Peter more than to the other apostles, for when our Lord spoke of the "rock," he spoke of the truth on which his church should be built; for any one who will examine the passage will see that it was not Petrus, but petra, rock, or rock of truth, of which the Saviour spoke, and Paul says, "that rock was Christ." As for the word "keys," it merely meant the admission of a person to or his rejection from the visible church on earth; that is, meaning the spiritual, not the corporeal discipline of the church. But this church power of mere discipline of membership was no more given to Peter than it was to the other apostles; no one was superior to the others; they were all on an equality. But the popish interpretation involves a double absurdity, for they take it literally, as they take the figurative expression, "This is my body," literally; and then, according to their own showing, Peter would be a literal rock, as the bread, or "wafer," in their interpretation is made a literal body. Peter was not constituted the head of the church. No such head, temporal or spiritual, was appointed in the New Testament. Popery commences its succession with the chair of Saint Peter at Rome; but there was no such chair. There is not a scrap of history, profane or ecclesiastical, to prove that Peter ever was at Rome, and from the above facts and proofs there was no papal see and no papal succession

* See Mosheim, Third Century.

of that apostle. The pontifical succession, therefore, is the sheerest imposture. Any minister of the gospel or bishop has the same reason to call himself Pope, and assert himself to be the universal head, spiritual and temporal, of the church. Throughout Greece, the Ionian Islands, etc., all the priests are called pope, such as Pope John, Pope Adrian, &c., consequently, independent of any additional proof, popery, with all its mummeries and iniquities, is a human invention, without one primitive plank to stand on, or even a cobweb for its support.

Here we might rest the argument, for any one may see that the Word of God is the only authority on this subject. If that says not one word nor gives the slightest hint about popery, as a part of the Christian system, we need pursue the argument no farther. And when we add to this the total absence of all primitive cotemporary authority—for which we refer the reader to Mosheim's Ecclesiastical History, Haweis's Church History, Dupin's Auteurs Ecclesiastiques, and other undoubted historians—the argument is complete, and we might be satisfied to scorn the hollow pretensions of popery; but we now proceed to show that the whole of the above alleged facts are sustained by the most barefaced

Forgeries.—In the first place, it is proper to notice certain documents called "Apostolical Constitutions."

These so-called Apostolical Constitutions were a collection of church regulations, attributed to the apostles, and pretended to have been collected by St. Clement, whose name they bear. They were designed to augment the power of each minister or bishop in his own church. They appeared first in the fourth century, but have been changed and corrupted in successive periods. They consist of eight books, and 250 octavo pages; but it is worthy of notice, as a very significant fact, that not a word is mentioned in them of the supremacy of the Pope or of the Church of Rome over other churches. They give the names of all the apostles, and represent them as performing ministerial duties, but never give even a hint at the supremacy of Peter or at his superior rights. Nothing, from the beginning to the end of the book, can be found to favor in the slightest degree any superior name, title or claim of the Church of Rome or of the supremacy of the Pope. That they were forgeries, is manifest from the following proofs:

First. That no mention is made of them by Irenœus, Origen, Eusebius, or by any historian, Christian or profane, until the third and fourth centuries.

Second. In this period the bishops had assumed authority and powers which never belonged to them, and to which they had no right. Superstition had begun to mar the simplicity of worship, and the people were overawed by the pride and arrogance of the priests who could easily deceive them.

Third. There are many things in them different from the New Testament, and even contrary to the design and genius of Christianity, and the "Constitutions" carry on them, *prima facie* evidence of forgery.

Fourth. Upon the character and writings of Cyprian; the papacy chiefly rest for the origin of popery and these, "Constitutions," which never speak a word about popery. But a work published by Longman & Co., London, written by the Rev. J. Shepherd, shows the forgery of Cyprian's writings, in the most convincing light. He not only pronounces the whole of Cyprian's writings to be forgeries, but he denies the very existence of Cyprian!

The references to him in Jerome and Eusebius, are Interpolations. The life of him by Pontius is an ill written fiction. Mr. Shepherd has critically examined every scrap of history in the early ecclesiastical periods of the church, and by the proofs which he has collected, arrives at these conclusions.*

But, forgeries, as they may be, let it be remembered, that they contain nothing to give the smallest countenance to the pretensions of the Pope or the Church of Rome. Having given the first or elementary forgery, which prepared the way for the enormous power of the popes in after periods, we come now to

THE SECOND FORGERY.—This is the greatest forgery ever perpetrated on earth. The Roman or Western empire was destroyed by barbarians from the north, under Odoacer, King of the Heruli, in 476. Fifteen years before that, the Bishop of Rome, whom the papists in their false catalogue of popes, call Leo I., *first* made Peter the fabulous basis of papal ambition.† From this period to the year 800, Rome was sometimes under the control of barbarians, and sometimes under that of the Emperor of Constantinople. Four important facts are here noted:— 1. The bishops of Rome, during all these periods, had no temporal possessions; they were not temporal rulers of Rome, nor of any provinces. They were subject to the control of barbarians, or that of the Emperor of Constantinople. 2. Their chief business was to wrangle with the bishops of Constantinople for some kind of spiritual authority. 3. The bishops of Rome, at the time of the inroads of the barbarians and the destruction of the Ro-

* See Grab's Answer to Whiston; Saurin's Ser., vol. ii., p. 185; Lardner's Cred., vol. iii, p. 2, ch. last; Doddridges' Lec. 119.

† See Ranke's History of the Popes; Wilkes, also.

man empire, came near losing their place altogether, at Rome. 4. The emperors had supreme civil authority over the bishops at this period; and, the emperors *alone*, and not the bishops, called general councils of the church, and no pope or legate then existed to preside in them. By considering these facts, and the ambitious design of the priesthood, and the growing prevalence of ignorance, superstition, and vice, among the people, the reasons for these forgeries will appear evident. The first general council called by the emperor, was that of Nice, A. D. 325. This fact of the emperor calling it, and not the minister or bishop of Rome, nullifies all the present claims of the popes of Rome to any power over the churches or bishops; and also cuts off all their authority for appeals to their usurped "See." A small provincial council, it is true, called to meet at Sardica, the metropolis of Lacia, in Illyricum, after the above general council authorized an appeal to the Bishop of Rome. "But, a provincial council, Rome being judge, has no lawful right to rescind or repeal the canons of a general council. And the council convened afterwards by the Emperor Theodosius, at Constantinople, condemned the proceedings of the Council at Sardica." Hence the popes, in some way, must contrive frauds for their usurpation and to establish their power.

This *second* important *forgery*, of which we are speaking, is a pretended donation from the Emperor Constantine the Great, in the year 324, of the city of Rome, and all Italy, with the crown, mitre, etc., to Sylvester, then bishop of Rome. So the first annunciation to the world of this pretended "donation" was not made till near the close of the eighth century, in an epistle of Pope Adrian I. to the Emperor Charlemagne, in which he exhorts him to imitate the liberality of the great Constantine. According to the legend, "the first of the Christian emperors was healed of the leprosy and purified in the waters of baptism by St. Sylvester, the Roman bishop, and never was physician more gloriously recompensed."*

Thus for nearly five hundred years from the time this pretended donation was given, history was silent—the world knew nothing of it—the bishop of Rome had no civil or temporal power. And all of a sudden, after a lapse of nearly five centuries, and when the bishop of Rome wanted some better authority, some pretended donation, some prop to stand upon, this forgery was cunningly and shrewdly manufactured for the purpose; and on this stupendous imposture the temporal usurpation or the temporal power of the pope of Rome is based! †

When this fictitious donation and other false decretals were imposed upon the world, Mosheim states that the corruptions and profligacy of the clergy had reached the most enormous height, and the people were shrouded in darkness. Said Mabillan, a very learned theological French writer of the seventeenth century, "not one priest in a thousand in Spain could write a common letter of salutation to another." A little later, Alfred the Great, King of England, declared that "he could not find a single priest south of the Thames who understood the ordinary prayers, or could translate latin into his mother tongue." We need not wonder then, that the forgeries were perpetrated, and that they corresponded

* Gibbon.

† See Mosheim, Eighth and Ninth Centuries. Hallam's Middle Ages, pages 380 to 460. Teraboschi, Storia, della Litteratura, tom. iii.

to the corruptions and knavery of the priests and the blindness and credulity of the people.

THIRD FORGERY.—Another most barefaced imposition, by which the above false decretals and other forgeries are palmed upon the world to establish the imposture of the popish "See," is contained in a volume by Severinus Binius, published at Cologne, 1618, authenticated by a bull of Pope Paul V., sanctioned by the Emperor of Germany, and approved and licensed by the Romish censors of the press. The front page contains a pictorial border, "at one of the four corners of which, on the top, Peter with his keys and coat of arms is represented as seated beside the three persons of the Trinity; at the other, is represented the pope with a sword wielding temporal power; on the right side, the church is holding a cross, the Pope's triple crown and keys; on the left side, religion with a crucifix, and over each, the Holy Ghost is painted as a dove. At the bottom, the Pope surrounded by and at the head of his bishops, is represented as treading on a prostrate band of so-called heretics, and over them, in latin, the inscription, 'They are dead who sought the church's life.'" This audacious volume, with its pictorial imposture, agrees well with popery. It verifies the description. The Mystery of Iniquity, 2d Thess. ii. 7. And mother of harlots and abominations, Rev. xviii. 5. Now let us read the title page. It is as follows:

Councils, General and Provincial, Greek and Latin, so far as known. Also Decretals, Epistles, and Lives of Roman Pontiffs; all by the study and labor of Severinus Binius, D.D., Presbyter of the Metropolitan Church of Cologne. Revised, enlarged, and again illustrated with Notes, and arranged in an historical method. To

S. D. N. Paul Pope. By John Gymnicus, 1618, *with the favor and privilege of his Royal Majesty.*

In these forged decretals there is a long epistle from the pretended Pope Clement to James, the Apostle at Jerusalem, establishing all the present claims of the pope of Rome. Successions, keys, supremacy, and the dogmas and canons, which complete this whole masterpiece of Satan and finish the building of Babylon, the pope and hierarchy of Rome.

Proofs of these Forgeries.—First, The internal evidence. The utter absurdity in supposing them to have been written in an age in which they profess to have been written, that is, during the first and second centuries. They omit all that is proper to that age. They contain numerous contradictions and false dates. The style of one man appears. They contain peculiar Latin words, and the style of the middle ages, which were not known in the first age. The Christians in the early age in which these epistles and decretals profess to have been written, were weak and suffering horrible persecutions, and yet they are not adapted to console them, but are only intent in rearing a Romish hierarchy to gratify the lust, pride, arrogance, and power of the popes of Rome. It is as if Thomas Aquinas, a voluminous Romish writer in 1270, had described the battle of Waterloo in 1815, in the style of the present day, or of Pius the IX., and his decrees of the *Immaculate Conception* of the Virgin Mary, or the doings of Archbishop Hughes in 1858. It is the same as if Erasmus in 1520, had written about the American Revolution, and Washington, and railroads, steamboats, and spinning jennies.

But one of the grossest blunders is, in trying to link the chair of the Pope to Peter. "The forger makes

Clement say that Peter, before his death, enjoined it on him to write to James, brother of our Lord, at Jerusalem, and inform Him of all the facts. Now, it is well known, that James died seven years before Peter, and yet, Peter, it seems, did not know this fact, and is made to enjoin Clement to write to a dead man!

Well might this blunder stagger Binius, who, Jesuit-like, says either Clement did not write the epistle, or that the name of James crept into the letter instead of Simeon. "But James is introduced, not only in the letter, but in the body of the work, and not only in one letter, but in two."

Second. Baronius, a great Romish authority of the sixteenth century, abandons the defence of these transparent and notorious frauds.

Bellarmine, a cardinal, and the champion of the Roman cause, abandons their defence. Fleury, the great French historian and papist, not only abandons their defence, but most clearly establishes their falsehood. David Blondell, at Geneva, in 1628, annihilates the whole fabric and completely refutes Surianus and Binius.

Notwithstanding all the evidences of the forgeries and their exposure, yet, the Popes of Rome cling to them, and on these base and wicked impostures the whole monstrous system of popery rests!

Thus the Papacy has built up the hierarchy of Rome, manufactured Peter's chair, placed the Popes, from the eighth and ninth centuries, in it, and instigated the cruel and bloody dogmas of persecution against all who disbelieve and oppose such fabricated wonders and knavery.*

* See Dr. Geddes on Popery, vol. ii. and iii. Hallam's Middle Ages, pages 50 to 80. Mosheim, Eighth, Ninth, and Seventeenth Centuries. Fleury's Eccle. His., vol. xvi. Cardinal Baronius Eccle. Annals, Eighth and Ninth Centuries.

Thus we have seen that there was *no temporal, spiritual*, or *universal pope*, or *any pope*, during all the time of the apostles, and during all the time of the early fathers—that popery is a *novelty*, gradually emerging through priestly corruption, worldly thirst for power, and frauds and forgeries of the most wicked and transparent character.

That the very name of pope, and the existence of popery were not known for several hundred years after the Christian era—that the first Christian minister or bishop to whom the name of pope (papa) was given, was Sommachus, and this not until the sixth century—that the *first* annunciation to the world that the Pope was a temporal bishop of Rome, *was not made until near the close of the eighth century*, and for the very plain reason, that the *forgeries* upon which this *temporal usurpation* was based, were *not completed;* and *then* it was introduced, says Gibbon, "by an epistle of Pope Adrian I. to the Emperor Charlemagne," in which a pretended "donation of the city of Rome and all Italy," was given by Constantine, in the fourth century, to Sylvester, then a bishop of Rome! *So that nearly five hundred years interval elapsed between the pretended gift and its publication to the world.*

Here then, we have the *origin of the temporal usurping* power of the apostate church. From this period, the temporal and spiritual power of the Romish hierarchy appeared in all its superstitions. Shortly after, in the eleventh century, we see Hildebrand, or Pope Gregory VII., mounting the papal throne in all the pride of royal power.

This fanatical and ambitious monk, "whose name is proverbial for imperiousness and wickedness, was the poisoner," says Rankè, "of popes; and, in the accomplishment of his schemes for his despotic elevation, had buried eight pontiffs, who were the instruments of his policy and the tools of his ambition."

Having thus shown the rise and establishment of popery by authentic history and chronology, we shall now show the *dates* when the various main parts of the scaffolding or structure of this temple of Babylon were reared, which will be a confirmation of the whole of the preceding evidences, and will clearly establish our proposition, viz.: that *Popery from its foundation is a novelty in religion and a mere human invention.*

Auricular Confession is a *novelty.* It was established by the Council of Lateran, 1215; and this enactment was made twelve hundred years after the Christian era! By the confessional, the priest obtains dominion over the conscience, and there is an end to personal liberty; and if the priest controls in the confessional the conscience of the nation, then, farewell to national liberty.

Baptism of the bells is a *novelty;* it was first introduced by Pope John XIII., in 972. This is a foolish farce, and a blasphemous perversion of the holy ordinance of Christian baptism, ordained only for human beings. The ceremony of baptism in this papal church takes place in private, wherever the child is presented. "Sometimes the font is represented with John the Baptist pouring water on the head of Jesus Christ, from an oyster shell, while the Saviour stands half immersed in the water. The mixture of salt water and two different kinds of sacred oils, which are required to make a good water of baptism, is prepared on 'holy Saturday' in each year, which is the day before Easter Sunday. It takes about five hours to make it. Popery has chosen to improve on the gospel mode as practised by St. John the Baptist and the Apostles, when on earth; then, the pure water of the stream, was all they required."

The child is first exorcised, to drive away evil spirits; then it promises, through its sponsors, to give up *Satan;* next, it has soda-salt put in its mouth (given as the salt of wisdom), with one kind of oil a cross is made on the forehead; with another kind, a cross on the shoulders and breast—the liquid from the fountain is then poured over the child's head, three times—then the priest hands the sponsor the end of his white stole, and says in latin, "Receive the white stole to be brought spotless before the Lord." The sponsor then, on his knees, recites the "Credo," according to the formula of the Jesuit Bellarmine, as they say it during mass. And the child is evermore a member of the Roman Catholic Church, or under its eternal curse as a heretic.*

The *use of Images* is a *novelty*. It was not fully established until the ninth century. This violates the second commandment, and is a heathenish practice.

"In 1837, the 27th of July, the ancient wooden statue of St. Anna having worn out, a new one was purchased from a dealer in saints, and was that day inaugurated at Ravenna, in Italy. The programme of the exhibition was hung in all directions. On the ground before the church were booths of the dealers in saints, Madonnas, rosaries, relics, Christs, of every material and description. Then, there were dealers in everything to eat and drink that the appetites of the multitude might be satisfied. There are numbers of priests there, who have no charge of a church, but live by selling masses to the highest bidders on solemn occasions. They were paid that day

* Gajani.

fifty cents, and a good dinner. Then there were clerks, destined for priests; they got five cents and a dinner. There were many hasty masses said that day, but at eleven o'clock a *solemn* one was sung, and then the procession formed. A plaster statue of Christ was borne by a young girl; four others followed, with candles; then followed men, women and children, attended by overseers, armed with sticks. These overseers were a brotherhood, clad in long white "cappe" and red cowls. After them followed the young priestly clerks, etc. All this crowd of poor ignorant creatures were singing in what they called latin praises to St. Anna. St. Anna's statue was borne by six young men, and under a canopy, borne by other six men. There was the old curate in pontifical robes; old priests; young clerks, who were burning incense and offering smoke of it to the statue with their censers. When they stopped by a large oak tree, an altar was found erected for the purpose. St. Anna was set on the altar, and all knelt in the dust to worship her statue! The old curate also knelt a few moments, and then rising before the rest, ordered the bearers to move the statue here and there, so as to form a cross in the air, while he pronounced his latin benediction. Then began the firing of five hundred mortars at measured intervals.

"Feasting and separation of the crowd followed, until four o'clock, when vespers were performed and the service closed by making a sign of the cross with a wafer, said to be the real body and blood of Jesus Christ; but the people evidently were more interested in the wooden statue of St. Anna than with the body and blood of Jesus Christ. From the church a large baloon was seen suspended, with the painted image of St. Anna, the object and date of the feast inscribed on it. At sunset, fireworks were exhibited, closing with St. Anna's portrait skilfully illuminated." *

The *doctrine of Purgatory* is a *novelty.* It was not established in Rome till 1450, by the Council of Florence. "This is a capital contrivance of the priests to get money from their votaries, and they have made millions by this crafty device. One day, a cardinal, disposed to be talkative, began to pose his chaplain, and try the extent of his profound theology. 'How many masses, I pray you,' said he, gravely, 'will it take to pray a soul out of purgatory?' The chaplain was struck dumb at the weighty question. After painful silence, during which he had rummaged every corner of his brain and exhausted his knowledge of the Fathers, he frankly told the truth—not usual in Rome—that he could not tell his eminence; that it was prodigiously beyond his depth.

"'Well, I will tell thee,' said his eminence, with a condescending air, while the chaplain was all eye and ear to receive the awfully important discovery, 'it will take as many masses to relieve a soul out of purgatory as it will take snow-balls to heat our oven.'" †

Signor Gajani relates, that his grandfather directed in his will, that the interment of his corpse should be without pomp or ceremony. The father-curate called immediately after the old man died, denounced the family for not having been called to assist the dying and administer the sacraments, and threatened to deny him the rights of burial. But, the burial took place, just as the will directed. Next day a bill written in latin was presented, and in these words: "*Pro funere non facto ducenta scutatorum;*" that is: "For not having made the solemn burial, two hundred dollars." And this the priest

* Gajani. † Gavin.

actually had the right to do, as the lawyer consulted soon showed, that there was a statute enforcing such impostures, and the bill was paid.

This right, to compel the payment of whatever sum the curate may assess, for not burying the dead in the boundaries of his parish, is called "black stole, or dress," in the same manner that he raises contributions for marrying or baptizing, in consequence of his "white stole." Beside, they teach, that the payment of this outrageous extortion will help the dead to escape the pains of purgatory! According to the doctrine of the Romish church, there are four places in the other world, where human souls may go, viz.: *Cœlum*, *Infernum*, *Purgatorium* and *Limbus*. In this last place were confined the souls of the holy Fathers before the advent of our Lord; then it was *Limbus Palium;* but at the ascension of Jesus Christ, the holy Fathers were removed to their places *in Cœlum;* and then, in order that such a place should not be empty, it was decreed that Limbus should be the mansion for little children who died *without baptism*, to stay there confined until the day of judgment; and since then, the place is called *Limbus Infantum.* Here is the climax of *novelties!*

The *priest's celibacy* is a *novelty* in the Christian world. It was introduced by that tyrant and atheist Gregory VII., in 1074. This is directly contrary to the Bible, which it says "Marriage is honorable in all;" and priests make no exception, for a minister or bishop is spoken of as having one wife.

Transubstantiation, is a *novelty.* The dogma was established by Pope Innocent III., at the Council of Lateran, 1215.

Gregory VII. wrote two epistles against it in the eleventh century.

Transubstantiation, means the conversion of bread and wine into the real body and blood of Jesus Christ, by the few mystic words uttered by a priest; and that the wafer is converted into Christ every time the mass is celebrated; this is contrary to the Bible, which says, Christ was only offered *once*.

The popish doctrine, which relates to the mass, with its two elements of transubstantiation and propitiatory sacrifice, is the most blasphemous in practice, and the most fatal in doctrine of all the papal impostures. The abominable presumption of priests making as many Christs as they please, and offering them to God as victims of a sacrifice, is the pivot on which the whole papal system turns. Reason, with which God has endowed his creatures cannot but reject it! The doctrine is, that, by the virtue of the sacraments, the bread and wine is actually and substantially changed into the body and blood of Christ, together with his soul and with his divinity.

The Romish Church invented the imposture of this sacrament, because it could not in any other way inspire a superstitious faith. What did our blessed Saviour say on the subject? His testimony should settle the question.

"The words that I speak to you they are spirit and they are life."*

"The kingdom of God is not meat and drink; it is the spirit which quickeneth; the flesh profiteth nothing."†

To eat and drink is to believe, to be united to Christ, by the work of the Spirit, and has nothing whatever to do with matter; corporeal substance is only a type of the spiritual.

This doctrine of converting a wafer into God omnipo-

* St. John, vi. 63. † Romans, xiv. 17.

tent was introduced by Eutichus, a heretic, whose dogma was presented to the Church by Pope Innocent III., who had it confirmed by the Council of Lateran, 1215.

Take away the imposture of transubstantiation, which sacrifices our blessed Lord every time the mass is celebrated, and the grand essential of popery is destroyed.

Jesus said, "I am the bread that came down from heaven." Who supposed when he said so to his disciples, "Verily, verily, I say unto you, except ye eat the flesh of the Son of Man, and drink his blood, ye have no life in you," that they thought of eating the actual substance of their Lord and Master?

Every one who takes the sacrament of mass is a Christophagus or Christ-eater! The taking away of the wine, or the holy cup from the people, is a *novelty*. This was sacriligiously done by Felix, a priest of Rome, in 490. After him Gelasius, a bishop, in the fifth century, pronounced it an impious sacrilege.

The *invocation of saints* is a *novelty*. It was established in the ninth century. This is a vain imagination, for the saints are never represented in Scripture as objects for invocation. To regard such invocation they must be omnipresent, an incommunicable attribute of God. Besides it is an idolatrous worship.

The *adoration of relics* is a *novelty*. It was introduced about the time of the invocation of saints. Even at this day, there are exhibited in Romish churches the "Virgin's comb" and "locks of hair," "Peter's chair," the "rope with which Judas hung himself," the "dice used by the soldiers in casting lots," some of the "blossoms of Aaron's rod," "one of the fingers of the arm of St. Simon," a "drop of the Virgin's milk," "the spear and shield of Michael," some of the "tail" of

Balaam's ass, four "heads" of John the Baptist, and other wondrous relics.

Among the relics still held in veneration in the Romish Church is the famous Prœputium D. N. Jesu Christi, or the circumcision of the humanity of Christ, preserved in a small town, Loretto, twenty-five miles west of Rome, called Auguillara diocesis of Nepi. It is kept in a precious shrine, exposed to veneration in the church of its name, which is richly endowed by donations of several popes, sovereigns, and princes, etc.

This poor town has for ages been the resort of deluded papist-pilgrims, to worship the "Holy House." It is said to be the very house of the "Holy Virgin," formerly standing at Nazareth. The pope gave, in a latin bull, an explanation of the remarkable change of place, saying that on a dark night angels carried the holy house from Nazareth, and set it down at Loretto! This night was found to be the 10th December, 603, and the papists have a feast called "The Passage of the Holy House," in celebration of the event.

The worshipers walk on their knees to the spot. There are two hundred wax lights burning day and night before the statue of the "Holy Virgin" and her Son. This statue is a piece of black wood, with two ugly heads, almost devoured by worms. It is the heathen god, Isis. The iron key, with which she locked the door when she went out on business, is on one side; on the other side is the *very* wooden cup from which she drank.

"The bones of St. Quietus," dug up in Rome and sent to the Romish priest in Hoboken, New Jersey, is now worshiped by the "faithful" here in the United States.

Infallibility is a *novelty*. Gregory VII., in the eleventh century, the Council of Lateran and that of Trent, 1660, and Pighius, Albert, Gielser, Bellarmine, and other popish writers, and Clement VII., and popes down to the present time, created the Pope infallible, because, as they say, he is in the place of "God," and he must of necessity be infallible.

It is a fact well known, that at the council of Lateran in Rome, the four deputies from the city of Bitonti, in the kingdom of Naples, were admitted to an audience by Pope Leo X., and who, after kneeling three times before the Pope, had to address him with these words in latin: "Lamb of God who taketh away the sins of the world, have mercy upon us;" "Lamb of God who taketh away the sins of the world, have mercy upon us;" "Lamb of God who taketh away the sins of the world, grant us *thy* peace!"

For this doctrine of the Pope's "infallibility," see the great popish writer Bellarmine, De Pontiff, Liber iv, Cap. 3 and Cap. 5; the Canon Law in the Gloss, and a work, among others, in common use at Rome, called "Classical Books."

Festivals and *saints' days* are a *novelty*. They include, in Rome nearly all the days in the year. The "Feast of Candlemas," or Purification; "Feast of the Ass," of "Lady Day," or the Annunciation; of "All Saints and all Souls," and of "Vigil, or Wakes," and others, had their origin in the fourth century, and in subsequent periods.*

Indulgence is a *novelty*. Boniface VIII., in the fourteenth century first introduced *indulgence* in these words: *Pœnarum remissionem*, and Polydore Virgil,† a famous Romish authority, says: "Then the use of pardons,

* Buck's Theo. Dic.

† Polydore Virgil, Invont. Rerum lib. 8, cap. 1.

which they call Indulgence, began to be famous." This "Indulgence" is a capital and most artful device of the priest to get money. In granting "Indulgences," the priest gives absolute pardon of sins or absolution for the time specified, whether it is ten or fifty or a hundred days, or five, ten, or fourteen or fifty years! In other words, like absolution in the "Confessional," they are a license for sin; and as papists have permitted the priests to suborn their conscience, so they permit them to tax their purses! But, "who can forgive sins but God?"

Absolving from an oath is a *novelty*. Gregory VII., 1080, issued a decree against Henry IV., in which he uses these words: "I release all Christians from their oath of allegiance to him." Hallam, in his Middle Ages, says: "The most important and mischievous dispensation (contained among the forged decretals,) was that from *promissory oaths*." Sismondi, in his history of the Italian Republics, furnished instances of this as a recognized and every-day practice.

In the letters of an Independent Irishman, addressed to Bishop Fitzpatrick is the following passage:

"Says Bishop Kenrick, 'No faith with heretics;' and says Bishop O'Connor, of Pittsburgh, 'Religious liberty is merely endured until the opposite can be carried into execution without peril to the catholic world!'"

The *use* of *holy water* is a *novelty*. It was first established by Leo II., in the seventh century, that is, in the year 680. It was invented among other superstitious fancies, such as "tapers at noon day," and "charms" to keep off diseases, so that, "the stupid multitude were persuaded that a portion of stinking oil taken from lamps

* Mosheim.

which burned at the tombs of martyrs, had a supernatural efficacy to ward off dangers."* In the same manner, the practice of crossing the forehead with holy water, of wearing the rosary or beads, to count the prayers said, is the invention of the priests to delude the devotions of simple papists.

The *name given to the pope*, calling him *God* is a *novelty*. Clement VII., 1523, and his cardinals in their letter to Charles, blasphemously declared that the dominion of God and the popes are the same.†

Urban VI., 1095, established the dogma that *no faith is to be kept with heretics*, which is a *novelty*. This dogma has been put in practice whenever Rome had the power to do it, from that period to this, by persecutions, etc.‡

The *persecuting dogmas of popery* are a *novelty*. Pope Innocent VII., in 1405, issued a bull "to crush the heretics like venemous asps." The oath which every Romish bishop takes, enacted by Pope Gregory VII., in 1070, binds the bishop to persecute and make war against heretics or protestants, and all who differ from and reject the dogmas and superstitions of popery.

The exterminating bull of Pope Alexander III., in 1160, was in these words: "We, therefore, subject to a curse the *perverseness of heretics* (*protestants*)."

The bull of Lucius III., in 1184, was in these words: "We condemn all manner of heresy and *decree any laymen, if he be heretic and disobedient* (to the pope), to condign punishment—that is, to tortures and death." Any one decree of a pope is always unchangeably in force, as

* Mosheim. Wilkes' Lives of the Popes. **Rankè.**

† Troisard, tom. iii. p. 147.

‡ Sismondi's History of France.

well as a dozen. The notes in the Rhemish Testament, sanctioned by the Romish bishops and clergy generally, declare the same persecuting tenets. In note on Luke ix. 55, it declares, that neither is the church of God (i. e. of Rome) blamed by God for putting heretics (protestants) to death!

In note on Heb. xiii. 17, it says: "When Rome puts heretics (protestants) to death—their blood is not of saints, nor is it more to be accounted of, than that of thieves, man-killers, or other malefactors."*

Immaculate Conception is a human invention, a four years old *novelty* of Pius IX. The pious belief of this dogma, is something old, however, since it was controverted between the dominicans and franciscans, from the time of Thomas Aquinas and John Duns Scotus, (thirteenth century,) but no pope until Pius IX., dared to enact it. This blasphemous mockery of creating the Virgin Mary a *divinity*, is the last climax of popish imposture.

The word of God says, that, "the wages of sin is death," and as Mary died, consequently, Mary was a sinner. Mary said, "My spirit hath rejoiced in God my Saviour." Now, if Christ was her Saviour, she rejoiced in being redeemed from sin and saved in heaven. And yet the pope decrees that salvation or damnation depends on the belief or rejection, of this impious fiction.

"Mother of God," used by the papists, is an ignorant appellation. Mary, a creature, could not be the mother of *divinity*. She was the mother of the *human*, not of the *divine* nature,—which would be an absurdity and an impossibility.

We have now revealed before us this temple of Baby-

* Bower's Lives of the Popes. Rankè.

lon. We see the periods when the scaffolding of this monstrous papal Juggernaut was reared by ambitious popes, and their subsequent emissaries, who assisted in raising the superstructure.

NOTE.—We have now proved that the Pope of Rome is an usurper; and that the whole edifice of the papal hierarchy rests on impostures, fictions, and pagan superstitions. The Holy Bible which contains the revealed will of God to mankind never alludes to a *pope*, to *auricular confession*, to *purgatory*, *transubstantiation*, to *saints*, *images*, *relics*, or absolution from sin; through outward works by any human priest or prelate. Neither does it refer to *inquisitions* to punish the human race—nor of madonnas and plaster casts of Jesus Christ our Saviour, *weeping* and *speaking* in the churches of the pope. These are some of the reasons why the Holy Scriptures both in the Old and New Testament, is a "prohibited Book," and the reading of it punished by the hierarchy, as a mortal sin.

Liguori, a canonized saint, teaches, that devotion to *Mary* is more beneficial than to *Jesus!* His miraculous ladders wrought into an altar-piece at Milan, represents Mary at the head of one, helping her votaries into heaven, and our Saviour at the top of the other, whose worshippers are *falling back to the earth!* The canons and professors of Romish theology, admit, that the *Virgin* was more *compassionate* than our blessed *Redeemer*, (the only intercessor between God and man!) Seymour's "Mornings among the Jesuits at Rome," p. 46. Long before the Pope of Rome claimed or assumed the title of *universal* ruler of the world, there were two thousand ministers or bishops in the Christian world and over *two hundred and forty* millions of Christians.*

* Bishop Hopkins on the Primitive Church.

CHAPTER II.

THE ROMISH CONFESSIONAL.

Cardinal Fleury—Jesuit Authors—Confessors seduce their Penitents—Maynooth's Class-Book—Priests' Questions—Llorente—Mother Aguada—Béguine Nuns—Barthelemi des Bois—Father Mena—Ricci—Nuns of St. Catharine—Solicitations in the Confessional—Antiquities of Paris—Abbé Mengrat—Fenelon—Paul Courier—The Upholsterer's Wife—Elizabeth Bavent—Girard and La Cadiere—Company of Jesus—Trial in France, 1843—Sterbini—What is in the Holy Office—The Confessional, how it endangers liberty—Escobar—Dalle—Cicisbeism—Muratori—Taxes on Sins—Sanchez—Raymond—Sættler—Moulet—Abandoned Women—Bouvier—Politics—The President Assassinated, by order of a Romish Bishop—La Confession—Coupeé—Education—Marriage—Reserved Cases—Rev. Pierce Connelly, former Rector of Trinity Church, Natchez.

Cardinal Fleury has justly said: "It is a species of falsehood to tell the truth by halves." Nobody is obliged to write history, but whoever undertakes it, is bound to tell the entire truth. If the manifestations of truth produce scandal, it is lawful; it is more useful to produce scandal then to avoid the defence of truth. To make the public feel the seriousness of the evil of Roman Catholic confession, we do not vaguely make deprecatory charges, but shall give the textual terms of the maxims professed in Roman Catholic Works, so far as delicacy would permit. We further explicitly state—what no Romish bishop or priest in the United States dare deny—that every author from whom we quote, is acknowledged as authority by the Roman Catholic church throughout the world. Jesuits write and publish only by their society.

In the Constitution of the Society of Jesus, part 7, ch.

4, art. 11, p. 70, we find: "Whoever is endowed with the talent of writing books, conducive to the common good and shall compose any such; nevertheless shall not publish them, except the General shall previously see them and subject them to the judgment and censure of others; that if they shall seem good for edification, they may come before the public, and not otherwise."

Now, Saint Thomas Aquinas says: "If a man knowingly read or retain, in print, or carry about in any way whatsoever, books containing the heresy of heretics and apostates, or treating of religion, he is *excommunicated with an excommunication reserved to the supreme Pontiff*." Dens, tom. vi, p. 307. But when confessors seduce their female penitents in confession, it is only necessary that she should change her confessor! The confessor, on the other hand, is not censurable in any degree, unless he falls oftener than "three or four times a month," when it becomes a reserved case for the archbishop or pope! The Romish church explicitly *denies* that it co-operates with chastity:

Obj. He that makes a vow of chastity, vows not to co-operate with, or consent to any sin against chastity.

*Ans. That is denied.**

We find by the decrees of popes, the fathers and councils, that sins were divided, subdivided and minutely specified, nay, many were imagined, that never had taken place in order to increase the power of the confessional. Whether in the United States, where Romish priests dictate every day their orders and the opinions to which the people ought to submit, and where, as absolute masters of consciences, they command without control and with-

* *Obj.* Vovens castitatem vovet non co-operari aut consentire ulli peccato contra castitatem. *R. Id. Negatur* Dens. tom. iv, p. 377.

out appeal; they are not granting in their own names, as God, absolution to each other's victims, seduced through the immoral instruction which females receive at the confessional, is a question confidently submitted to the reader.

The frequency of confession, and the facility of absolution, renders the tribunal all the more dissolute. In Maynooth Class-Book, *Tract de Matrimo*, p. 482, a book which forms a part of the education of the priests in our country, we find questions of the most revolting character are submitted to married women, too horrible to be mentioned; and to these direct questions on her mortal sins, she is compelled to give direct answers, "for if she refuse," says this authority, "it does not appear that she can be excused from that perverse obstinacy, which renders her unworthy of the benefit of absolution." "In every carnal sin, let the circumstance of marriage be expressed in confession. Are the married at any time to be asked in confession . . . . . etc. *Answ.* Yes, particularly *women* . . . . . but the question is not to be put abruptly, but to be framed prudently; for instance, whether they have quarrelled with their husbands; what was the cause of these quarrels, etc., etc.*

"Prudent confessors are wont, and lay it down regularly, to ask from all young women going to be married . . . . . etc. And since young women are more under the influence of modesty, we are wont for that reason to hear the betrothed husbands first . . . . . etc."†

The only principle of morality which we can find, after a thorough research into the papal imposture, is the zealous care with which the church studies to avoid *scan-*

* Dens, tom. vii, p. 150. † Dens, tom. v, pp. 239–40.

dal; and as the confessional gives to the priest so thorough a knowledge of the character of his victims, very little comparatively is ever betrayed. Hence, we find that even when a confessor has fallen oftener "than three or four times" in a month, which constitutes a reserved case, he receives no censure, but a simple negation of jurisdiction: so, in fact, the practice of seduction, is winked at by the Romish clergy. "Wherefore," says Dens, (tom. vi, p. 287): "Carnal sin with a novice, or a nun, or any other, bound by a simple vow of chastity, does not constitute a reserved case, nor is a religious man or priest comprehended, (in the reserved case,) so that a free woman, (query, lay women,) transgressing with a religious priest, does not incur this case (of reservation)." Here we see, that the priest (provided he is religious,) may be a perfect libertine.

It is impossible to give the reader a correct idea of the immoral trash which they blasphemously teach as theology, but whoever will follow us through these pages shall learn enough of the sad story of the Papal impostors, and out of their own books they may judge whether "confession opens the gate of heaven," as they say Saint Chrysostom vauntingly asserts. Llorente observes, "A woman, young and weak, gives, by the confession of the faults she has committed against the sixth (seventh) precept in the Decalogue, the most frequent opportunity for the attempt of which the confessor becomes guilty." This respectable ecclesiastic had had in his hands the *procès-verbeau* of the acts and judgments pronounced by the Inquisition of Spain, of which he was for a long time secretary. We will relate a few facts from his unquestionably authentic testimony:

In the Carmelite Convent, in the city of Lerma, in

1712, a girl of noble family, born at Corello, took the veil. For twenty years she intrigued with the provincial and other friars, and on account of her ecstacies, impostures and miracles, her accomplices determined to build her a convent! Mother Aguada, the name of this abbess, lived the most vicious life, while her reputation for sanctity so increased every day that people flocked to her from neighboring countries to seek her intercession with God!

The man who seduced this girl into every excess of corruption and fanaticism, was a provincial monk of the bare-legged Carmelite order. His name was Juan de la Véga. "He had been," says Llorente, "the spiritual director and accomplice of Mother Aguada, was thirty-five years old, and at his trial, evidence appeared that he had had five children by her. His conversation had corrupted other nuns, by making them believe that what he advised them to do was genuine virtue. He had written his life of Mother Aguada, and spoken of her as a model of sanctity."

A niece of this Mother Aguada entered her convent at the age of nine years, and soon was this child instructed in her evil doctrines. The lesson was successful, and on the trial of her aunt before the Holy Inquisition, she revealed the whole of her guilt, saying she thought all she had done was lawful, as her aunt and her confessor so taught her, and she had the highest opinion of their virtue, as Mother Aguada was called a saint! "We see," says Llorente, "extreme moderation in the inquisitors when there is any question about punishing the prodigious number of infanticides committed by the monks and nuns at the Convent of Corello, of which Aguada was foundress." If the witnesses are to be believed, there were not less than twenty attempts at abortion, and more than thirty murders committed upon infants after birth, several of whom were not baptized. But unparalleled as was the case, the Holy Office displayed its graciousness and mercy, so often vaunted in its decrees.*

On the same page, Llorente, whose sincerity and honesty on this subject is beyond all question, remarks, "Since the Inquisition meddles with what passes in convents, it is surprising that, after so many irregularities of this kind, with which its archives are filled, but of which decency does not permit us to give an account, it has not resolved to deprive monks of the direction of the convents of women."

We find an account in Llorente's book of a Capuchin friar who was a spiritual director and adviser of an establishment of seventeen Béguine nuns in Spanish America, and who corrupted thirteen of that number. He made these blessed nuns to understand that Jesus Christ had appeared in the very act of confession, in the consecrated wafer, and directed him to tell the "nun before him that she could sin with her confessor, and then she should have a dispensation from Him, and must never speak of it, even to another confessor, to avoid scandal." The friar further told her that Jesus Christ had directed this that she might grow in holiness! So the thirteen were severally destroyed, and "as to the confessor," says Llorente, "the Inquisition feared to put him in its prisons for his outrage on these women (forced to be nuns in spite of themselves), as it would show that the Holy Office interferes with the convents,

* See Llorente's Historie de l' Inquisition d' Espagne, tom. iv. p. 33, et seq.

which they wish to keep concealed, so they merely shipped him to another convent at Madrid!"

In a work called "Causes Célèbres," par Richter, t. xi., p. 74, two remarkable trials, the result of the confessional, are recorded. "The College of Jesuits," says this author, "had property in Caparacena, two leagues from Grenada, entrusted to friar Barthelemi des Bois. This Jesuit became enamored with a man's wife, and determined to possess her. He employed her husband in cultivating the lands, and doubled his wages, that he might accomplish his wish. The husband becoming jealous and suspicious, concealed himself in the house, and so managed to surprise the guilty priest, and put him to death. The civil law allowed a man this right after he had heard the criminal conversation with his wife, but the rector of Grenada preferred a complaint for the murder of the Jesuit, and the witnesses heard on the husband's side were compelled to retract! The wife was proved to be aged, though she was but twenty-eight, and the case was so managed, that the poor husband was condemned and hung! To the honor of the pious and chaste confessor, the Jesuits had the trial, thus purged, printed, together with the definite judgment.

Father Mena was another Jesuit, who wore a threadbare dress and a large chaplet. He used to confess a simple-hearted girl at Salamanca. He told her, one day, that God had revealed that she must become the confessor's wife! The innocent girl did not enter the snare at that moment, but consulted the doctors of the University, (as father Mena knew she would, and whom he had already acquainted with his design,) and they told her simply to follow the advice of her confessor. The devotee thought it was the will of heaven, and married her confessor. He went on as before with all his external acts of piety. He had several children by his wife, whom he kept shut up in a lonely spot at hand. This Jesuit father was at length denounced to the Inquisition. The Jesuits undertook his defence, and finding the case so well proved, they resorted to artifice to save him. Physicians certified he was ill; and thus they got him transferred to the college of the Inquisition, to be cured! They then pretended he was dead; and made a figure of wood, with hands and feet of pasteboard, dressed in the Jesuit garb; put it on a bier; the bells were tolled, and every ceremony gone through for the burial of the effigy.

In the meantime, the real father Mena, mounted on a mule, had hurried to Genoa, where he openly taught the laws of Moses to the Jews!

Ricci, bishop of Pistoia, left in possession of his family, the facts, acts, correspondence, and orders of the Grand Duke of Leopold concerning the confessional in the convents of Tuscany. M. de Potter, to whom the whole was communicated, has published them in a work, called, "Vie de Scipion de Ricci, èrêquedo Pistoie et Prato." The scandalous conduct practised by the monks in those convents were made known by six nuns, who petitioned Leopold on the subject. "I do not state anything," says Ricci, "of which I have not proofs." We here find that the monks passed their time in the private cells of the nuns, and the grossest libertinism prevailed in all the convents. The Jesuit who first practised his familiarities, would tell the nuns they did a virtuous action in submitting to what was repugnant to them!

The nuns in the convent of Saint Catharine of Pistoia, stated the infamous practices of their confessors and superiors. These men kept keys and entered the chambers of the nuns just when it suited them. Such as allowed themselves to be led by the counsels of these confessors, were gratified in every whim and caprice, and others were obliged to outrage their consciences by the same course, or undergo an endless persecution. In the report of the wardens of the same convent, it is stated, that when the confessors went to administer consolation to the dying, they would eat and sleep in the convent, and dine with whom they pleased. This was the practice of every father and prior, who successively performed the duties. Their maxim was, that God has forbidden hatred and not love! "Without a miracle," says the prioress of the convent Peroccini, "no one can frequent their company without at length yielding to this species of diabolical temptation. The priests are the husbands of the nuns, and the lay-brothers of the lay-sisters."

A certain nun, when solicited by her confessor, said, "I testified to him the fear and scruples which they excited within me." He replied, "I must tell you plainly, you are a precious simpleton; follow my advice, you will thank me for my lessons, and your scruples will cease."

These facts are scandalous, but for this reason they should not be concealed from the public. Under a pretext of religion, these iniquities are practised and provoked! It is time the people of our country had more light upon these offences.

Let it be fully understood that all this sin and shame has been brought about by the confessional in the convents. Can you see, then, any difference between them and those of the present day founded in our land, and under the same authority? If there be a country where the people should be free from such outrages as these debasing institutions, ought it not to be the United States of America?

José M. Samper, an editor and representative of the people of New Grenada, a *Roman Catholic himself*, writes, in 1858, of the dissolute character of the Romish priesthood in Spanish America: "We can affirm that the great majority of the New Grenada clergy, beginning with the convents of Bogota, and many of the secular ministers of this city, *live in permanent concubinage*, scandalizing society. We have seen a curate go out with his concubine, leading his children under an umbrella, to administer the eucharist to the sick, half dressed, without pantaloons. We have *known* many curates with large families of acknowledged children. We have known curates destroy innocent women, by taking advantage of their office. We have *known* a curate who, having a daughter, had progeny also by her, and by his *grand-daughter;* and another who has a family by his sister," etc., etc., etc.

If such are the dissolute practices of Romish theologians in the southern parts of our continent, who can doubt that the same course of libertinism is secretly taking place every day in the United States?

This seduction of women through the confessional is peculiar to no country: it is common to all—and must be from the unchanging nature of the Romish system.

In the Antiquitiés de Paris, in the time of Cardinal legate Jacques de Vitre, it is stated that priests made no scruples in going from an intrigue to say mass.

Clemagis, a secretary to pope Benedict XIII., wrote of the convents in 1430. "The bishops of France," said he, "permit curates, for a certain contribution, to keep concubines; and the canons bring up publicly the children of those whom they keep as their own wives. As to the convents of women, there is now no difference be tween making a young girl take the veil, and exposing her to the greatest degradation."

This work contains the most revolting and atrocious facts: we will state a few.

The newspapers had spoken of the priest, Roubignac who used to invite young girls to his house, and fascinated one at the age of nineteen so far, that he covered her body with hair-cloth furnished with iron points, and reduced her thus almost to death, for the purpose of his own base actions. This infamous priest found a welcome asylum after this, in the Jesuit house at Toulouse! The next abominable case to which we turn in those pages, is that of Abbé Mingrat. He was zealous for good works. He would not allow so much as a bare arm to appear at church, and was anxious to establish the purity of the *ancien régime!* To this end, he had a school in the house of his aunt, for young girls, in which he prepared them for mass. Presently two of them, attracted his attention. He invited them to his house. They went singly, or together. One of these girls, the only daughter of President de Neuilly, a girl of fourteen, became a mother! The father brought an action, but the priest only laughed, and the clergy interfered; and in spite of the French parliament, president, and daughter, he was created by the pope, Bishop of Senlis!

Here is another case. Forty years since, some young ladies were educated in a convent, near Nogent-le-Rotron, under a saintly prêtre-abbés, who confessed, catechised, and taught them. It was discovered that he had corrupted several of the girls, and when there was any prospect of detection, he poisoned the one whose situation might expose him, and then watched her, and kept every one away, under pretense of confession or dying exhortations, never leaving her till she was dead, coffined and buried.

Abbé Mingrat now occupied another field, and we find him entering the house of a turner, whose wife was one of his devotees. But she was reputed virtuous and it made no scandal. One evening she came rather late to confess and after detaining her a long while, he sent her to his aunt's. He took a different direction and arriving there before her, compelled her to enter. No one can tell what occurred, except that she was subsequently taken out dead, and her body thrown into the river Isère.

These fragments floated and were one by one picked up and the body recognized, as well as the bloody knife left in the grotto. Then it was at once remembered that he was the seducer of President de Neuilly's daughter, etc.

What think you reader then happened, the case was fully stated, and all the facts published, in spite of the clergy. But, the church was determined to save him. The Grand-Vicar of Grenoble, Abbé Bochard preached upon rash judgment saying, "Brethren beware! Such a one may appear guilty who is obliged by his honor and life to remain silent upon the crimes of another, and insinuated that the woman's husband had committed the murder, and the confessor Mingrat, was the martyr to the secrecy of the confessional!" The proof was too refulgent, and the criminal, though known to be Mingrat, could not be touched; for they held that he was, the "Lord's anointed."

* It is well known, that the priests in cases of murder in this country, have refused to depose as witnesses under our civil laws: alleging the secrecy of the confessional.

"Should a priest happen," says Fenelon, "to commit a fault, people ought modestly to cast down their eyes and remain silent." This has been, and ever will be their maxim, in every age, and every country. Paul Courier has described in the most animated manner, and with most logical reasoning, the dangers of priestly confession. "What a life," he exclaims, "is that of a priest! What a condition! Love and especially marriage are forbidden, yet women are given up to them! They may not have one, but they may live familiarly with all. This is but little; but their confidence, their intimacy, their secrecy of their private actions, of all their thoughts, is given to him. The innocent little girl, hears from the first, the priest, who soon calling her, converses with her apart; who, first, before she can err, speaks to her of sin. When schooled, he marries her; when married he still confesses and *governs* her. He precedes the husband in her affections, and ever stands his ground. What she does not confide to her mother, or avow to her husband, a priest *must* know; he demands and knows it; yet will he not be her lover. Indeed, how could he be? Is he not in holy orders? He hears a young woman whispering to him her faults, feelings, wishes, weaknesses; he inhales her sighs, without feeling any emotion; and he is five-and-twenty!" *

"The pope pardons everything in priests but marriage; and would rather have them unchaste adulterers, debauched assassins, like Mingrat, than married. Mingrat kills his mistress; he is defended from the pulpit; here, they preach for him; here, they canonize him; but if he married one—what a monster! He would never find an asylum.

* Will American men weigh well these sentences.

"Now, reflect and see if it be possible ever to combine in the self-same person two more contrary things than the duty of the confessor and the vow of chastity. What must be the fate of these poor young men, between the prohibition of possessing what nature impels to love and the obligation of conversing intimately, confidentially, with the objects of their loves?"

"But why does a man turn priest, some will say, when he is susceptible of such impressions. Do you think they make themselves what they are? They are brought up from infancy by the papal militia; they are seduced and enlisted; they pronounce that abominable vow never to have a wife or a family before they understand it; otherwise they ought to be seized and transported to some desert island. Girls and women are given up to them to govern! These thousands of priests have the gift of continency vested in their gowns, and are henceforth as if they had no longer either sex or bodies! Do you credit it?"

The trial of Elizabeth Bavent, a nun of the Convent of Saint Elizabeth de Louvieres, seduced in the tribunal of confession, is very remarkable for the immoral and superstitious character it presents of the priesthood. She was early initiated, and became a nun at the *turning* box. She was handed over to two confessors, and they both taught her that no immoral action she could commit through the confessional, was contrary to piety and religion. She was irreproachable in her conduct until the age of twelve years, when she entered the convent of Saint Francis on account of her devotional turn of mind; but was soon hurried away by her boundless confidence and blind submission to her confessors. She, at the suggestion of Picard, her villainous confessor, made a donation of her body to the devil! In describing the position in which she was kept, she says: "No one in the house was ignorant of that man's attachment to me; of his privacy, or of my frequent visits to his room, at his instance. . . . But the nuns turned a deaf ear, and would never allow me to go and confess elsewhere; though I entreated them in the hope that an honest man might find a remedy for my poor conscience and tell me what I had to do." Her tranquility and resignation under the inflictions of her confessor and the nuns, is very astonishing. They refused her the most necessary things of life; which she bore unmoved, thinking her faults deserved "she should be in hell." "They refused me even a bit of linen, says she, to put to my ulcerated breast, and I heard the superior say, with my own ears, '*Let the wretch die if she will!*'" After being made the victim of the inhuman bishop, who had been her confessor for fifteen months, he pronounced sentence against her on the calumnious testimony of a nun—by which she was made prisoner all her life—being compelled to fast three days in the week on bread and water.

Poor Bavent was put in prison, first for four days in a subterraneous dungeon, a horrible place, on the testimony of another debauched nun. On being delivered from the dungeon, she gave up to despair and stabbed herself. Reduced by the loss of blood, she became extremely weak; her wound festered in her body, but all the remedy she used was a little cold water, having nothing else. She asked repeatedly for a confessor, but was always refused. Three days after this attempt upon her life, she got some glass, ground it, and swallowed it by degrees, taking nothing else for days, in order to hasten her death.

"No one could ever imagine all I endured," says Bavent, "during my imprisonment at Evreux, which lasted five years; *three and a half* of which I passed in the dungeons, either in the cellar or above. There I fasted my three appointed days on bread and water, without mercy, and I was badly enough fed on the other days. I was taken out three or four times more dead than alive; and at times of despair, I went five times, seven days, without eating or drinking. They ordered me to be visited by divers physicians and surgeons, four times at least, having inflicted on me rather violent torments; and my head being pricked about and covered with blood and swelled like a bushel. For a long time no one came near me or spoke to me, and M. de Louchemp, (the confessor they had given her, who declared against her,) even kept, by order of M. de Evreux, the keys of my dungeon, fearing lest the turnkeys should give me a little air. The filthy state of my dungeon was insupportable. All I say is true. I cannot say all. But what afflicted me still more, was my suffering conscience, which they did not attempt to relieve; for I asked for a confessor a hundred times, but could obtain no other than the penitentiary, whom I could not endure."

The guilty confessors triumphed over this seduced victim, as usual, and the girl suffered the extreme penalty of their vengeance!*

* Professor Morse furnishes the following testimony of a French Jesuit: "As soon as the young girl—for I speak peculiarly of their confession—enters the confessional, 'Bless me, father,' she says, kneeling and crossing herself, 'for I have sinned,' and the priest mumbles, 'Dominus sit in ore tuo et in corde,' etc.—'The Lord be in your heart and lips, that you may confess all your sins.' (This confession amounts to nothing, for it becomes a mere listless habit.) If she is an ugly, common country girl or woman, she is soon dispatched;

Richter, in his work on the *Causes Célèbres et Intérêssantes*, p. 11, gives an account of a law-suit, the most noted affair of the kind that ever occupied the tribunal of the kingdom:

"All Europe resounded with the names of Girard and La Cadière; all Europe read the writings published on both sides; everybopy awaited the sentence with impatience; it astonished everybody, and nobody was satisfied."

This notoriety arose from the accused being of the Society of Jesus. The Jesuits follow their policy strictly,

but, on the contrary, if she is pretty and fair, the holy father puts himself at ease; he examines her in the most secret recesses of her soul; he unfolds her mind in *every sense*, in *every manner*, upon *every matter*. This is the way which *theology* recommends us to follow in our interrogations: '*Daughter*, have you had bad thoughts? On what subject? How often? etc. Have you had bad desires? What desires? Have you committed bad actions? With whom? What actions?' etc. I am obliged to stop. Many times the poor, ashamed girl does not dare answer the questions, they are so impure. In that case, the holy man says to her: 'Listen, daughter, to the true doctrine of the Church; you must confess the truth, all the truth, to your spiritual father. Do you know that I am in the place of God; that you cannot deceive Him? Speak, then, reveal your heart to me, as God knows it. Will you not? Yes. Begin; I will help you;' and then begins such a diabolical explanation as is not to be found but in houses of infamy, I suppose, or in our theological books. This is so well known, that I have often heard of wicked young men saying to each other, 'Come, let us go to confession, and the curate will teach us a great many corrupt things which we never knew;' and many young girls have told me in confession that, in order to become acquainted with details on those matters, pleasing to their corrupt nature (and ruined morals), they went purposely to the confessional, to speak about it to their spiritual father."

never to leave one of their order in trouble. These men are the embodiment of cunning, immorality and hypocrisy; they are enterprising, audacious, greedy of dominion, and skillful in using the confession to rule the minds of men, to corrupt women and to enrich themselves. Father Girard was an exceedingly homely Jesuit; yet he had singular power in fascinating women. In this way, by great profession of sanctity, his influence increased, until he was made rector of the royal Seminary of the Nevay, at Toulouse. Maria Catharine Cadière was born in 1709, and was the daughter of a devout widowed mother. She was handsome, her figure was fine, her neck beautiful, with a fair complexion, dark eyes and hair, and an animated countenance. Her education was defective; and she was more than twenty-one before she could write. Father Girard seeing that she loved praise and was inclined to be a saint, improved her taste by the ascetic books which he put into her hands. He directed her to *quietism*, as an infallible means of success. Finally he pursued his practices, until he told her she must look on him as God, and submit to whatever he required of her. He was at the same time enticing other girls, through the confessional, and one of them was soon to be a mother. This Jesuit soon persuaded the public that La Cadière performed miracles, as well as himself. In a word, he having sacrificed her to his licentiousness, wanted to sacrifice her to his ambition, by securing a reputation for making saints.

It now became necessary for La Cadière to lay her complaint before the lieutenant of Toulon. The bishop forbade all the confessors from hearing Cadière, until she retracted all her charges against father Girard! She was made to drink salted wine to effect this, while she remained in her mind steadfast to what she first stated. Every thing jesuitical ingenuity could devise was brought against that nun on the trial; and the Jesuits so managed, that every witness was first instructed by them, as to the mode of deposing; they suborned witnesses against her, and silenced her own. The disconsolate mother of the nun, seeing her overwhelmed by such powerful influences, addressed four petitions—to Cardinal de Fleury, to the Chancellor, to the Keeper of Seals, and the Secretary of State.

Not one of these petitions availed her anything. The seducer of her daughter continued his career of vice, continued all his sacred duties and his preaching, attended by the bishop, and the official, his judge, while the poor girl was shut up in the monastery, under the direction of another Jesuit, who was subject to Girard. The mother sent another petition to Cardinal de Fleury, stating these facts and appealed to his intercession; but, not one word did she hear from him. In fact, the Jesuits had turned the whole testimony of the nuns and others in the convent against Cadière, and in favor of Girard, on pain of torture, with which they were threatened! In one of Girard's letters to the abbess of the convent at Toulon, he made this request: "Let the young lady write home, without her letters being read, and my answers returned to her without being seen." Then, he would give two letters to his messenger, one of which contained only spiritual counsel, to pass through the hands of the abbess, if she should require it; the other, with his true sentiments, to go direct into the hands of his penitent. These letters he afterwards took back from the nun, retaining her own, which he refused to give up, as containing secrets of conscience.

The definite conclusion of the *parquet* was to the effect that La Cadière had abused religion and counterfeited the saint, and afterwards the *possessed*, for which she was ordered to be given over to the hands of the executioner to be hanged at Place des Prêchems; after first being put to extraordinary torture to extort more about the accomplices of her crime. But the court finally rendered sentence on the accused parties. The Jesuit got off with impunity; the girl was not hanged, the decision being revoked, and she was sent home to her mother.

On leaving the prison she was called upon by the distinguished people of the place, and earnestly congratulated on her safety. Jesuit hatred could not endure this, and she was ordered to leave the town of Aix the same day, by the authorities. But she suddenly *disappeared*, and no one ever could tell what became of her.

This diabolical combination for the purpose of maintaining the honor of the priesthood and of the confession, should be a warning to us all.

Another instance of popish tyranny resulting from the confessional, may be seen in the trial which occurred in the court of Assizes of Vienne, in France, the 18th November, 1843.

Nine nuns and two novices were accused of forcibly detaining and ill-treating a young woman named Genevieve in the conventof the Good Shepherd. The nuns appeared in the court attired in their convent dress, with sanctimonious demeanor. To add to the blasphemous character of these women, they had assumed the names of the Mother of the Saviour, the Mother of Mercy, the Mother of the Holy Spirit, the Mother of Charity, etc.

In the course of the trial a number of the most respectable witnesses testified to having frequently heard agonizing cries of distress proceeding from the convent.

The surgeon and six witnesses testified as to the girl's condition on her release. "I attended her," said the physician, "and found bruises on her chest, and a sore on her side as large as the palm of my hand."

Genevieve appeared in court so ill that she had to be supported by two persons, and made oath to the following statement:

"Not being able to bear the regulations of the convent, I often demanded to quit it; I was told that I must remain there a year at least. One day, when I was very sick, I wished to retire from the class; the Mother of the Saviour would not permit me. The Mother of the Holy Spirit and the Mother of Charity dragged me by the hair, and the Mother of the Seraphim beat me. At another time I could not repeat my lesson, I was taken to a dungeon. I had then been three weeks in the convent, and was told I should never quit it. On the 25th of July, the Mother of the Saviour came to tell me I must rise, and dragged off the bed clothes; she took me by the hair and severely kicked me. I was dragged by the arm from one end of the dormitory to the other. Many threw themselves on me, and I was dragged down to the dungeon. I know not what occurred as they dragged me to the dungeon, for I fainted. When I recovered I found myself in the dungeon, stripped of my clothes. The Mother of the Saviour and the Mother of St. Matthew tied my arms behind my back. The Mother of Mercy then kicked me several times. I continued in the dungeon from Tuesday until Thursday. I was afterwards taken to the convent door and left on the steps.

A woman, who passed by, pitied me, and took me to the house of Madame Piat, who procured me admittance to the hospital, where I yet remain."

The nuns and their doctor were the only witnesses called for the defence, and they escaped as guiltless, except the Mother of Mercy, who was sentenced to three months' imprisonment.

In 1849, when the Republic of Rome threw open the doors of the Inquisition, L. De Sanctis* says: "With Sterbini we went to this horrible place to examine the papers. We came to ten great volumes full of denunciations made by confessors; and often had the artful priest employed his ferocious eloquence in persuading the dying men to denounce their friends. In this manner were denounced nearly all the political men in the Roman States. In the closet of the Inquisition was found a letter written by Cardinal Bernetti, in 1828, begging the father commissory, in the name of the Pope, to aid in finding out a conspiracy which the police had failed to detect. Appended to this letter was the decision of the Inquisition, that the confessional was the best means to effect such discoveries. The Holy Office, however, begged the Pope not to allow a confessor to absolve a conspirator until he had denounced the persons to their tribunal; which was done. We came," says this author, "to another shelf containing revelations, as they are called, respecting *solicitations to evil.* We turned over the leaves of these numerous volumes filled with horrible crimes: here a confessor had seduced a whole convent of nuns by means of confession, and had a greater part of them mothers; there, a confessor at the institution called

* Formerly Curate of the Magdalene, Professor of Theology in the Roman University, and Qualificator of the Inquisition.

Conservatory of Divine Providence, under the mask of piety, had ruined sixteen of the most beautiful young girls; and of similar facts there were thousands.

"I recollect, besides, the case of a confessor who had been accused seventeen times of solicitations to evil, but had never been punished, because he was a most zealous accuser of sectaries and heretics."* (p. 255.)

"Penitents, in accusing themselves of their own sins, reveal several sins that are foreign to them: men, what relates to their wives; wives to their husbands; servants what concerns their masters; masters things relating to their servants, and so on; one against another."†

Women have always been used as the best instruments for revealing what they knew, as their devotion to their confessor, whom they look upon as God, will not allow them to refuse him anything. This intimate confidence leads to every immoral act, without *éclat*. This was well understood by the long experience of those men who made

* It is the duty of the subordinates in the Roman Catholic Church to reveal to the superiors whatever facts and sins by which benefit will accrue to the Church. Every parish priest in the United States reports weekly to the bishop of his diocese the progress of his work for the Church, in all particulars; also, the feeling and action of Protestants towards them. These reports are then transmitted to the Pope, when, they are duly recorded and alphabetically arranged, and become the subject of deliberation as to the next edict in the premises. It is in this way that the moral, social and political character of our country is penetrated, and the Pope made familiar with the secrets of American families in connection with the government of the country. There is not a political office, from a petty municipality to the Presidency of the Republic, that is not thus interfered with. This mode of exposing the secrets of their neighbors, as well as the penitent's own, is fatal to liberty but good for the Church.

† See S. Toletanus, Instruct Sacerdot, ad Pœnit, tom. iii., c. 6, art. 3.

the system of confession. Thus Escobar quotes numerous facts, which he says he had known of this kind; among others, that of a confessor who had an intimacy with three girls and their mother, having seduced them at the tribunal of confession.

Mr. Mahoney, a Romish priest, when examined before a Committee of the House of Commons, in England, on the Mortmain Acts, stated that a "very nefarious use was made by convents, and by other parties having the patronage of certain marriage portions, which dying sensualists are urged to give in reparation for their sins. The consequences were anything but satisfactory to lovers of decency.

How many of the successive generations of *foundlings* are due to this system cannot be estimated, especially, as "all these girls who chose nunneries are entitled to dower in preference to those who merely ask it to marry." In other words, a woman, instead of being allowed to return to virtue, is seduced into a convent to live in sin with the bishop and other confessors. It is not human to place a priest where he is *allowed* to fall, and suppose him innocent. Reader, commit your daughter to the soldier or hussar, who can marry her, rather than to a Romish priest.

Another scandal which should be mentioned in connection with confession, is that denominated *cicisbeism*, a custom which is particularly practised among the higher classes in Italy, especially in Rome, Florence and Naples.

* See Escobar, Tracta de Confess. Selec, in exordio.

This mode of adultery is openly practised in the sight of Europe, and has been for more than two centuries. A husband and wife observe the laws of marriage during the first year, but it is a thing, of course, that after this period the wife takes a lover under the name of *cicisbeo*, and the husband becomes the *cavaliere servente* of another woman. This sinful practice is authorized by the priests, who constantly give absolution to the persons who present themselves at a confessional; and this not once a year, but ten or twelve times a year, if devotion induces the guilty parties to enjoy the benefits of the grace attached to this sacrament. Such are the fruits of this confession, so beneficial to morals !*

That the reader may better understand the fatal effects of cicisbeism, we quote an author who presents its consequences: "The peace of families," says Sismondi, "was banished from all Italy; no husband any longer regarded his wife as a faithful companion, associated with his existence; no man any longer found in her a support in adversity, a saviour in danger, a comforter in despair; no father durst affirm that the children who bore his name were his own, and no one any longer felt himself tied to his child by the sentiments of nature. Incessantly annoyed in his own house by the *friend* of his wife, and separated from a part of his family, pent up in convents, he was considered only as the administrator of his fortune; and it was not because women had lovers, but because it became a law that they *must* have them, that the Italians ceased to be men."†

It was in the general council of Lateran that Innocent

* C. P. De Lasteyrie on Auricular Confession, p. 264.

† Sismondi, Hist. des Repub. d' Ital.

III. established sacerdotal confession, and caused the custom of receiving money for the administration of the sacraments.*

We find in a work, "Muratori," (a ritual of sins, and the cost of pardons,) that any sin can be redeemed by the payment of money, in place of the penance.† Every imagined crime is laid down, and the penance prescribed; so the penitent believed that he fully satisfied Divine justice when he paid his money to the priest, who said a few masses for the same, and told him "that God does not judge twice, but that, having submitted to their confessor, their sins are blotted out forever."‡

It is only in the rituals or penitentials that the nomenclature of the commutation of penalties, and that of the taxes imposed on penitents by the pope, bishops and monks, is to be found. This matter is kept secret in the present day, though undoubtedly still prevailing wherever there is a penitent or confessor of the Romish Church. Pope Nicholas said, in 1366, when consulted about it, "Laymen have no right to judge the acts of the priesthood."§

Pope Leo X. ordered the catalogue of sins to be drawn up in Rome, and the sums to be paid for absolution. The ecclesiastical budget is called, "Taxes of the Apostolic Chancery," and "Taxes of the Holy Apostolic Penitentiary."

We give the reader a few specimens which are found in the work:

"Remission given to a rich man for the wealth he has absconded with, 50 ducats; for a poor man, 20 ducats.

* Historiæ du Councile de Trente, par Fra Paola Sarpi, i. 11.

† Muratori Antiqui Mediævi, p. 724.

‡ Murat., p. 728. § Murat., p. 741.

For a layman not to be bound to observe fasts of the Church, and to eat cheese, 20 ducats. For an indulgence to visit the body of Jesus Christ, when it is publicly exposed, 12 ducats. For absolution of any one who has been intimate with a woman in a church, or done any other harm, 6 ducats. For destroying a virgin, 6 ducats. For the absolution of a concubinage, and dispensation of irregularities, 7 ducats. For the absolution of him who has killed his father, mother, brother, or sister, or any of his lay-relations, 5 or 6 ducats! For an absolution for spoilers, incendiaries, thieves and homicidal laymen, 8 ducats. For absolution of a woman who causes her child to perish, 5 ducats. For allowing a ship to convey merchandise to infidels, 100 ducats. For enabling the king and queen to procure indulgence, as if they had been to Rome, 200 ducats. For absolution of a king who has visited the Holy Sepulchre without the pope's permission, 100 ducats."

The reader will here observe, that the most enormous crimes, many of which are too shocking to mention, are taxed much lower than the most insignificant practices prescribed by the Court of Rome. These prescriptions, all originating with confession, end with the following: "*Pro mortuo excommunicato, par quo supplicant consanguinei littera absolutiones venit, ducat* 1, *carl.* 9."

So, the Pope, exalting himself to a level with God, gives absolution to the dead in a state of excommunication, and a soul in the lowest pit of hell can be got back by paying the Holy Penitentiary at Rome the sum of one ducat nine carlines! By virtue of these two words, *te absolvo*, accompanied by plenary indulgence and a few pieces of money, people obtained, and still do, forgiveness and remission of crimes, however enormous they may be, and even have the dead hurled from hell, and placed in all the delights of paradise! So teaches the Holy Mother Church!

Tanchez, the Jesuit, wrote a work which was printed in 1592, at Genoa, "De Matrimonio," in which he unveiled the mysteries of marriage. This book, a true school of debauchery, was dedicated to the Archbishop of Grenada, and was approved by the Roman Catholic censors, with so much delight, that in the license we find this language "Legi, perlegi maxima cum voluptate." From the famous work of this Jesuit, cases of conscience have been manufactured, and the licentious details with which the priests and bishops pollute the seminaries and the minds of those who are appointed to direct consciences, are drawn.

Albert-le-Grand had fathomed this same indelicate subject in the thirteenth century, in his "Commentary on the Fourth Book of Sentences." He pleads as his excuse for writing of conjugal duties, the horrible avowal that they must be heard in confession: "cogentibus monstris quæ in confessione audiunter."

Theophilus Raymond, a Jesuit, who, lived in the middle of the seventeenth century, commends Albert for having unveiled to the casuists, the turpitude of conjugal duties!

The chief pleasure of these writers seems to be in assimilating the hidden mysteries of religion, with the animal functions inherent to mankind, and no language can describe their excessive vileness.

Another, equally scandalous as these to which we have referred, was published by a priest named Sœttler, and reprinted by a professor of theology, with the title "Joannis Gaspari Sœttler sextum Decalogi prœceptum," etc. Here is the translation: "Extracts of Universal

Moral Theology on the sixth (7th) precept of the Decalogue relative to the Obligations of the Married Life, and divers points concerning Marriage, by J. G. Sœttler; with Notes and New Researches, by J. P. Ronsselet, Professor of Theology in the Seminary of Grenoble."*

In pages 17, 23, 28, and 37, cases of conscience and questions upon unheard of crimes, are so disgusting that it is impossible to mention them in any language. The very title of the book is enough to show its loathsome character.

Another work, which is in the hands of the young in the Romish seminaries of our country, to corrupt their morals, is called "Compendium Theologiæ Moralis," etc. In this we find a formal attack *against our institutions and liberties.* In commending this to the earnest observation of the reader, we translate: "Abridgment of Moral Theology, extracted chiefly from the works of B. Ligouri, by Moullet, ex-Professor of Moral Philosophy, printed with the permission of the Superiors."† With ingenious subtlety and distinctions, the author authorizes murder, theft, adultery, and other crimes. He supposes a case in which a person, came to be confessed after he had heard that all Christian sects were equally good, and all lead to salvation, and he believed that to be true; but now asks whether he had sinned in so hearing and believing. This is the answer of the Jesuit theologian: "You are guilty of heresy, if, knowing that the Catholic Church teaches the contrary, you think that any one may be saved in any of the communions which are termed Christian; and because you have manifested *this voluntary* error, you have incurred, by so doing, your damnation."

* Cary, liber, edit. 1840, pages 192. † Fribourg, Labartrovi, 1834.

Observe further, "The agent obeying his chief with a good intention, acts meritoriously, though, by so doing, he acts against the laws of God, —'quam vis materialiter agat contra legem Dei.'" (p. 38.)* It is from these rules and similar instructions from confessors, that the Roman Catholic subjects of these United States are trained to support the supremacy of the pope of Rome.

Our authority also thus justifies perjury: "If any one accuses himself at the sacred tribunal of penitence for having taken an oath, the confessor ought to ask him if it was his intention to swear, that is to say, to call God to witness; for people often use judicatory formulas without any intention of taking an oath."

The author next instructs young confessors upon their duty when abandoned women reveal the story of their shame, in all its detail, and tells them—that it is of no consequence what the effect of the recital may be on them; provided they do not consent! He adds: "It is equally safe to the conscience of the confessor, to read what may be written on luxury or debauchery, in *books on morality!*" After saying, that he who by fraud, solicitation, address or promise of marriage, betrays a woman, is bound to make reparation *only* in case the thing is made public; he adds: "If, however, his crime has remained absolutely secret, it is more than probable that, in his conscience, the seducer is bound to make no reparation." (p. 406.)

In vol. II., p. 333, there is a combination of infamy,

* It is with such maxims, that the confessors have excited the Ravaillacs, Saint Bartholomew's massacres, insurrections of the people against legitimate authority, and the civil wars which have defiled Europe with blood, and excited all that spirit of encroachment and intolerance which animates the Romish priesthood

which no other class of men, but Roman Catholic theologians could conceive! "For a marriage to be valid, there must be an internal mutual consent; for marriage is a legitimate contract that is essentially true of two persons. If, therefore, the consent of either party were feigned or fictitious, the marriage would be void." (Vol. ii., p. 216.)

We now come to the work of Mr. Bouvier, which is designed for the instruction of the seminaries and colleges which are founded or directed by Jesuits. The book bears this title: "Institutiones Philosophiæ ad usum Collegiorum et Seminariorum. Autore J. B. Bouvier, episcopo Cenomanensis, sexta edit. Parisiis, Meguinion, Junior, 1841." Bouvier was appointed Bishop of Mans, and afterwards created a Roman Count by Pope Gregory XVI.

From the extracts we shall give from this work, the reader will be abundantly able to discover, what at this day, are the principles of morality, religion, philosophy, and politics of the Romish bishops and priests of the United States; and what will be the results of confession and education entrusted to men and women who are secretly teaching such doctrines.

As regards politics, the Bishop of Mans thus instructs: he terms the sovereignty of the people an impious principle which has given rise to deplorable calamities: "Ex quo lugendæ provenerunt calamitates." Supreme authority proceeds from God and can proceed only from God, because civil power is but the image of paternal power, which proceeds evidently from God. God alone can exercise supreme authority, because He alone is superior to it (that is the priests in his name).*

It is a legal proverb in Rome "Legislator von tenteur." The Lawgiver is not bounded.

There is nothing the prince may not do when circumstances require it. Princes are not properly bound by any civil laws, for they could be bound only by laws made by others. Now, that cannot be, since they own no superior in temporal matters; and their own laws cannot oblige them, because no one obliges himself. (p. 605.) Subjects ought, whenever the legitimate prince may order it, to take up arms against the usurper, combat, overthrow and expel him, if he can. Nay, more; any individual ought to kill him as a public malefactor, if the legitimate prince should expressly command it.*

The editor of the "Roman Catholic Review" in this country, rightly expounded this Romish doctrine when he said, "the Pope is the proper authority to decide whether the constitution of this country is, or is not, repugnant to the laws of God." Now, as we see by the established dogma of the Romish church, any individual might, with a safe conscience, perpetrate any enormity against the interest of the state, with impunity. "In these 'Philosophical Institutes,' the obscenity is so abominable, that the bishop, after directing confessors how to put questions to the other sex on the validity of matrimony, directs them to an infallible means to preserve themselves from danger. This is by a prayer addressed to the Holy Virgin Mary, of which he gives the formula.

We have now made the reader acquainted with the works on moral theological philosophy, which are put at this present time in the hands of every priest in the Roman Catholic seminaries of the United States, as the rule they are to follow in the direction of the souls con-

* Arma assumere, illum espugnare, vincere et espellere, si possint; imo privatim illum tanquam publicum malefactorem occidere, si legitimus princeps id expresse jubet. (p. 628.)

fided to their care. By examining the writings of Car dinal Tolet, Fillicius, Tambourini, Emmanuel Sa, Escobar, Businbaum, Molino, Toletanus and other Romish authors, it is found that cases of conscience and inquisitorial curiosity forms the most important branch of their theology, by seeking the most secret thoughts of the mind.

There is a work called, "La Confession Coupeé, or, an easy method of preparing for particular and general confessions; invented by the reverend father Saint Christopher Leuterbrever, a friar of the order of St. Francis: with a treatise on the most common sins among married people." (Paris: 1739. 18mo.) This book is put into the hands of children called to make a general confession, at the time of first mass.

It contains some thousands of sins, with which children are made acquainted, many of which grown persons should be ignorant all their lives. "Each sin is printed on one side only of the leaf, cut into little slips which could be raised and folded to point out the sins of which any one might be guilty!" Cardinal Fleury thus shows the depravity of the confession: "With regard to sins which could be excused, the remedy is an easy absolution. Sometimes he is told that he sins indeed, but that the remedy is easy, and he may sin every day, by confessing every day." Would the people be afraid of the ague, if it could be cured by merely swallowing a glass of water? Or, would any one be afraid to rob or murder, if he could get off by washing his hands? Confession is almost as easy, where you have only to whisper a word in the ear of the priest, without fearing a postponement of absolution; without any painful expiation, or the necessity of missing the opportunity. You may wear a scapulary, tell your beads or say some famous prayer every day, without forgiving your enemy, restoring ill-acquired wealth, or quitting your concubine.*

With a view of ascertaining sins of which the penitents are ignorant, the confessors teach them the knowledge of them. It is this knowledge of vice, so imparted, that leads to all the immoralities between priests and women: opportunity invites to crime, both parties being sure that no revelation of their guilt will be made, while they are equally interested in keeping the secret.

"When is it lawful for the confessor to make use of the knowledge acquired in confession? *Answer*: When the sinner is by no means discovered; also, when no grievance is occasioned to him or another; in fine, when nothing intervenes to render confession odious.†" In like manner, if he should learn from confession that, heresies are being spread in his parish; that certain vices and sins are creeping on, he will be able by general instructions and monitions, to guard the faithful against such sins, so as not to reveal the person.‡

"But is the condition of educating the offspring in heresy repugnant to the substance of matrimony, namely, that the sons may follow their heretical father in his sect, and the daughters their Catholic mother? *Answer*. Daelman observes, that, if the Catholic party entering matrimony under such condition, directly intended the education of her offspring in heresy, the marriage would be invalid; whence it is supposed, he says, that she only obliges herself not to prevent such education."

Then after giving the opinions of other Roman Catholic theologians, to the same end, Dens proceeds:

* See Fleury's Discours sur l' Histoire Ecce disc. viii., n. 14.

† Dens, t. vi., p. 238.

‡ Dens, t. vi., p. 238.

"In the meantime, this kind of stipulation is null, since it is repugnant to the obligations of parents; and although some endeavor to excuse such compact, whilst the Catholic party only obliges herself to permit such education for the sake of avoiding greater evil in a community where Catholics and heretics lived mingled together; however, we must say with Pontius, Braunman, and Reiffenstuel, that such marriage with express or tacit compact, or under the condition, 'that either all, or any of the children, for instance the males, be educated in the sect of their heretical father' is *always* and *everywhere* unlawful, most iniquitous, and grievously sinful, against the natural obligations of parents, and against the divine and ecclesiastical law; for every parent is bound piously to take care that the offspring be educated in the true faith, and acquire the necessary means for salvation; therefore she is bound by no obligation to permit the education of her offspring in a *damnable sect!* Nor does the usage and custom openly existing in several places, make against this; for this compact is against divine law, against which even immemorial custom operates nothing." (Dens, t. vii., pp. 144–5.)

"Take notice that if a Catholic knowingly contract marriage with a heretic, he cannot on that head separate himself from her, because he has renounced the right of divorce; except however, unless promised her conversion, and would not stand to her promise: in like manner, if the Catholic knows that he is in imminent danger of losing the faith, by cohabiting with the heretic. (Dens, t. vii., p. 180.) Here we learn, that, if a Protestant woman, who has married a Roman Catholic, refuses to renounce her religion, at the dictation of the priest, the marriage is invalid, and the husband may sue for a divorce.

So that any Catholic can dissolve his marriage with a heretic, by telling the priest, his faith is in danger!

"What is understood by reserved cases? *Answer.*—Certain sins, the sacramental absolution of which the superior specially reserves to himself. This simple reservation is not a censure, since it is not properly a punishment, but a simple negation of approbation or jurisdiction. (Dens, t. vi., p. 263.)

"Who can reserve sins? *Answer.* That superior for whom it is competent to grant approbation or jurisdiction to absolve from sins. The Supreme Pontiff determines the reserved cases for the universal church; the Bishop for his own diocese; the superiors of regulars can reserve cases for their own subjects, but according to the limitation of Clement the VIIIth." (Dens, t. vi., p. 270.)*

Rev. Pierce Connelly, M. A., was formerly a clergyman of the Episcopal Church of the United States, and rector of Trinity, Natchez. It appears that more than fifteen years ago he became a Roman Catholic. The Earl of Shrewsbury stood sponsor for him on entering the Church of Rome, and he became his lordship's domestic chaplain. He has now renounced the communion of Rome, and with propriety addresses to the Earl of Shrewsbury his Reasons for abjuring the allegiance to the See of Rome.

Mr. Connelly says: "I know this same Church of Rome in its petty schemes of anarchy in families more hateful and more devilish than when it deals with nations. I have seen priests and bishops of the Church of Rome,

* Here in the United States, (as we have shown,) each Romish bishop, makes out his own formula for confession; reserving what monstrous sins he pleases, for his own absolution. This is printed and may be found in the pocket of every priest.

their own convictions disregarded, and all responsibility to God and society thrown off, in the instinct of hostility to man's natural relationships; in spite, too, in one instance, of the private commands of the Pope—I have seen them band together, for the mere sake of a legacy or a life-interest, to break down laws which are looked upon even by savages as the most sacred of all, divine or human.

"I have known a husband taught to deal double in the sacred matters of religion with his high-born wife, a brother with his high-born sisters, wives with their husbands and daughters, without number, with their trusting parents. I have seen clerical inviolability to mean nothing less than license and impurity. I have read to the pure and simple-minded Cardinal Prefect of the Propaganda a narrative written to a pious lay-friend by a respected Roman priest, of such enormities of lust in his fallen priests around him, that the reading of them took away my breath, to be answered, '*Caro mio*,' I know it, I know it all, and worse than all, but nothing could be done!

"I have known a priest, here in England, practice Liguori simply as an amateur of wickedness, just as he would try poison upon cats or dogs. I have known this creature get up, and very successfully, a miracle (I have proof in his own hand-writing) at the very moment when, as a brother priest satisfied me, he was experimenting in seduction, 'but nothing could be done!'

"I have known a priest received and honored at a prince-bishop's table, when the host knew him to have seduced a member of his own family! but *nothing could be done.*

"I have been mocked by dean and bishop for denouncing a young priest, in whose bed-room, and before there had been time to dress himself, in broad day, in England, under a convent-roof, I had myself found a young nun, apparently as much at home as her confessor was himself."

How many such sights might be witnessed in our country, could the convents be suddenly uncovered!

"In the rear of Allegany town," says the *Richmond Telegraph*, of 1846, "and in full view of Pittsburgh, is a Catholic nunnery, one of these schools of tyranny, superstition and pollution. An event has recently occurred which has suddenly scattered the priest and the whole community. A gentleman, residing in the east, had been induced by fair statements to place his daughter in the nunnery to be educated. Much time elapsed, he had often written to her, but no answer came. He set off for the nunnery to see her. The lady superior, accustomed to duplicity, told him she was not at home. He insisted on knowing where she was, and finally the abbess told him that she was sick in bed and could not be seen. He demanded a sight of her in a tone and spirit which the lady-superior thought it imprudent to resist, and being shown to her room, behold, there was the once healthy and promising daughter—*with an infant!* His indignation was so aroused, that he uttered threats in regard to the safety of the establishment, and the next morning not an individual was found there."

Mr. Connelly further says:

"I have been forced to let pass, without even ecclesiastical rebuke, a priest's attempt upon the chastity of my own wife, the mother of my children, and to find instead only sure means taken to prevent the communication to me of any similar attempts!

"This is a part of what has come within my own experience, but it is not the worst of that sad experience.

"I have seen priests of mean abilities, of coarse natures and gross breeding, practice upon pure and highly-gifted women of the upper ranks, married and unmarried, the teachings of their treacherous and impure casuistry, with a success which seemed more than human.

"I have seen these priests impose their pretendedly divine authority, and sustain it by mock miracles, for ends that were simply devilish. I have had poured into my ears what can never be uttered, and what ought not to be believed, but was only too plainly true; and I have seen that all that is most deplorable is not an accident, but a result, an inevitable result, and a *confessedly* inevitable result of the working of the practical system of the Church of Rome, with all its stupendous machinery of mischief; and the system is *irrevocable* and *irremediable!*"

"There are throughout Spain *Moral Academies*, which are colleges or assemblies of Father Confessors in which each proposes some moral cause which has happened to him in confession, with an exact and particular account of the confession, without mentioning the penitent's name. This question is propounded and each member delivers his opinion upon it. This is constantly practised every Friday. When the case is intricate and extraordinary, they send it to the great Academy, a college composed of sixteen casuistical doctors and four professors of divinity; by them the case is debated and the resolution entered on the Books of the Academy. I was a member," says Gavin,* "three years of the Academy of

* Anthony Gavin a secular priest in the University of Zaragosa, in Arragon, Spain.

Holy Trinity founded by the Archbishop of Gamboa. I was ordained before I was twenty-three years old, and at the same time licensed to hear confessions of both sexes. I entered this Academy as soon as possible and found that every member when chosen had to promise upon the word of a priest, to give the whole Assembly a faithful account of all the private confessions heard the week before, which have anything difficult yet not so as to mention the penitent's name. The secretary enters all the cases in a book, which is printed every three years. The Academy of Holy Trinity, is composed of twenty members; so each member becomes acquainted with many hundred private confessions, not made to himself. There is no confession which may not be lawfully revealed, (provided the confessor does not discover the penitent,) and the only reason for enjoining and keeping secrecy, is the hazard the penitent may run by the discovery.

"Among the private cases recorded in the Academy's book, is that of a woman, who leading a life of infamy with the priests, went to confess to escape the censure of the Church. 'I went,' she relates, 'to an old father he was easy and gave me a certificate of confession on my promising to pay him a pistole, without inquiring into the matter and without it, I satisfied the curate of the parish. But last year, I went to confess and the confessor was very strict; he would not give me absolution because I was a sinner, but I gave him five pistoles for ten masses and then he told me, that a confessor's duty was to take care of souls in Purgatory, and upon that account, he could not refuse me absolution. So by that I escaped the censure of the church. I stole from the church a chalice by the advice of the said confessor, and he used the money I got for the silver, and I did converse with him unlawfully, several times, in the church. To this, I must add an infinite number of sins, in thought, word, and deed, etc.' The confessor had destroyed this woman and made away with the property willed her, by her father. But the reverend Fathers of the Academy decided, that the friar had nothing of his own, and at his death was obliged to leave everything to the convent, therefore he was not to blame; and as to the woman, she was not required to make any restitution. In the fourth case of private confession, was that of a priest about to die in 1710. "My thoughts" says he, "have been impure since I first began to hear confession. . . . . My actions have been the most criminal among mankind."

"Every priest had a list of the handsomest women in his parish, and when he had a fancy to see any woman remarkable for her beauty in another parish, the priest sent for her to his own house. So we served one another for twelve years. Our method has been to persuade their fathers and husbands not to hinder their spiritual comfort. I have spared no woman for whom I had a fancy, and many of other parishes, I cannot tell the number!"

"The case of the sacrament's dog was another before the Moral Academy for discussion. It appears that in a Dominican convent, a woman went to receive the sacrament, accompanied by her lap-dog; and as the dog looked up and began to bark, the friar dropped the wafer into its mouth, instead of that of his mistress. In the alarm of both lady and friar, the reverend prior of the convent was called, who ordered the cross and two lighted candles to be brought, and had the dog carried in the form of a procession to the vestry, and there to be retained until he had digested the wafer, and then he must be killed. The devotee objected to the killing of her dog; the case came before the Inquisitors, and to the grief of the woman, the dog was sent to the Inquisition!" *

We conclude our citations from Romish writers upon the confessional, with the following: "What is the seal of the sacramental confession? It is the obligation or duty of concealing those things which are learned from sacramental confession." Can a case be given, in which it is lawful to break the sacramental seal? *Answer:* It cannot; although the life or safety of a man depended thereon, or even the destruction of the commonwealth; nor can the supreme pontiff give dispensation in this; so that, on that account, this secret of the seal is more binding than the obligation of an oath, a vow, a natural secret, etc.; and that by the positive will of God."†

We shall find this strong language to mean that the priests keep the secret or not, as it promotes the interest of the church! "What answer, then, ought a confessor to give, when questioned concerning a truth, which he knows from sacramental confession only? *Answer: He ought to answer that he does not know it, and, if necessary, to confirm the same with an oath! Objection:* It is in no case lawful to tell a lie; but that confessor would be guilty of a lie, because he knows the truth; therefore, etc. *Answer:* I deny the minor, because such a confessor is questioned as a man; but now he does not know that truth as a man, though he knows it as God, says St. Thomas, and that is the free and natural meaning of the answer; for when he is asked, or when he answers outside confession, he is considered as a man. Here we observe, that the vile priest asserts that he is God, while hearing a penitent!

* Gavin. † Dens, vol. vi.

"What if a confessor were directly asked whether he knows it through sacramental confession? *Answer:* In this case he ought to give no answer; reject the question as impious; or he could even say, absolutely not relatively to the question, I know nothing; because the word I restricts to his human knowledge." *

"But if any one should disclose his sins to a confessor, with the intention of mocking him, or of drawing him into an alliance with him in the execution of a bad design? *Answer:* The seal does not result therefrom, because the confession is not sacramental. Thus, as Dominick Soto relates, it has been decided at Rome, in a case in which some one went to a confessor with the intention of drawing him into a conspiracy against the Pope.† In fine all things are reduced indirectly to the seal, by the revealing of which the sacrament would be rendered odious, according to the manners of the country and the changes of the times; and thus Steyart observes, that some things are at one time opposed to the seal, which at another time are *not* considered as such." (Dens.)‡

"Does a confessor, relating the sins which he has heard in confession, act contrary to the seal? *Answer:* If the sinner or person can by no means be discovered, not even in general, nor any prejudice to himself happen therefrom,

* Dens. † Dens.

‡ So, we find, that while the seal would prevent a Romish priest from disclosing a conspiracy, which was designed against the lives of the citizens or government of the United States, he is free to violate it at any time, when the Pope or the interests of his church require it. Hence a papist can enter a confession of his intention to take the life of a particular individual, either by assassination or poison, in our country, and return after the commission of the deed, make a confession of the fact, and be absolved from the crime!

he does not act contrary to the seal, because the seal has reference to the penitent or sinner." Dens.

"Lastly take note, that since the restriction is made to carnal sins, the confessor will be able to give valid absolution to his accomplice in other sins, namely, in theft, in homicide, etc.* A confessor has seduced his penitent to the commission of carnal sin, not in confession, nor by occasion of confession, but from some other extraordinary occasion: is he to be denounced? *Answer: No.* If he had tampered with her, from his knowledge of confession, it would be a different thing; because, for instance, he knows that person, from her confession, to be given to carnal sins.† For which reason, Steyart reminds us that a confessor can ask a penitent, who confesses that she has sinned with a priest, or has been seduced by him to the commission of carnal sin, whether that priest was her confessor, or had seduced her in the confessional."

On the absolution of an accomplice. "Let it be observed, that in case of danger of death, no confessor, though he may otherwise have the power of absolving from reserved cases, may or can absolve his accomplice in any external mortal sin against chastity, committed by the accomplice with the confessor himself." This case of an accomplice is *not* placed amongst the reserved cases, because the bishop does *not* reserve the absolution.

We learn, further, that while the penitent is bound not to disclose what she has heard from the priest in the confession, the priest is bound only by his interest. The confessor, as we are informed by Dens, begins, by saying he is bound to inviolable secresy, but ends by showing that there is no secresy whatever. It is beyond all ques-

* Dens. † P. Antoine.

tion the inviolable secresy enjoined on penitents, which has and must ever cause the gross immoralities of the confessional. In this way, this specious pretence that the confessor holds out of his obligation to secresy, which has deceived and beguiled mankind, and is now doing it in these United States.

This theological book of Dens, like all the Romish authors, is published in the Latin language, but it can be found in the Catholic book-stores in our country, where any scholar may procure and read it. It is in the hands of every Romish confessor in our land.

CHAPTER III.

CONVENTS EXPOSED BY ROMISH WRITERS.

The Age required—Examination—Ceremony—The Consecration of Nuns—Romish Authority—Black Veil—Nuptial Character—What Takes Place—The Polluting Character—The Ring—The Veil—The Crown—Eastern Custom—The Prayer—The Curse—The Mass—The Breviary—The Abbess—Confessional—Penance—Gother on Mortal Sin—What a Nun should do when there against her Will—The Nuns' Danger—Confessor may Fall—The Bishop makes his Form of Confession for this Country—Virgin Nuns' Spouse—St. Mary De Pazzi—Nuns Immaculate—Horrors of Marriage—The Grate—The Suffering—The Saints Fortunes—Abnegation of Self—no Will for Nuns—External Mortification—Sanctification of the Eyes—Of the Appetite—Hearing—Smelling—Touch—Flogging Nuns—Torture Against Sleep—Poverty—Danger of Relatives—Secrets of the Convents—Love—The Grate to be Shunned—The Prison—Spiritual Reading—Confess Fully—The Girl who Concealed—The Eucharist is God—Holy Mary—Her Gorshipers—The Rosary—Indulgence—The Abbess—Rigors—Theatricals—Law should Break them up.

THE tender age of sixteen, is all that the Council of Trent requires, in a male or female, in order to make a profession of the monastic life! (See Session xxv. chap. xv.) At the same Session, chap. xvi., we read: "that if a monk or nun, through force or fear, should take the vows under the age appointed by law, they shall not be heard until within five years of their profession!"

The poor child whose physical system is yet undeveloped, then has the duties and cares of married life freely discussed, and denounced by the bishop, as interfering with her soul's health.

Thus wooed and won, a young and handsome girl, the daughter of a nobleman in England, entered the cloister of her own choice! An eye-witness described the scene as truly affecting. The church was strewn with flowers to the altar—the strangers gazed—the cardinal gave his blessing—the priests, their flattery—the friends, their tears; and, for that ceremony, the deluded girl was a great heroine! Every eye was moistened as she chanted, in soft recitative, her irrevocable vows! Her diamonds were taken from her beautiful hair, which hung in luxuriant tresses on her shoulders. The grate to entomb her was opened! The abbess and her black train of nuns, welcomed her in their choral strain. She renounced her name and title; and under the solemn benediction of the cardinal, and the last embrace of her friends, she passed to that bourne from whence she was never to return.

A panel behind the high altar now opened, and she appeared at the grate again, despoiled of all her jewels and elegant attire, with her beautiful hair all shorn from her head, by the merciless sisters—who hastened to invest her with the sober robe of the nuns—the white coif and the novitiate veil.

She was last seen at the little postern gate of the convent, to receive the sympathy, the praise, and the congratulations of friends; who were expected to pay their compliments to the new "spouse of heaven!" But this, reader, is but the outward pomp, and is as much as a Protestant can ever see. Now, let Liguori and other Roman Catholic authorities tell the rest.

The ceremony to which we have alluded, was the taking of the white, or first veil. How is it with the black veil? We shall see. In the *Pontificate Romanum*,* we

* Pontificate Romanum, Pars Prima De Benedictione et Consecratione Virginium, Brussels, 1735. Fayes' Romish Rites, and Officers and Legends, London, 1839.

learn the form of the Consecration of Nuns. It says: "That the evening before the day of the benediction, or on the morning before, the pontiff vests himself for mass, and the virgins are presented in some convenient place, where he questions them, individually, as to their purpose to remain virgins; and each one apart, by herself, concerning her life and conscience, and her *carnal integrity*." They are also questioned in regard to age; as to whether they are five and twenty, but the age varies in different countries. The rubric then states how the vestments, jewels, rings, etc., to be blessed, are laid first on the Epistle side of the altar; matrons are appointed bridesmaids, and a pavilion is erected in the church, where the nuns assemble and are clothed in these hallowed vestments. Mark the *nuptial* character of this ceremony.

After mass the Arch-presbyter profanely chants: "Ye wise virgins, make ready your lamps; behold the bridegroom cometh; go ye forth to meet him."

The virgins hearing his voice, light their wax tapers, and, two by two, advance and are presented upon their knees, before the pontiff, by the arch-presbyter, who says: "Most reverend father, the Holy Catholic Mother Church demands that you vouchsafe to hallow and consecrate these present virgins, and *espouse them* to our Lord Jesus Christ, the Son of the Most High God."

The mitred pontiff says to the Arch-priest, "Dost thou know them to be worthy?" and being satisfactorily answered, he says to all standing around: "The Lord God and our Saviour Jesus Christ helping, we elect these virgins now before us, to bless them and consecrate and espouse them to our Lord Jesus Christ, the Son of the Most High God." Then the pontiff calls the virgins in chant, saying, "*Venite;*" they answer in latin, "And now we follow;" and rising, one by one, they proceed to the entrance of the choir and kneel outside. Then the pontiff calls on them a second time, in a louder tone, "*Venite.*" They answer, "And now we follow with the whole heart," and proceed to the centre of the choir, and then kneel. A third time the pontiff calls them, in a still louder voice, "*Venite filiæ, audite me:*" "Come my daughters, and I will teach you the fear of the Lord." They, rising, answer chanting: "And now we follow with the whole heart; we fear Thee: we seek to see Thy face. O Lord, confound us not; but do unto us according to Thy loving-kindness, and according to the multitude of Thy mercy." Chanting, they come nearer, and ascend to the presbytery and kneel before the pontiff and lowly bend their heads almost even to the ground; then, each raising her head slightly, chants: "Raise Thou me up, O Lord, according to Thy Word, that iniquity have no dominion over me." Then they rise, and the matron arranges them in a circle around the pontiff, who publicly interrogates them as to their vow of virginity, saying:

"Will you persevere in your purpose of holy virginity?"

They answer. "We will." Then each one kneels successively, and putting both her hands, joined between his hands, he says; "Dost thou promise ever to keep thy virginity? *Ans.*: "I promise." The pontiff: "Thanks be to God."

Each kisses his hand, rises, returns to her place and kneels. He then says to all: "Will ye be hallowed and consecrated, and espoused to the Lord Jesus Christ, the Son of the Most High God?" They all answer: "We will." The Litany and *Veni Creator*, follow. Then the virgins retire to their position, and the pontiff puts off his mitre and after various long collects, crossings, and hallows, proceeds to sprinkle the vestments of the virgins, which are then carried to their pavilion; where the virgins having divested themselves of their daily garments, put on the blessed ones. The pontiff then hallows the veils of the virgins; then he sprinkles the same; next, the rings—the marriage rings—saying:

"Creator Lord, send Thy bene†diction upon these rings; that those who shall wear the same, being fortified with celestial virtue, may maintain entire faith and unbroken fidelity, and, as the spouses of Jesus Christ, may guard the vow of their virginity and persevere in chastity." This is all repeated in latin.

The pontiff next hallows the necklaces, etc., and when these hallowings and sanctifications are through, the virgins, arrayed in the blessed vestment, the veils excepted, return, two and two, to the pontiff, chanting the Responsory, "The kingdom of this world, and all secular adorning, I have despised for the love of our Lord Jesus Christ." "R. Whom I have seen, whom I have loved, and in whom I have believed, in whom I have delighted." "My heart hath uttered a good word; I speak of my works to the King."*

Then the virgins are arranged by their bride-maids before the altar, on their knees, in the presence of the pontiff, their faces bent to the ground. The pontiff, without his mitre, rises, and facing the virgins, with his hands stretched out before his breast, repeats several prayers. We select some passages. "Look down, O Lord, on these thy handmaids, who, placing in thy hand the vow of their continence, make an offering of their devotion

* This last passage is a mistranslation of xiv. Psalm.

unto thee, from whom they themselves have received the desire to make this vow. For how else could their mind, compassed with mortal flesh, get the victory over the law of nature, the freedom of license, the force of custom, and the stimulants of youthful age?"

The following passage of this polluting service cannot be given in literal English:

" . . . . From the fountain of thy bountifulness has flowed this gift. That while the blessing still remained on holy matrimony, there should exist souls so sublime as to loathe . . . . (see Note A,) and earnestly to desire the sacrament of marriage, and yet not to imitate what is done in the marriage state, but love what is denoted thereby."

Again, "Blessed virginity confesses Him who is her Author, and rivalling the integrity of angels, has devoted herself to the *bridal chamber and the bed* of Him, ... who is the spouse of perpetual virginity, like as is the son of perpetual virginity."

The preliminaries ended, the pontiff sits, having put on his mitre. The virgins rise, and the first pair are presented by the bride-maids to the pontiff, before whom they kneel lowly, and having vowed to persevere in their purpose, the pontiff puts the veil over the head of each successively, saying, "Receive then the sacred veil whereby thou mayest be known to have condemned the world, and truly and humbly, with the whole endeavor of thy heart, to have subjected thyself as a *wife to Jesus Christ for ever*, who defend thee from all evil and bring thee to life eternal. Amen.

The two being veiled, remain on their knees, and sing, "He hath set his seal upon my forehead, that I should *admit no lover but Him.*" And so on, two by two, until all are veiled; after which he calls them, chanting in latin. "Come, my beloved, to be *wedded*; the winter is past, the turtle is singing, and the flourishing vines give smell." Here the virgins are again presented to the pontiff, two by two, by the bride-maids; and then taking the ring and the virgin's right hand in his left, and putting the ring on the ring-finger of her right hand, he espouses the same to Jesus Christ, saying to each severally, "I espouse thee to Jesus Christ, the Son of the Supreme Father, who keep thee *undefiled.* Therefore, receive the ring of faith, the seal of the Holy Ghost, so that thou be called the spouse of God, and if thou serve him faithfully, be crowned everlastingly. In nomine Pa † tri et Fi † lii et Spiritus † Sancti. Amen."

This done, the two still kneeling, sing, "I am espoused to him whom angels serve, and at whose beauty the sun and moon do marvel." The same is done by all until the whole are wedded; and now kneeling on their knees, they all at the same time lift up their right hands on high and show them, singing, "With his own ring hath he wedded me, my Lord Jesus Christ, and hath adorned me with a crown as his spouse."

The pontiff rising in his mitre, faces them, and says: "God the Father Almighty, creator of heaven and earth, who hath vouchsafed to choose you to an *espousalship* like that of the blessed Mary, mother of our Lord Jesus Christ, hal † low you; that in the presen ce of God and his angels, you may preserve, untouched and undefiled, the virginity you have professed, and hold on your purpose, love chastity, and keep patience, that you may merit the crown of virginity. Through the same Christ our Lord. Amen."

Next follows the ceremony of crowning, which anciently in the Western and to this day in the Eastern churches, is as essential a part of the marriage ceremony as the putting on the ring.

After this is done, the virgins rise and chant: "Lo, what I longed for, I now enjoy; what I have hoped for, I now hold; I am joined in heaven to him whom I have loved while on earth, with my whole devotion." Then the pontiff joining his hands before his breast, pronounces over the virgins two benedictions, while they stand, lowly bending their heads. A few extracts from these benedictions will be sufficient. "O God prepare them under the governance of thy wisdom for all the work of virtue and glory, that overcoming the enticements of the flesh, and rejecting forbidden concubinage, they may inherit the indissoluble *copula* of thy Son Jesus Christ our Lord." "Let the showers of thy heavenly grace extinguish in them all hurtful heat, and kindle up in them the light of abiding chastity; let not the modest face be exposed to scandal, nor negligence afford to the incautious occasions of falling." "God . . . . . make you strong when frail; strengthen you when weak, and govern your minds with piety, direct your ways, etc., that, when you enter the *bed-chamber* of your spouse . . . . . he may discover in you nothing hidden, nothing filthy, nothing corrupt, nothing disgraceful . . . . . that when the day of repayment of the just, the retribution of the bad, shall come avenging fire, may find in you nothing to burn, but divine goodness what to crown, as being those *whom a religious life has already cleansed in this world;* so that when about to ascend the tribunal of the eternal king, you may have protection with those who follow the lamb and sing the new song without ceasing; there to receive the reward after labor, and remain forever in the regions of the living. Amen."

The benediction over, the pontiff sits down and pronounces his curse on any who may draw away from the banner of chastity, or on any who may purloin their goods, or hinder them from possessing their goods in quiet. This is the curse.

"By the authority of Almighty God and his holy apostles, Peter and Paul, we solemnly forbid, under pain of anathema, that any one draw away these present virgins or holy nuns from the divine service to which they have devoted themselves, under the banner of chastity; or that any one purloin their goods or hinder their possessing them, unmolested: but if any one shall dare attempt such a thing, let him be accursed at home and abroad; accursed in the city and in the field; accursed in waking and sleeping; accursed in eating and drinking; accursed in walking and sitting; cursed be his flesh, his bones and from the crown of his head to the soles of his feet, let him have no soundness. Come upon him, the malediction, which by Moses in the law, the Lord laid on the sons of iniquity. Be his name blotted out from the book of the living, and not be written with the righteous. His portion and inheritance be with Cain the fratricide, with Dathan and Abiram, with Ananias and Sapphira, with Simon the sorcerer, and with Judas the traitor, and with those who have said to God, depart from us, we desire not the knowledge of thy ways. Let him perish in the day of judgment, and let everlasting fire devour him, with the devil and his angels, unless he make restitution and come to amendment. *Fiat, Fiat.* So be it, so be it." Next, mass and the offertory is observed. That is, a lighted candle is presented to the pontiff, by each nun. Then they are ordained to the faculty of beginning the sacred hours. The pontiff "sits down, having put on his mitre, and delivers to them the breviary, which they touch with both hands, while he says: "Receive ye this book, that ye may begin the canonical hours and read the office in the church. In the name of the Fa † ther and of the † Son and of the Holy † Ghost. Amen."

Last of all (after other ceremonies,) the virgins return to the gates of the monastery, where they kneel before the pontiff, who present them to the abbess, who also kneels, while he says: "Take care how thou keepest these virgins, who are consecrated to God; and that thou again present them to him *immaculate;* as thou shalt render account for them before the tribunal of their *husband*, the judge that is to come.*

We have now, with some slight abridgment, given the service of the final consecration of nuns; a ceremony which is taking place in every nunnery between the nuns and the bishop.

The nun being now fully espoused, and the Breviary put in her hand, we naturally wish to know more of that interesting work. It is the service-book of the popish church, consisting of the offices of matins, prime, third, sixth, nones, vespers, and complines; that is of seven hours, to accord with the saying of David, Psalm cxix., "Seven times a day do I praise thee." We shall soon see how these lessons in the Breviary, praise God; first remarking that so inestimable is the value put upon the last revision of this work, which was done under Pope Urban VIII. in 1631, that the Romish church commands it to be read by all of both sexes who have professed in any of the regular orders; and all deacons, sub-deacons, and

* "Pontificale Romanum, Pars Prima de Benedictione et Consecratione Virginium." Brussels, 1735. Foye's Romish Rites and Offices. Lond. 1839.

priests, are bound to repeat in public or private the whole service of the day out of the Breviary, on pain of mortal sin. We have seen that the nun has been especially enjoined to this office of opening the canonical hours.

In the service appointed for August 30, we find the Legend of St. Rose of Lima, who, it states, "at the age of *five* made a vow of perpetual virginity, and both before and since, Pope Clement the Xth enrolled her in the catalogue of Holy Virgins." In the pope's bull of canonization, he states that "on Palm Sunday when Rose was absorbed in meditation, in the chapel of the Blessed Virgin of the Rosary, *her lover* thus addressed her: 'Rose of my heart, be *my love.*' The virgin trembled at the sweet voice of her Divine Spouse, and at the instant, she heard the voice of the mother of God, *wishing her joy* and saying, '*Rose, it is no mean honor which this my son proposes to you.*'"*

For 15th October, St. Teresa Virgin. The lesson says, that this virgin "used to weep over the darkness of infidels and heretics; and to appease the wrath of Divine vengeance, she used to dedicate to God for their salvation the voluntary tortures of her own body. She saw an angel transpiercing her heart and soul with a fiery dart, and *heard* Christ say to her, giving her his right hand, 'Thou shalt be henceforth zealous for mine honor, as my wife indeed!'" She was canonized by Pope Gregory XV., 1614.†

The absurd fable of the spiritual espousals of St.

* The bull which canonized this saint, is dated 12th of April, 1761, and is signed by Clement and thirty-five cardinals. See Bullarium Magnum. Fol. Lux. 1727. The translation is by Rev. P. Townsend Ponell.

† See Acta Sanctorum Octobris. Brussels, 1845.

Veronica, who is said to have lived from 1660 to 1727, the details of which are such an admixture of puerility and profanity, that we refrain from copying them. It is palpably evident, however, that such impious fabrications, although belonging to a past age, yet possess a living interest with Romanists of the present time, since we find Cardinal Wiseman, in 1846, endorsing them, in the following words: "This spiritual union with certain devout souls, God has been pleased to manifest to them by mere visible signs, *accompanied by formalities like those used in ordinary marriages.*"*

As this Breviary is the only *Bible* of the convents and nunneries of the United States, the reader will find more of its amorous and impure teachings in the Supplemental Chapter of this volume. Having seen the *latest* instructions of the Cardinal Archbishop, we turn now to the nun's "*Confessional.*" This is more important, from the fact that it is the confessional which begins with childhood, and assumes its most blighting influence just as a girl is becoming a young woman, which induces her to take the step which cannot be retraced; for when once the victim takes the veil, she is marked as a slave for ever.

We give the teaching of the Roman Catholic Church on this subject:†

PENANCE EXPOUNDED.

Q. What is the fourth sacrament? *A.* Penance.

Q. What warrant have you for doing acts of penance?

* For more information of the Breviary, see *Supplemental Chapter*.

† "An Abridgement of Christian Doctrine, with Proofs of Scripture for points controverted." Dublin, 1838. The preface is signed H. T. (Dr. Henry Tuberville, D.D., of the English College of Douay,) and the little book was re-published by the Rev. J. Doyle, D.D. This is a standard Catechism of Roman Catholics.

A. First, Apoc. ii. 4: "Thou hast left thy first charity; be mindful from whence thou art fallen, and *do penance.*" Secondly, Matt. iv. 17: "And Jesus began to preach and to say, Do ye penance, for the kingdom of heaven is at hand."

Q. What is the matter of the sacrament? *A.* The contrition as expressed, and confession of the penitent.

Q. What is the form of it? *A.* I absolve thee from thy sins, in the name of the Father, and of the Son, and of the Holy Ghost.

The catechiser goes on to say, what the effects of penance are: that it reconciles us to God, and either restores or increaseth grace. It proceeds:

Q. What is confession? *A.* It is a full, sincere and humble declaration of our sins to a priest, to obtain absolution.

Q. Is there any special good or comfort to man from confession? *A.* Very great, because to a mind laden with secret griefs, the best of her comforts is to disclose her case to some faithful friend; so to a soul laden with secret sins, one of the greatest comforts and best remedies possible is to have selected persons, ordained for that end by Christ himself, men of singular piety and learning, and *not questionable by any law*, of what they may hear in confession, to whom one may confess his sins, with an assurance both of comfort, correction and direction, for the amendment of his faults.

Q. What are the necessary conditions of a good confession? *A.* That it be short, diligent, humble, sorrowful, sincere and entire.

After explaining some of these conditions:

Q. How entire? *A.* By confessing, not only in what things we have sinned mortally, but also how often, as near as we are able to remember.

Q. What if a man do knowingly leave out any mortal sin in his confession, for *fear of shame?* *A.* He makes his whole confession void, and commits a great sacrilege, by *lying to the Holy Ghost*, and abusing the sacrament.

Q. How prove you that? *A.* By the example of Ananias and his wife, Sapphira, etc.

This popular exposition is strictly and carefully grounded on the highest authority of the Church of Rome—the Council of Trent—to which we will refer.

"*Sessio XIV. Cap. v. de Confessione.*—From the institution of the sacrament of penance, already explained, the Universal Church has always understood that the entire confession of sins was also instituted by the Lord, and is of divine right necessary to all who have fallen after baptism; because that our Lord Jesus Christ, when about to ascend from earth to heaven, left priests, His own vicars, as presidents and judges (sacerdotes sui ipsius vicarios reliquit, tanquam præsides et judices), before whom all the mortal crimes into which the faithful of Christ may have fallen should be brought, to the end that, according to the power of the keys, they my pronounce the sentence of remission or retention of sins. For it is certain that priests could not have exercised this judgment, the cause being unknown; neither, indeed, could they have observed equity in enjoining punishments, if they should have declared their sins in general only, and not rather specifically and singly. Hence it is gathered, that all the deadly sins of which after a diligent examination of themselves, they have consciousness, must needs be enumerated by penitents in confession, even though those sins be most hidden, and committed only against the two last precepts of the decalogue, which sometimes wound the soul more grievously, and are more dangerous than those which are committed outwardly. For venial sins, by which we are not excluded from the grace of God, and into which we more frequently fall, although they be rightly and profitably, and without any presumption declared in confession, as the custom of pious persons shows, yet may be passed over without guilt, and be expiated by many other remedies. But whereas all mortal sins, even those of thought, render men children of wrath, and enemies of God, it is necessary to seek also for the pardon of them all from God, with an open and modest confession; wherefore, while the faithful of Christ are anxious to confess all the sins which occur to the memory, they without doubt lay them all open before the mercy of God to be forgiven. But they who act otherwise, and knowingly keep back certain sins, set nothing before the divine bounty to be remitted through the priest. . . . It is certain that in the church nothing else is required of penitents, but that after each has examined himself diligently, and *examined all the folds and recesses of his conscience*, he confess those sins by which he shall remember that he has in a deadly manner offended his Lord and his God; whilst the other sins, which do not occur to him after diligent considering, are understood to be included as a whole in that same confession; for which sins we confidently say with the prophet, '*Ab occultis meis, munda me, Domine.* From my secret sins cleanse me, O Lord.'" . . .

"*Cap. VI. De ministro hujus Sacramenti, et Absolutione.*—But as respects the minister of this sacrament, the Holy Synod declares all these doctrines to be false, and utterly alien from the truth of the Gospel, which perniciously extend the ministry of the keys to any other men soever, besides bishops and priests. . . . It also teaches that *even priests who are held in deadly sins, through the virtue of the Holy Ghost, bestowed in ordination*, exercise the function of remitting sins, as the ministers of Christ, and that they *think erroneously who contend that this power exists not in bad priests.* But although the absolution of the priest is the dispensation of another's bounty, yet it is not a bare ministry only, whether of announcing the Gospel or of declaring that sins are remitted, but it is *after the manner of a 'judicial' act*, which by sentence *is pronounced by the priest as by a judge.* And, therefore, the penitent ought not to flatter himself concerning his own personal faith, as to think that, even though there be no contrition on his part, or no intention on the part of the priest acting seriously and absolving truly, he is nevertheless truly and in the eyes of God absolved on account of his faith alone; neither would faith without penance bestow any remission of sins, nor would he be otherwise than most negligent of his own salvation who should know that a priest but absolved him in jest, and should not sedulously seek for another who would act in earnest."

It will be observed that the penitent is to examine all the folds of his (or her) conscience;* and in order that no fold should be left unexamined, the church of Rome places in the hands of all her members—boys and girls just reaching years of puberty—certain questions or heads for self-examination. They may be found in any Roman Catholic manual of devotion, such, for instance, as "Challoner's Garden of the Soul." We cannot think

* Modesty must not interfere. De La Hogue *De Pœn*, says: "Pudorem illum prorsus humanum quantuscumque sit, a Pœnitente superandum esse, et nolenti denegandum esse absolutionem."—P. 168. Coyne's Dublin Ed. 1825.

of polluting our pages by transcribing the directions which a Roman Catholic bishop wrote, and which Roman Catholic bishops now place in the hands of Roman Catholic young American ladies, as a manual of devotion.

They will be found under the heads for self-examination upon the sixth (that is the seventh) commandment. The "Garden of the Soul," it must be remembered, is written by a bishop, is universally recommended, and is described "as the most popular prayer-book of the Roman Catholics."

We have also before us "A manual for Confession and Communion for those who frequent the Oratory of St. Philip Neri, King William Street, Strand," and from it we shall learn the kind of authority with which the confessor is represented as being invested:

DIRECTIONS TO BE OBSERVED IN MAKING THE CONFESSION.

1. "Having prepared yourself for confession, go to your confessor with great humility and modesty, and imagine to yourself that you are about to present yourself before Jesus Christ himself, who sees the depth of your heart, and will one day judge you. If you are obliged to wait, keep yourself all the time in devout silence and recollection, and renew your act of sorrow for your sins. Fancy yourself a criminal bound with chains, who has been tried and convicted, and is called before the judge whom he has insulted and offended.

2. "When at the feet of your confessor, kneel down with the greatest reverence and humility, imagining that you are at the *feet of Jesus* crucified, who desires to hear from your own lips, a sincere confession of all your sins, and is ready to pardon you for them, if you really repent of them, and to wash you in His own most pre-

5

cious blood, by means of His minister and the sacramental absolution. It is, indeed, true, that while the Word of God declares that "it is a shame even to speak of these things which are done in secret," popery not only authorizes sin, but gives occasion to practice it. What must be the effect of these books, which furnish the daily meditations of the professed penitents? Where is the self-respect of a woman who can prostrate herself at the feet of a man, and unveil the most secret and hidden feelings, as to God? Think, oh! think of the purity put upon such a test, called to violate the very instincts of nature, in making such a recital to a man! Dangerous at any time, but oh! how awful for those espoused nuns thus incarcerated, to be examined and re-examined, sifted and searched every day by men, who are themselves under professed vows of celibacy! The Rev. John Gother, a Roman Catholic, writing on confession, says:

"That in all mortal sins, he (the penitent) discovers the number, that is, how often he has fallen into each sort of sin; there being a great difference betwixt committing a sin twice or thrice, and twenty or thirty times . . . "That he explain such circumstances as change the nature of the sin, or at least considerably aggravate it; and, therefore, because there is a great difference betwixt robbing a church and another place; betwixt cheating or stealing five shillings and five hundred pounds; betwixt a married person and a single; in sins of impurity, etc., etc." He also gives minute directions for examination on the sixth and the seventh commandments.

St. Alphonsus M. Liguori, Bishop of St. Agatha and founder of the congregation of the Most Holy Redeemer, was born 1726, and died 1787. He was canonized with five others, by the late Pope Gregory XVI. in 1839.

This saint wrote a book, to which we have before referred, "The True Spouse of Christ, or, the Nun Sanctified by the Virtues of her State." As he is the model saint of Cardinal Wiseman, of England, and of all the Romish hierarchy in the United States, we proceed to give this high authority upon many important facts.

At page 549 he heads a section thus: "*What ought a person to do who finds she has become a nun against her inclination?* I answer: If at the time of your profession you had not a vocation, I would not have advised you to make the vows of a religieuse, but I would have advised you to suspend your resolution of going back to the world, and casting yourself into the many dangers of perdition found in the world. I now see you placed in the house of God, and made, either voluntarily or unwillingly, the spouse of Jesus Christ. I add: grant what you say is true; now that you are professed in a convent, and that it is *impossible for you to leave it*, tell me what you do wish to do. If you have embraced religion (i. e. become a nun), you must now remain with cheerfulness. If you abandon yourself to melancholy, you must lead a life of misery, and will expose yourself to great danger of suffering a hell here, and another hereafter. *You must then make a virtue of necessity.* And if the devil has brought you into religion (i. e. a nunnery) for your destruction, let it be your care to avail yourself of your holy state, for your salvation, and become a saint." Being asked his opinion regarding a person who had become a nun against her will, St. Francis de Sales answered: "It is true that this child, if she had not been obliged by her parents, would not have left the world; but this is of little importance, provided she knows that the *force* employed by her parents is more useful to her than the per mission to follow her will; for now she can say, 'If I had not lost such liberty, I should have lost true liberty.' The saint! meant to say, that had she not been compelled by her parents to become a nun, she would have remained in the world."

This canonized Jesuit has furnished various features of this system, which shows the most tremendous power wielded by the priest. To conceal anything from him from *fear* or *shame*, is called lying to the Holy Ghost; to him is given the absolute power to remit sin; the entire conscience must be revealed to him; the manuals in the nun's hands presuppose her guilty of things at which her purity recoils. She interrogates herself; have I done so and so? and how often? Then follow the indecent questions from her confessor, drilled in the same school of impurity.

The Romish authority admits there are nuns against their will. Take one of this class, forced into a life against which her nature recoils; with no sympathy, debarred the association of her fellow prisoners; ground down to a life of servile obedience; obliged, for the least deviation or omission of an Ave Maria, to kneel for hours, to kiss the ground before her superior's feet; to lick a cross upon the floor; to eat her food like a cat,* from a dish placed on the ground, without using her hands; the confessional, then, is the only relief her pained heart can positively find; the confessor, then, her only friend!

Dens' Theology, the text book of every Romish bishop and priest, has a clause headed: "On Just Causes for Promoting Sensuality." "Just causes," says Dens, "are

* To eat with cats is a punishment literally practised in the Capuchin monastries. The culprits sit on the ground in common with the cats, of which there are always a number in these houses.

the hearing of confessions; the reading of cases of conscience drawn up for a confessor; necessary or useful attendance on an invalid; but," he adds, "the confessor so affected, by the hearing of confessions, ought not on that account, to abstain from hearing them." The same writer has a chapter on the "proximate cause of sin." It is defined to be that which brings a moral or probable danger of mortal sin. He mentions several cases, as drunkenness, or conversing with a young woman. In this book it is deliberately taught, that it is only when a confessor falls as often as two or three times a month, that he is in any danger of *mortal* sin. Once a month is clearly allowed.

Another fact unknown to Protestants is, that every confessor, secular or regular, must have a license from the bishop before he can hear confession in a diocese.

The directions called Pagelle, differ according to the bishop's jurisdiction.

We have two specimens of these licenses, granted in 1836 and 1838, in Naples, and signed by two bishops. In these licenses we find special allusion to the danger of the confessor, as well as the reserved cases, in which the bishop reserves to himself, the power to absolve.

The power thus invested in the bishops is absolute. Not merely to exercise the right of enforcing their unchanging system of polluting theology, as Dens' or Bailey's, but to improve by Jesuit ingenuity, the means of enforcing their despotism upon the whole country.

In the work of St. Alphonsus M. Liguori, called the "Nun Sanctified," we read chapter 1, "On the excellence of virginity consecrated to God, in the religious state." Virgins who dedicate themselves to Christ, by commending to him the "lily of their purity," are as dear to God as his angels. Besides, whoever consecrates her virginity to Jesus Christ, becomes *his* spouse."

"A religieuse on the day of profession, is espoused to Jesus Christ, for the bishop says to the novice, 'I espouse thee to Jesus Christ; may he preserve thee inviolate. Receive, then, as his spouse, the ring of faith, that if thou serve him with fidelity, he may give thee an eternal crown.' We learn from St. Ambrose, that the virgin St. Agnes, when offered for husband the son of the Roman prefect, answered, 'she had found a better spouse.'"

He gives a number of instances where saints refused the crowned heads of Europe, Louis XI., Ferdinand XI., Henry Archduke of Austria, in order to espouse Jesus Christ!

Page 4 treats of the misfortunes of the married state, the associations of the family, the horrors of young children and servants, and says: "The greatest misfortune is to be in continual danger of losing the grace of God, and their own immortal souls."

Page 10: "To preserve her body and soul free from stain, a virgin must chastise her flesh, by fasting, abstinence, by disciplines, which is the saintly name of *scourging*, and other penitential works.

Page 522: "In correcting the religieux, attend to two things. The first is, not to have recourse to *chastisement*, (*i.e.* whipping) I mean *severe chastisement*, (*i.e.*, they may be whipped a little) unless when it is absolutely necessary for the amendment of a sister, or for the example of others, and then, of course, whip them severely.

"*Severe remedies*," he adds, "are applied to diseases otherwise incurable." So the Abbess flogs at her discretion!

Chapter II., "On the advantages of the Religious

State," St. Bernard is quoted. Page 19: "Is not that a holy state, in which a man lives more purely, falls more rarely, rises more speedily, walks more cautiously, is bedewed more frequently, rests more serenely, dies more confidently, is purged more quickly, and rewarded more abundantly." On each of these heads St. Alphonsus elaborates. "A religieuse performs these duties by obedience, that is, by the holy will of God. For in her rule, and in the *commands of her superior, she hears his voice.*" Page 23: "Jesus refreshed his spouse at prayers, communion, in the holy sacrament, and in the cell before the crucifix!" Page 26: "A religieuse in the convent enjoys a foretaste of paradise, *or suffers an anticipation of hell.*"

That is *to be* FORCED AGAINST THE INCLINATIONS OF NATURE, by the will of others!!! To be *distrusted, despised, reproved, and chastised by those with whom we live;* TO BE SHUT UP IN A PLACE OF CONFINEMENT, FROM WHICH IT IS IMPOSSIBLE TO ESCAPE;—in a word, it is to be in CONTINUED TORTURE WITHOUT A MOMENT'S PEACE. Page 26.

Page 28: ". . . Why wear the habit of a religieuse, if in heart and soul you be a secular? Why wear it, you Jesuit St. Alphonsus! why wear it? Because you have told her she cannot take it off; you have just told her *it is impossible to escape.*"

Page 32: "The religieuse suffers to render herself more acceptable to God. I hold as certain, that the greater number of seraphic thrones vacated by Lucifer and his associates, will be filled by *religieux.* Out of sixty, enrolled during the last century, in the catalogue of saints and honored as the blessed, all, with the exception of five or six, belonged to the religious orders."

Chapter III., "The religieux should belong entirely to God. The Redeemer bears every imperfection more patiently than a divided heart. 'Receive,' said the bishop at consecration of the veil, 'that thou admit no lover but him.' The church commands the religieux to change their names at their profession, that they may forget the world. If an earthly object steal into her heart, she should say: 'Begone pernicious affection, for another lover more noble, more faithful, and more acceptable than you has loved me before I could love him, and has taken possession of my soul: my spouse is the Lord, the king of heaven and earth; I am espoused to him whom angels serve.'" Thus are they taught to love the Lord Jesus Christ as a human suitor!

Page 37: "Who can behold virgins of noble family and splendid fortunes* despising the pomp and pleasures of the world, and shutting themselves up in a convent to live in poverty and abjection; who, I say, can behold these holy virgins, without exclaiming, 'This is the generation of them that seek the Lord.'"

Chapters V. and VI. are "On the danger to which an imperfect religieuse exposes her salvation." Page 75: "Oh, God! how many religieux are there, who, because they do not disengage their hearts from certain earthly attractions, never become saints." Page 85: "A religieuse should examine if they arise from familiarity with any person, within or without the monastery."

* One nun does not know the name of another: it is sister Mary Joseph, or sister Mary Magdalen. The property of wealthy nuns is immediately renounced to the convent, as well as their name. Immense wealth has thus accrued to these polluted institutions in our own country. It is in wealthy families that Jesuits make their insinuating addresses to entrap young ladies.

Chapter VII., "On abnegation of self-love," says: "If you receive a letter, abstain from opening it for some time. . . . If you desire to read the termination of an interesting narrative, defer it until another time. . . . If you feel inclined to look at an object, to pluck a flower, suppress these inclinations, for the love of Jesus Christ. . . . Father Leonard, of Port Maurice, relates that a servant of God performed *eight acts of mortification in eating an egg*, and, as a reward, eight degrees of grace, and as many of glory, were bestowed upon her." Page 99: "Nothing is more injurious than to be guided by their own will. 'Whoever,' says St. Bernard, 'constitutes himself his own master, becomes the disciple of a fool.'" Page 113: "Consider, in obeying your *superiors, that you obey God himself*, and that, in despising their commands, we despise the authority of our Divine Master, who has said, 'He that heareth you, heareth me.'—Luke x: 16. . . . When a religieuse receives a precept from her prelate, superior or confessor, she should immediately execute it, not only to please men, but principally to please God, whose will is made known to her by their command. In obeying their directions, she is more certain of obeying the will of God, than if an angel came down from heaven to manifest his will to her." Page 114: "It may be added, that there is more certainty of doing the will of God *by obedience to superiors, than by obedience to Jesus Christ, should He appear in person and give his commands;* because, should Jesus Christ appear to a religieuse, she would not be certain whether it was He that spoke, or an evil spirit." Page 122: "In a word, the only way by which a religieuse can be a saint, and be saved, is *to observe* her rule; *for her there is no other way that leads to salvation!!*"

(Jesus says, "I am the way: no man cometh to the Father, but by me.") Page 143: "The fourth and last degree of obedience is to obey with simplicity. St. Mary Magdalene de Pazzi says, 'Perfect obedience requires a soul without a will, and a will without an intellect." Page 145: "To regard as good whatever superiors command, is the *blind obedience* so much practised by the saints, and is the duty of every religieuse." Page 147: "To try the obedience of their *subjects*, superiors sometimes impose commands that are inexpedient, or even absurd. St. Francis commanded his disciples to plant cabbages with their roots uppermost."

Chapter VIII. treats of the "External mortification of the senses." Page 149: "Our Lord once said to St. Francis, of Assium, 'If you desire my love, use bitters as sweets and sweets as bitters." Page 151: "If we read the lives of saints, and see the works of penance which they performed, we shall be ashamed of the delicacy and of the reserve with which we chastise the flesh. In the lives of the ancient Fathers, we read of a large community of nuns who never tasted fruit or wine. Some of them took food only once every day; others never eat a meal, except after two or three days of rigorous abstinence; and all were clothed, and even slept, in hair-cloth. I do not require such austerities from the religieuse in the present day; but is it too much for them to *take the discipline several times in the week?*—to wear the chain round some part of the body till the hour of dinner? —not to approach the fire in winter—to abstain from fruit and sweetmeats, and, in honor of the Mother of God, to fast every Saturday on bread and water, or at least to be content with one dish? If you cannot (from ill-health) chasten your body by positive rigor, abstain, at least, from some lawful pleasure." Page 156: "To animate your fervor in the practice of mortification, I shall here place before your eyes what St. John Climacus saw in a monastery called the Prison of Penitents: 'I saw,' says the saint, 'some of them standing the whole night in the open air, to overcome sleep. I saw others with their eyes fixed on heaven, and with tears begging for mercy from God. Others stood with their hands bound behind their shoulders, and their heads bowed down, as if they were unworthy to raise their eyes to heaven. Others remained on ashes, with their heads beneath their knees, and beat the ground with their foreheads. Others deluged the floor with their tears. Others stood in the burning rays of the sun. Others, parched with thirst, were content with taking a few drops of water to prevent death. Others took a mouthful of bread, and then threw it out, saying, 'He who has been guilty of brutish actions is unworthy of the food of men.' Some had their cheeks furrowed by continual streams of tears, and others their eyes wasted away. Others struck their breasts with such violence that they began to spit blood; and I saw all with faces so pallid and emaciated, that they appeared to be so many corpses."

Then comes a section "On the sanctification of the eyes, and our modesty in general." Page 159: "'Through the eyes,' says St. Bernard, 'the deadly arrows of love enter.'—Sec. 13. St. Bernard, after being three years a novice, could not tell whether his cell was vaulted. The saints were particularly cautious not to look at persons of a different sex. St. Hugh, bishop, when compelled to speak with women, never looked them in the face. St. Clare would never fix her eyes on the face of a man. She was greatly afflicted, when, raising her eyes at the elevation of the host, she once involuntarily saw the face of the priest. St. Louis Gonzaga never looked his own mother in the face. For once looking deliberately at a woman who was gathering ears of corn, the abbot, Paster, was tormented for forty years by the temptation against chastity." Page 162: "Except in looking at such objects (sacred images, etc.), a religieuse should in general keep the eyes cast down. In conversing with men, she should never roll the eyes about to look at them, and much less to look at them a second time." Page 164: "A religieuse should be modest in her walk. 'Let your gait,' says St. Basil, 'be neither slow nor vehement.' Your walk, to be modest, must be grave—neither too quick nor too slow.'"

"On the mortification of the appetite," page 169, "Saint Gregory relates, that a certain nun, seeing in the garden a very fine lettuce, pulled and eat in opposition to her rule. She was instantly possessed of the devil, who tormented her grievously. Her companions called to her aid the holy Abbot Eqnitius, to whom the demon said, What evil have I done? I sat upon the lettuce; she came and eat it." Page 170: "Besides, he who gratifies the taste readily indulges the other senses; for, having lost the spirit of recollection, he will commit faults by indecent words and unbecoming gestures."

"On the mortification of the senses of hearing, smell, and touch," page 180, says: "Every fault committed by the indulgence of *touch*, exposes the soul to the danger of eternal death." Again: "*Hair clothes* are of various kinds; some are made of strong coarse hair, and others are bands or chains of brass or iron wire. The former may be injurious to persons of delicate constitutions, as Father Scaramelli remarks, they inflame the flesh and weaken the stomach. The latter may be worn on the arms, legs or shoulders, without injury to the health, but not on the breast or body. These are the ordinary species of hair cloth, and may be safely used by all. St. Rose of Lima, used a long hair shirt interwoven with needles, and carried a broad chain around her loins. St. Peter of Alcantara, wore on his shoulders a plate of iron, which was covered with sharp projections that kept the flesh in a continual state of laceration. Would it be too much for you to wear a small band of iron from morning to the hour of dinner?"*

Page 181: "*Disciplines* or *flagellations* are a species of mortification strongly recommended by St. Francis Sale, and universally adopted in religious communities of both sexes. All the modern saints, without a single exception, have continually practised this sort of penance. It is related of St. Lewis of Gonzaga, that he often scourged himself unto blood three times a day. Surely then it would not be too much for you to take the *discipline* once in the day, or at least three or four times in the week. *Vigils* or *Watchings* consist in the retrenchment of sleep. Of St. Peter of Alcantara we read, that for forty years he slept but one hour, or at most an hour and a half each night." Page 182: "The saints have not only curtailed sleep, but practised various mortifications in the manner of taking repose. The venerable sister Mary Crucified, of Sicily, used a pillow of thorns."

A religieuse should not seek a bed of down; if a straw bed be not injurious to her health, why should she require a mattrass of hair? St. Francis Borgia was obliged to

* This, reader, is rather harsh treatment for delicate American ladies; but here is the most unquestionable authority that they do it who are veiled victims.

remain all night under the snow which fell heavily. "Be assured," said the saint, "that though I suffered much in the body, I have been consoled in the spirit by the reflection that *God rejoiced in my pains!*"

As this "Nun Sanctified" is the book of St. Alphonsus Liguori, which has been translated and published for the use of English and American nuns and postulants, we wish every citizen of our land to understand more about it.

In the Roman Catholic Directory for 1846, p. 167, it is stated that before St. Alphonsus was canonized in 1839, all his writings, whether printed or inedited, were more than *twenty* times rigorously discussed by the sacred congregation of rites, which decreed that not one word in them had been worthy of censure. It is no wonder, then, that this recently made saint is the peculiar favorite of Cardinal Wiseman, and the Romish authorities of the U.S.

Rev. Blanco White, once a Roman Catholic, whom Dr. Newman describes "as year after year *holding the Lord in his hands*, dispensing *Him* to his people," and of whom he says: "I have the fullest confidence in his word, when he witnesses to facts, and facts which he knew:" "who had special means of knowing a Catholic country, and a man you can trust."* Mr. White's testimony was published in 1826 in three octavo volumes. "I cannot," says he, "find tints sufficiently dark to portray the miseries which I have witnessed in the convents. Crime, in spite of the spiked walls and prison grates, is there. The gates of the holy prison are for ever closed upon the inhabitants; force and shame await them wherever they might fly; the short vows of their profession, like a potent charm, bind them to one spot of earth,

* *See Lectures on the Present Position of Catholics in England, by John Henry Newman, D.D.* 1851.

and fix their *dwelling upon their grave.* The great poet who boasted that "slaves cannot live in England" forgot that superstition may baffle the most sacred laws of freedom. Slaves *do live* in England, and multiply daily by the same arts which fill all the convents abroad. In vain does the law of the land stretch a friendly hand to the victim; she may be dying to break her fetters; the mark of slavery is burnt by the Church into her soul, without the *possibility* of repenting of vows made for a whole life, of which she has seen but the dawn!

Page 206: " . . . The nun who leaves her relatives in effect and affection, shall obtain eternal beatitude in heaven, and a hundred fold on earth; she will leave a few, and find many sisters in religion; she will abandon a father and mother, and in return shall have God for her father and Mary for her mother." St. Benedict, who is regarded as the model for all monastic rules, recites the fifth commandment thus: "Honor all men," (instead of "Honor thy father and mother, that thy days may be long in the land which the Lord, thy God, giveth thee.") Page 206: "Hence, convinced that attachment to relatives is displeasing to God, the saints have sought to be wholly removed from them. For my part, says St. Teresa, I cannot conceive what consolation a nun can find in her relatives. By attachment to them she displeases God. When your parents and friends come to the grate, they certainly cannot make you a partaker of their worldly amusements; for you cannot go beyond the limits of your enclosure. Ah, if you keep aloof from them, what torrents of consolation and happiness would your spouse, Jesus, infuse into your soul."

"I saw," says Blanco White, "my own sister enter one of the gloomiest convents of Seville, where the nuns were obliged to sleep on a few planks raised about a foot from the ground, where the use of linen was forbidden near the body. The nuns wore coarse open sandals, through which the bare foot was exposed to the wet and cold; where the nearest relations were not allowed to see the face of the recluse, nor have any communication, except on certain days, when in the presence of another nun, and with a thick curtain close behind the double railing which separates the inmates of the convent, the parent, brother, or sister, exchanged a few unmeaning words with the dear one, whom they had lost forever. I choke now with feelings of indignation as I recall the picture of Father —— sitting near my sister, where, in the presence of my mother, I was betrayed into a burst of indignation which darkened the priest's brow, and convinced me he was thinking of the Inquisition. I saw this sister once more; she was on her death-bed. In my capacity of priest I heard her last confession. When shall I forget the mortal agony, with which not to disturb her dying moments, I suppressed my gushing tears, until with faltering steps I left the convent, making the solitary street where it stood, reëcho the sobs I could no longer contain.

"Another sister was left to me, but at the age of twenty she, too, misled by Catholic impressions, left her infirm mother in the care of servants and strangers, and was shut up in a convent, where she was not allowed to see the nearest relative. With a delicate frame, requiring every comfort, she embraced a rule, which denied her those of the lowest class in life. A coarse woolen frock fretted her skin, her feet had no covering that they might be exposed to a brick floor, a plank her bed, and an unfurnished cell her dwelling. I have often endured the torture of witnessing her agony at the confessional. I left her when I quitted Spain, dying much too slowly for her own relief. I wept bitterly for her loss two years later, yet I could not be so cruel as to wish her alive."

"Of all the victims of the church of Rome, the *nuns* deserve the greatest sympathy. The real nunnery is a byeword for *weakness of intellect*, and the *nun*, the superlative of *old woman*. I have seen the human mind in all stages of debasement, but souls more polluted than some of those professed vestals of the Church of Rome, have never come under my observation.

"The undisguised disclosure of many victims in confession assures me, that the policy of Rome reckons on the alarming feelings of *delicacy*, as a security against the publication of facts, which would raise a formidable cry of indignation in countries not completely under the authority of the pope, and I feel bound to bear witness to these terrible results, to which the Roman Catholic Church is utterly indifferent."

We make no comment on the above evidence, from the pen of a witness, who appears with a certificate of character ftom Rev. John Newman, D. D.! Every sensible mind will apply it to the convents of his own country.

The next Roman Catholic author, from whom we quote, says: "Nunneries are not sanctuaries of God, but receptacles for . . deeds. . It is the same thing *to put a nun's veil on a girl, as to expose her to public prostitution.*" "Nuns in *every place, and under all circumstances*, follow the *example* of the monks and priests who are placed over them."

In the Præcepta Antiquæ Diœcesis Rotomagensis,"

* See Clamenques' De Corrupto Eccl. Brown's Ap. Lond. 1690.

Sacro Sanct. Concil., vol. xiii, col. 1341, the 41st Precept is as follows: "Priests are strictly forbidden to have living with them, any offspring which they may have begotten, *to avoid scandal*—propter scandalum." A princess and a canonized saint, St. Bridget, daughter of the royal Birger of Sweden, after being the mother of eight lawful children, devoted the rest of her life to founding monasteries. In the fourth book of her Revelations, cap. 33, she says: "The monks are not ashamed, but openly boast, when their favorite mistress, is to become a mother."

At page 361 we read this significant passage: "*Would to God that in all monasteries there were grates of punched iron*, such as we find in some observant convents."

There no protestant parent or guardian could obtain an interview with their victims. What an awful account will the abbess have to give to God, who introduces open grates, or who neglects to make the companions attend. In one of her letters, St. Teresa wrote this sentence: "The grates, when shut, are the gates of heaven; and when open, they are the gates of danger." And she added: "A monastery of nuns, in which there is liberty, serves to conduct them to hell, rather than to cure their weakness."

"Oh, what rapid progress in the divine love does the religieuse make who never goes to the grate. In your intercourse with seculars, you should not only guard against all affectionate expressions, but should be very grave and reserved at the grate. St. Mary Magdalene de Pazzi wished her nuns to be as uncultivated as the wild deer: these are her very words. In a monastery of the venerable Sister Seraphina da Carpi, two females began to talk of a certain marriage; the attendant at the turn* heard

* A sort of box, revolving on its axis, by which goods are passed into the nunneries.

the voice of Sister Seraphina, (who was dead,) saying: 'Chase away, chase away these women.'"

"On Solitude," (page 366:) ". . . . Whoever loves God, loves solitude . . . . . God speaks not at the grates, nor in the 'belvediere,' nor in any other place in which the religieux indulge in useless laughter and idle talk. The Lord is not in the earthquake. 'Non in commotione Dominus.'"

Page 367: "There is no one more deserving of pity than a nun, who being unable to go into the world, brings the world to herself, by conversing with seculars, and by seeking to learn what happens in the neighborhood."

"In a certain convent of St. Francis there was an idle brother going about the house; now troublesome to one, and again to another. The saint called him Brother Fly. Would to God, that in monasteries there were not Sisters Fly, constantly going about observing who is at the grate, or at the confession, who send and receive presents and the like. Such religieux would deserve, like flies, to be expelled the house, or *at least be shut up in a prison!*"

St. Alphonsus tells us for what purpose the prisons are needed; they are a part of the nunnery-discipline, for the Church of the Inquisition.

Chapter XVII., "On Spiritual Reading," but not one word is said of the Bible; except at p. 392, where we find this passage: "But before all, the apostle's prescribed spiritual reading to Timothy: 'attend unto reading.'" Now, this "Spiritual Reading," has nothing whatever to do with the Word of God.

The poor nun knows that her "Spiritual Reading" is the perusal of that infamous and polluting Breviary, which the bishop solemnly puts in her hand at her consecration.

At page 396, we find this passage: "How many saints have, by reading a spiritual book been induced to forsake the world and give themselves to God? It is known to all that St. Augustine, when miserably chained by his passions and vices, was, by reading one of the epistles of St. Paul enlightened with divine light; went forth from his darkness and began to lead a holy life. Thus, also St. Ignatius, while a soldier, by reading a volume of the lives of the saints, which he accidentally took up, in order to get rid of the bed to which he was confined by sickness, was led to commence a life of sanctity, and became the father and founder of the Society of Jesus, (†) an order which has done so much for the Church." We here see that St. Paul's Epistle is treated as the legends of St. Rose of Lima, or St. Teresa, in the Breviary! Page 397 on "Spiritual Reading" we read: "St. Phillip devoted all the vacant hours he could procure to the reading of spiritual books, and particularly the lives of the saints. If you ask me what book is most useful for a religieuse, first I tell you, to read the books you find best calculated to excite your devotion and to move you most powerfully to unite your soul with God. Of this character are the works of St. Francis de Sales, of St. Teresa, of Father Granada, of Rodriguez, of Sangiure, of Nieremberg, of Pinamonti, and other similar books; and particularly the Admonitions to Religieux, by the Fathers of St. Maur; and the Ascetic Directory of Father Scaramelli, a modern work, full of unction. In general, I advise you to lay aside works hard to be understood, and to read books of devotion, written in a plain and simple style. Be careful also, to read the subjects which will contribute most to your perfection. Among the rest, read frequently the lives of the saints, and particularly those who have been religious, such as the life of St. Teresa, of St. Mary Magdalene de Pazzi, of St. Catharine of Sienna, of St. Jane Chanlat, of the venerable Francis Farnese, of the venerable Sister Seraphina da Capri, of St. Peter of Alcantara, of St. John of the Cross, of St. Francis Borgia, of St. Aloysius Gonzaga, etc. Read frequently the lives of the holy martyrs, particularly of so many holy young virgins, who have given their lives to Jesus Christ. You can use the lives of saints, published by Father Crasset. Oh, how profitable is the reading of the lives of saints!"

There are other pages directing the way of spiritual reading; but except, in the two instances, to which we have referred; there is not the remotest hint whatever, that God ever gave any revelation to mankind! Not only is the Word of God kept from the poor helpless nuns, but the most pernicious poison is given in its place. Instead of the blessed Bible, which alone makes wise to salvation; the nuns and seculars read fables and blasphemy.

Chapter XVIII., is on the importance of confession, p. 403. "Every one knows that for a good confession three things are necessary: an examination of conscience, sorrow, and a purpose to avoid sin." Anything like loving a friend or relative, the nun is taught, keeps her from God. (P. 407,) "To St. Ludgard, whiles he was entangled in a dangerous friendship, Jesus appeared, and shewed her his heart grievously wounded. The saint began to weep at her fault, took leave of her friend, saying she could, love none other than Christ, to whom she was espoused." . . . . "But a nun, may perhaps be tempted to conceal a sin in confession. A certain nun may have a misfortune of falling into mortal sin; the devil endeavors to lock her mouth and to make her ashamed to confess her sin. Oh! God how many souls shall on account of this accursed shame, burn and burn forever in hell, or rather in the bottom of hell." In the Chronicles of the Carmelites (tom. iii, lib. 10, c. 34), it is related, that a young girl of great virtue consented to sin against chastity, she concealed the sin three times in confession and went to communion; after the third communion she fell dead. Because she was considered to be a saint, her body was laid in a particular part of the Church of the Jesuits; but after the obsequies were finished and the church closed, the confessor was conducted by two angels to the place of interment; she came forth, fell on her knees, and threw from her mouth into a chalice prepared for them, the three consecrated hosts, which had been sacrilegiously received and miraculously preserved in her breast. The angels stripped her of the scapular, and the miserable girl presented a horrible aspect, and was carried out of sight by two devils."

We come now to a long section "On Communion and reception of the Blessed Sacrament." "The other sacraments contain the gifts of God, but the Holy Eucharist is God himself." Again, at p. 453, "This paradise (of the holy sacrament) religieux can enjoy, in a special manner. It is true Jesus remains in the holy sacrament for all, but he remains particularly for nuns, his spouses, who enjoy his society, day and night, within their own very house. To visit Jesus Christ, seculars have to leave their houses and go to church, which is closed at night, and in many places is open only in the morning, but a nun need not leave her own dwelling in order to enjoy the society of Jesus Christ, he remains continually in the house in which she dwells. A nun, then, can visit him whenever she pleases, morning or evening, by day or night."

Page 445: "St. Phillip Neri, when he saw the most holy *viaticum* brought into his room, was all on fire with holy love, and exclaimed, 'Behold my love!' Do you say the same when you remain before the holy tabernacle? Consider that your spouse, shut up in that prison of love, is burning with love for you."

Page 454: "Our Lord complained to his servant, sister Margaret Alacoque, to whom he showed one day his divine heart, burning with flames of love for men, and said to her," etc. . . . "If he were to come into your church once a year, and remain only for a single day, surely all would contend with each other in paying homage to him, and in remaining in his loving company, and will you leave him alone, and visit him so seldom, because, in order to see you more frequently in his presence, he, in his goodness, remains continually with you?"

The 21st chapter is headed: "On Devotion to Most Holy Mary." This idolatry of the Virgin Mary is a grand feature in the nunneries and the training of nuns.

Page 479 begins, "Oh! how great the grounds of hope to the soul that trusts in the intercession of this great mother of God. Behold the works which the holy church applies to Mary on her festivals. . . . To inspire us with confidence in this great advocate, the holy church invokes her under the title of powerful Virgin. 'Virgo potens, ora pro nobis.' Hence, St. Theophilus, Bishop of Alexandria, has written, 'The Son is pleased that the mother should pray to him, because he wishes to grant her whatever she asks, in order to repay her for the favor received from her in giving him flesh.'"

Page 481: "But what is the principal reason why

Mary's prayers are so powerful before God? St. Antonine says, 'The prayer of the mother of God partakes of the nature of a command, hence it is impossible that she should not be heard.'"

At page 485 we read: "The Lord has constituted Mary the universal advocate of all."

Page 486: "St. Bridget heard our Saviour say to his mother, 'You would show mercy even to the devil, were he to ask with humility.' The proud Lucifer will never humble himself so far as to recommend himself to Mary, but were he to humble himself to this divine mother, and ask her aid, she would not cast him off, but would deliver him (the devil) from hell by her intercession."

Page 487: "The holy church wishes we should call this divine mother our Hope—'spes nostra salve.' The impious Luther said, 'God alone is our hope, and God himself curses them who place their hope in any creature.' Yes, but we hope in Mary as a mediatrix with God." The Bible, with which popery has nothing to do, says, "There is one God, and one mediator between God and man, the man Christ Jesus."—1 Tim. ii., 5. This blasphemy is urged with more minuteness at p. 489 as follows: "First, say every morning at rising, and every evening before going to bed, three aves, in honor of the purity of Mary, adding, 'O Mary, through thy pure and immaculate conception, obtain for me purity of the body and sanctity of the soul.' Salute her also with an Ave Maria, as often as the clock strikes, and whenever you leave or return to the cell, or pass by any of her images; and at the beginning of every action salute her with an Ave Maria—blessed shall be the actions which are commenced and terminated by an Ave Maria!"

"Secondly, do not omit to say the rosary every day, or

at least five decades of it. This is a devotion practised generally by all the faithful, even by seculars, and has been favored by the sovereign pontiff with immense indulgence. But observe, that to gain the indulgence or the rosary, it is necessary to accompany the recital of the rosary, which is kept by the fathers of the order of St. Dominick, and that the beads be blessed." "Do not let a day pass without reading a small portion of a book which treats of Mary. There are many of this kind—True devotion towards the Blessed Virgin, by Father Crasset." Several others are enumerated, and St. Alphonsus then says: "I, too, have written a work on the Virgin, entitled *The Glories of Mary*, of which several editions have been published."

Next we turn to the "Admonition to the Abbess," page 518: "Be particularly careful not to permit any particular friendship either among the sisters or with externs. Be careful not to allow persons employed in the monastery to bring letters or inconvenient messages to the religieux." The "mistress of the Novices," is thus instructed: "Not to permit the novices to be familiar with the religieux, or with the postulants, much less with each other; not permit them to read profane books, to indulge in vanity of dress, or to write useless letters."

The reader will understand that a *novice* is only trying whether she would like to become a nun, and wears the ordinary dress. Such are all girls who enter the convents of our country for the purpose, ostensibly, of education. The *postulants* are they who have declared their desire to become nuns, and are seeking admission; but it is only when these degrees have been gone through, and they becomes religieux, that the real picture is unveiled.

The following occurs at page 545: "What shall we say of the recreations practised in certain monasteries during the carnival, when some of the common exercises are allowed to be in private; the good order of the community and silence are not observed, and the nuns spend a part of the day in dancing, singing profane songs and other worldly amusements. If you are invited to take part in any little opera, avoid it as much as possible, and refuse absolutely, unless the opera be altogether sacred." Here we have the Romish authority, the St. Alphonsus, informing us that operas take place in nunneries. The confessor, of course, is the distinguished auditor! We have further authority for saying that comedies are regularly performed in nunneries. One witness deposes to having seen *La Vedeva Scaltra*, by Goldina, better acted in a nunnery than on the stage of a theatre.

Is it not the duty of our legislators to take immediate action on this subject in the United States? 1. Let every State pass a law which will compel every house in our land, in which communities of females, bound by religious vows, reside, to be registered and licensed.

2. That this register shall furnish the real and surname, as well as the conventual name by which the person is known in the sisterhood.

3. That a visiting committee, composed of the most reliable Protestant citizens, be charged with the duty of inspecting such houses as are in any given district.

4. That these visits shall be frequent, and without previous notice, and that the nuns shall be questioned, apart from the abbess, lady superior, priest or confessor, as to whether they voluntarily remain within their walls, and if by compulsion, to liberate them.

CHAPTER IV.

THE INQUISITION.

Cardinal Wiseman—Thomas Aquinas—Inquisition now—Bishops in the United States sworn to support it—All Inquisitors—Inquisition active under the English Government—Jesuit Treachery—Tyranny—The Foreign Consuls Tools of the Inquisition—The Ottoman Government—Keosse—The Past and Present Inquisition the same—Book of Death—The Process—Americans—Accusers to the Inquisitors—Parents—Children—Excommunication—The Wife—The Husband—Cruelties to Jews—Immoralities of Inquisitors—Bishop Potter, of New York—Pope's orders, How Given and Executed in the United States—Thomas Aquinas—England—Propaganda—Jesuits—Protestants—The Confessional in Rome—In the United States—Visiting Priests, &c.—What They Know—The Jesuits' Vow—Opening of the Inquisition—The Scene—The Building—The Corpses—The Hair—"Trap-Door"—Paintings—Prisoners—The Sight to the People—Bishop of Detroit—Importance—Numbers in Prison—Letters of Confessors—An Instance of Cruelty—Antonelli—The Priests' Crimes—The Chains and Links in the Neapolitan Government—Form of Arrest—The Gay Court of Rome—The Flagellation of Women—Haynau—Danger and Warning to Americans.

THE Inquisition, with all the ingenious cruelty and intolerance which characterized it during the barbarous ages, is yet actually and powerfully in existence. In an article on this fearful institution, published in Dublin, 1850, by Cardinal Wiseman, it was insisted that the Inquisition "is necessary for the present state of society, and the interests of religion!"

Thomas Aquinas, the leading theologian of the Church of Rome, teaches that: "It is much more grievous to corrupt faith, which is the source and life of the soul, than to corrupt money, which only tends to the relief of the body. Hence, if coiners and malefactors are justly put to death by the secular authority, much more may heretics, not only be excommunicated, but put to death."*

* See St. Thom., 2nd 9, xi, art. 3.

Now, if an enlightened mind should dare to disbelieve that the bread and wine is made the actual flesh and blood of the Lord Jesus Christ, by the few words a priest utters over them, he has corrupted the faith of the Romish church, as taught by its theology; and the inquisitor who has knowledge of the fact, lays hold of that man or woman, with sufficient cause to condemn the same to death, for the glory of God! Some may say, these were the barbarous practices of the Church of Rome in past ages: but now it is precisely the same, except that poisoning is resorted to, in place of the fire and faggots, for the disposal of heretics. This modern improvement has had the effect of deceiving the Protestant world, while the secret poisoning, or secret burning in ovens, of the inquisition, is just as effective, and causes no scandal!

Rome is the centre of the Inquisition, but by means of its missionaries, its dominion extends throughout the world.

If, therefore, Cardinal Wiseman or Archbishop Hughes, knew that any Romish subject under their jurisdiction, refused to believe, that the breathing the words "Hoc est corpus meum," by a priest, could transmute these elements into the real flesh and blood of our Lord, it would be their duty, if they had the power, to condemn that individual to death. They could not do less, to be consistent with their principles, with the logical and legal decisions of their theology, and be faithful to the oath by which every Romish bishop is bound.

"Every bishop who is sent in *partibus infidelium* (heathen parts), is an inquisitor, charged to discover, through his missionaries, whatever is done or said by others, in reference to Rome, with the obligation to make his report secretly. The apostolic nuncios are all inquisitors, as also are the apostolic vicars." Here then, Americans, you see the Roman Inquisition extends its authority throughout these United States. The Roman Inquisition and the Propaganda, are in close connection with each other.

The Pope has, within a few weeks, published an encyclical letter, addressed to all primates, patriarchs, bishops, and archbishops, requiring them to exercise strict watch over all ecclesiastics having charge of souls, in the United States and other parts of the world; and commanding mass to be performed, not only on Sundays and holy-days, but on every day throughout the year. This new decree, of June 28th, 1858, will tend, as it is designed, to increase the zeal of papists for the pope's Church, and thereby furnish to his *Inquisitors* in this part of his dominions, increased facilities for multiplying his power over this free country.

Even in India, in the dominions of the English, the work of the Inquisition goes on with power. "A Romish priest was sent there from Rome, in March, 1840, by the propaganda. He was a zealous bigot, and being able to speak the English language, he was soon promoted to the bishopric of Bombay, and sent as a chaplain to the military camp of Belgaum.

About this time, a Protestant clergyman named Taylor, performed a marriage ceremony for two Catholics, which greatly incensed the Romish bishop, as is usual, and he wrote the Protestant an insulting letter, which was kindly answered and accompanied with some Protestant books. The Catholic refused, of course, to read them, and they were returned. But, writes this Romish bishop, "God put it in the heart of Mr. Taylor, to call as he did on me. He spoke to me a new language, which I had never heard before, it was the language of a true Christian, (how a sinner is justified before God). This language, by the grace of God, touched my heart in such a manner, that I took a Protestant book and began to read. It was the "Spirit of Papacy," which opened my eyes, and I began to see the errors of the Church of Rome. Then, quite another man, I opened the Holy Bible, and became convinced that the Catholic religion is in perfect contradiction to the Word of God, and that the Protestant church was the church to which God called me; therefore I opened my mind to the Rev. Mr. Jackson, who was the military Protestant chaplain at Belgaum. He advised me to write to Dr. Carr, bishop of Bombay, which I did; and his lordship was pleased to answer me in a very polite manner, begging me to write my sentiments about the real presence of our Lord Jesus Christ in the sacrament, and a treatise on the spiritual powers of the Pope, which I also did; and then he wrote me to go to Bombay, where I embraced the Protestant religion, that is to say, the pure religion of the Gospel."

A Spanish Jesuit priest, named Francis Xavier Serra, whom I never saw before, called upon me in a secular dress, and, speaking the Italian language well, he told me he was an Italian layman, and, having heard I was an Italian too, he called on me; but he did not mention anything about religion, saying he did not care about it, but he was very kind to me.

He called on me four or five times, till, one day, being a very agreeable evening, he begged me to take a walk with him, which I did, and we went near the Catholic Church, and, to my surprise, I was taken by four men and forced to go to the vicar-general, where they forced me to write a letter to the Protestant minister, Mr. Valentine, in whose house I lived, and there state my intention to return to the Catholic religion, which, I am very sorry to say, I did. They then closed me in a room till Sunday, when the vicar took me by force to the pulpit, and dictated to me what I was to say to the congregation; and he obliged me to declare that I forsook the Catholic religion, for worldly motives, which was quite contrary to my sentiments. When night came, they took me from the room in which I was kept, and delivered me to a captain of a French ship as a prisoner, with the order to take care of me to Marseilles, where he delivered me to the bishop, who, with a French priest, sent me to Rome. From Rome, I was sent as a punishment to a convent at Perugia, where I remained for five years, till I regained my liberty, and returned to Rome: this was in November, 1848. You are not surprised to hear the treachery used towards me at Bombay, by that Jesuit, and by the vicar. The vicar, whose name is Father Michele Antonio, for his bad character, had been in jail for six months, by order of the British government at Bombay!

I live now in the most wretched state of mind, being from my heart a Protestant, yet I am obliged to serve Roman Catholic forms, which is quite contrary to my feelings. I am very sorry I had not in India the Christian courage which you* have demonstrated in Rome; but you must know they threatened me with brutal menace, and I was too young.

I am at present firmly resolved to fly from this Babylon and embrace again the pure doctrine of the gospel; to remain in the faith, by the grace of God, till my death, and to preach it throughout the world.

Here is a very plain case showing that the Inquisition

* Dr. Achilli, who was twice in the Inquisition, for abjuring popery and spreadig the Bible in Italy, 1849.

still exists, and how it acts through its emissaries and agents, even within the limits of the British government.

All that the public know of this persecution at Bombay, was the simple announcement that the priest recanted and had left the country. The treachery and tricks of the Jesuit and vicar were kept a secret, as it is their custom. It is well known that the Turkish governor grants no protection whatever to foreigners, so that the consuls of Austria, France and Naples oblige the bishops, by arresting whomsoever they will, and shipping them as prisoners of the inquisition to Rome. A most noted example occurred in Constantinople in 1847: "An Armenian priest, D. Giovanne Keosse, although an Ottoman subject, and born in Constantinople, was seized in the night, by four ruffians, from the Austrian embassy, and hurried on board a steamer, to be conveyed to Marseilles, and from thence to Rome, to be handed to the inquisition. This was done by order of the Armenian Catholic bishop.

Keosse was placed in the cabin of a steamer, but finding means to escape through a window into a boat, he embraced the precious opportunity, as the vessel was landing goods and passengers at Smyrna. He sought the protection there of the American consul, and being detected, abandoned the matter. Keosse, to secure himself from the inquisitors, knowing it was essential to his safety to get out of the power of the Ottoman government, went to Malta. The newspapers discussed the matter at the time, and some of them charged the embassy with acting in concert with the inquisition." Such occurrences may be found in all parts of the world where the Roman Catholic church has a lodgment.

"Rev. J. R. Dodds, an American missionary, sent out in the fall of 1856, to India, was recently driven from Zahleh, where he had gone to learn the Arabic language. So soon as he had taken a house for the residence of his family, one of the chief Greek Catholic priests visited him, and informed him, unless he left immediately, they would 'stone' him out of the town. A few days after, some ten or a dozen of that order of priests, with one of the French Jesuits, came with mules, and told him he must pack up and be off. They said they were acting under the orders of the bishop. The woman, an old Italian, who boarded Mr. Dodds, remonstrated, but she was severely beaten, and the American missionary was forced at a moment's notice to start for the mountains, with his wife and infant, a journey of eight hours, under a burning sun, to a brother missionary, who lived at Bhamdoon. Mr. Dodds then went to Beyrout and reported the case to Mr. Moore, the English Consul-general, who was acting as American consul. Mr. Moore took up the case with great spirit, and also sent an order to the chief Sheiks of the place to proceed to Bhamdoon and escort Mr. Dodds back to the town, and held them responsible for his future good treatment. The Sheiks agreed to this, and state that it was the work of the 'priests' alone."

"The inquisition of the present day in Rome, is the same that was instituted at the Council of Verona to burn Arnold of Brescia; the same that was established at the third Council of Lateran to sanction the slaughter of the Albigenses and Waldenses, the massacre of the people, and the destruction of the city; the same that was confirmed at the Council of Constance, to burn alive two holy men, John Huss and Jerome of Prague; that which at Florence subjected Savonarala to the torture; and at Rome condemned Aonio Palcario and Pietro Carnesecchi. It is the same inquisition with that of Pope Caraffa and of Fr. Michele Gheslieri, who built the palace of the Holy office, where so many victims fell a sacrifice to its barbarity, and where at the present moment the Roman inquisition exists. Its laws are always the same; the 'Black Book, or Praxis Sacra Romanœ Inquisitionis,' is always the model of that which succeeds it. This book is a large manuscript volume in folio, and is carefully preserved by the head of the inquisition. It is called 'Libro Nero, the Black Book,' because it is covered with that color, or as an inquisitor explained it, is 'Libro Necro,' the book of the dead."

In this book of death, the code of crime, the mode of accusing, and the punishment for every supposed crime, is given. Among the punishments for blasphemy against God, the virgin, the saints, or the pope, there is an instrument used, called "mordacchia, or bit," which is a contrivance to confine the tongue, and compress it between two cylinders of wood and iron, and furnished with spikes. This instrument not only wounds the tongue and creates intense pain, but it often so swells it as to cause the victim danger from suffocation. This, reader, is what a human being is doomed to suffer for speaking against the pope, which, in the papal church, is as unpardonable a crime as to blaspheme the holy name of God! This torture, and many similar ones, are in use at this present time. Cardinal Ferretti, the cousin of the present pope, used these means more than once when he was Bishop of Rieti and Fermo.

Every possible variety of ingenious cruelty has been practised by the Inquisition to torture and agonize its victims. We are writing of the Inquisition as it exists at the present time, and are fully prepared to prove that the laws of the institution are unalterable and in no respect changed. The advanced state of civilization forbids the same open and palpable display of its tyrannous power, lest such a revolt would take place as would endanger its very existence; but, while for this reason its severest penalties, have in some degree been outwardly restrained, yet they remain unalterably in force.

Regarding the method of conducting a process, the "Libro Necro" has this astounding page. "With respect to the examination, and the duty of examiners either the prisoner confesses, and he is proved guilty from his confession, or he does not confess, and is equally guilty on the evidence of the witness. If a prisoner confesses the whole guilt of which he is accused, he is unquestionably guilty of the whole; but if he confesses only a part, he ought still to be regarded as guilty of the whole; since what he has confessed proves him to be capable of the guilt, as to the other points of accusation. And here the precept is to be kept in view, 'no one is obliged to condemn himself,' 'nemo teneter prodere seipsum.' Nevertheless, the judge should do all in his power to induce the culprit to confess, since confession lends to the glory of God. And as the respect due to the glory of God requires, that no one particular should be omitted, not even a mere attempt; so the judge is bound to put in force, not only the ordinary means which the Inquisition affords, but whatever may enter into his thoughts, as fitting to lead to a confession."

"Bodily torture has ever been found the most salutary and efficient means of leading to spiritual repentance. Therefore, the choice of the most befitting torture, is left to the judge of the Inquisition, who determines according to the age, the sex, and the constitution of the party. He will be prudent in its use, always being mindful, at the same time, to procure what is required from it —the confession of the delinquent. If, notwithstanding all the means employed, the unfortunate wretch still denies his guilt, he is to be considered as a victim of the devil; and as such, deserves no compassion from the servants of God, nor the pity or indulgence of holy Mother Church: he is a son of perdition. Let him perish, then, among the damned and let his place be no longer among the living."

In this "black book" of the Inquisition, there is a transcript of proceeding in regard to the increase of crime. The crime is permitted to increase, when a victim is marked for death.

For example: a liberal sentiment, a doubt as to the infallibility of any dogma or tenet of the church; would be Jesuitically approved by significant smiles or gestures, until the party, so encouraged, is by expression or act, sufficiently criminal under their system, to be destroyed.

To establish the guilt of a prisoner, they have various modes; and the object in all cases is to mislead the accused and prevent his understanding the points, upon which he is charged guilty. For example, a person is accused of having taken meat on a Friday at the house of a certain friend. The informer summons all the family of that house for evidence; but they being accomplices, will not depose, against their guest. Then other persons will be summoued and inquiries made in regard to this family; and efforts will be made to find out other houses, where the accused had eaten; finally, the circumstantial evidence is so far ascertained, that the accused admits it;

while he remains silent, or denies the crime imputed to him. But, this is enough—the accused wants no more witnesses: judgment is pronounced. So, the Inquisition now practices, and whether the crime charged is confessed or not, the party is declared guilty, or as they term it, *reo convinto.*

The Inquisition declares that in matters of religion, it is the bounden duty of every one to become an accuser. Children are bound to accuse their parents, wives their husbands, servants their masters. The decrees of several popes, is, that whoever is acquainted with any offence committed against religion, whether from his own knowledge or hearsay, is bound within fifteen days, to make it known to an inquisitor, or vicar of the Holy office; but, in places where there is no Holy office present, as in the United States, the accusation, must be made to the bishop. The crime, whatever, it may be, not only attaches to the principal and accomplices, but to every one who knows of it and does not reveal it. A person belonging to the Church of Rome, who should listen to a discourse against any dogma of "Holy Mother Church," would be obliged to accuse the speaker, himself, and every one who heard him—and whoever knows that another has listened to a Protestant is under an obligation to denounce that person, to the Inquisition.

The punishment for non-observance of this duty is excommunication, which excludes the party from the benefit of all the sacraments and shuts him out, from the kingdom of heaven. Moreover, besides excommunication, he is liable to be imprisoned in the Inquisition and to suffer such other punishment as may be deemed necessary.

Think reader of a wife being obliged to accuse her husband, or a mother her child. Every offence which comes before the Inquisition is called an "offence against the Holy office;" and to get possession of a secret, every natural tie is disregarded and the confidence a man reposes in his wife may lead to his death! Such is the Inquisition, as now practised in Rome—the only difference between its present action, as already observed, and that of past ages is, that these iniquities are perpetrated with more caution, for the sake of saving the Holy See from the censure of the world at large.

There are many artifices used to induce persons to betray their friends to this Holy Inquisition! It is easier for a mother to betray her child, than her husband—and if a husband could know that his wife meant to open his secret thoughts, by which he would be arrested, tortured and condemned; perhaps to die—he would never allow her to go to the confessional. It is there, that the priest induces a woman often to betray her husband, or contrives a plot, to cast suspicion, and thus creates discord between them. The Court of Rome foresaw, the difficulty that might endanger the confessional in regard to the wife making an accusation against a husband, and so managed that she shall betray her husband, but without the least chance of his discovering her treachery. She is therefore instructed by her confessor to go to another town, where she is not known and there make her disclosures; keeping in secret that she is the wife of the accused, and concealing his real name, till the confessor has disclosed the whole affair to the Inquisition, which alone knows all the intricacies of the proceedings. And since it might happen, that the husband might know that his wife, under a false pretence, had gone to another place to see the inquisitors or the bishop's vicar; the Inquisition grants to other persons the privilege of receiving an accusation; making them sub-inquisitors for that single case, under the pledge of inviolable secrecy. We have at hand the most irrefragible proof, of this, as of everything, stated, in this work.

At Ancona, in 1842, two inquisitors had seduced certain wives for the purpose of inducing them to accuse their husbands; another inquisitor tried to persuade two young ladies to accuse their uncle in order to imprison him—the offence was, that the uncle forbade the immoral inquisitor from visiting his family.

This same inquisitor, Salva, sent forth to the world his edict against the Jews under his jurisdiction, on the 24th of June, 1843. This people were ordered to leave within the term of three months; to sell, all their possessions, under penalty of confiscation; within eight days, to abandon all their shops outside the Ghetto, which is enclosed by high walls, and is a part of the city in which the Jews were confined; and within three days to dismiss from their houses all their Christian servants, male and female, even to their children's nurses. They were prohibited to sleep one night out of the Ghetto; to take a single meal, or hold any communication with a Christian. These poor Jews were further debarred from buying or reading any prohibited book, under a penalty of one hundred crowns and an imprisonment of seven years!

The occasion of this diabolical edict is satisfactorily explained, by the following letter from Ancona:

"The Father Inquisitor Salva, is a person of very licentious habits, and at the same time very greedy of money.

He became offended at our women (the Jewesses) because they would not listen to his propositions; he allured, he threatened, but could never render them subservient to his desires."

"At length he took a fresh occasion of offence against us, because we refused to pay him a considerable sum of money, which he claimed, and not for the first time; saying his predecessors had had such donations, that it was for that reason, he had looked upon us favorably, and that, if we did not make similar acknowledgement, we need not expect any service or consideration from him. After due deliberation upon the matter, however, it was resolved that we should not give him anything; and now see what has happened!"

The personal immoralities of the inquisitors throughout the Roman States, are notorious and unquestionable. The predecessor of the Holy Inquisitor Salva, it is well known, extorted so much money and seduced so many women, that he finally had to fly from his position and retreat to Tuscany.

An inquisitor sows discord between man and wife, and to suit his purpose, demoralizes the wife, to make her the base betrayer of her own husband!

Every archbishop who is true to the theology of Thomas Aquinas, and faithful to his oath to support the canon laws of the Inquisition, would put to death, if he could, all heretics everywhere.

These Romish prelates are sent to the United States, as to *heathen parts*, *in partibus infidelium*. They are sworn to the pope, to watch every opportunity to aid the Inquisition; which they secretly do. To help this *holy* work, and bring the human mind in complete subjection, is the work of all belonging to the monastic orders. In these, neither the will nor the understanding, can possibly be exercised, apart from the *superior*. Every one so trained, must believe that there is *no hope or mercy in heaven*, but in blind obedience to these superiors, be they who they may; and who alone, according to the Romish doctrine, are *responsible* for his acts! Was there ever a more consummate plan devised to effect the greatest possible evil? Any common mind can perceive in the *actual* existence of the secret Inquisition in our midst, the danger which imperils the lives and liberties of this people!

Look at the work of the Inquisition in England, on the passage of the emancipation bill, in 1829. The Jesuits immediately returned there, and since then, we have seen numbers of clergymen of the Church of England, go over to the Romish church. Look at the wounds inflicted on Protestantism by the tractarians and Puseyites! These Jesuits are here in our midst; in the best society of the land, as teachers of languages and private tutors. They are trusted by many respectable families; sit at their tables, and converse with their children. It is a notorious fact, that these Jesuits are preferred as the best teachers, and are more sought after than any others!

They are not able to destroy Protestantism in the United States, but they excite variance between the sects, and then tauntingly declare that the "Protestants cannot exist much longer; they will destroy themselves."

The principal object of the inquisition is to possess itself of the secrets of every class of society. This is its operation in the United States; and the Jesuits here are the right arm of its power. Its agents enter into the domestic circle, watch every action, listen to every conversation, and seek, as far as possible, to penetrate the hidden thoughts of the whole people. The secret officials of this Romish police are everywhere. They are far more successful than government spies, because with them, no door is closed, no curtain drawn, no veil or shadow cast over a secret or mystery. What is not learned from men, is obtained through women; what the father does not reveal, the son will disclose; and what the master may attempt to conceal, the servant will make known. The confessional gives the Jesuit a secret at once, that the spy of a government might not ascertain in a year, if ever. The confessional is the first and paramount instrument; and besides this, much is learned even through the children in the schools.

Every morning, at the break of day, twelve reverend fathers ascend the steps of the church of Gesu (Jesuits) in Rome, as the doors open at day dawn. They are dressed in their robes and surplices, and seat themselves in the confessional chairs. Then come servants of both sexes, old men and women, who are used to stirring early, shop-keepers, and working men of all kinds. They come to give an account of their sins, and of other people's business, of which they know more than of their own. In less than one hour, all the affairs of the city are related to these twelve confessors, and are carefully registered and discussed at home, as cases of conscience. The same is practised in the church of St. Ignasius, St. Andrew, and St. Vitate, and all others belonging to the company.

That order is in our midst, and the same means to obtain a knowledge of our private and domestic history, is being as sedulously used here, as in Rome. If you have any connection whatever, with those who belong to the Roman Catholic church, you are more or less endangered, according to the influence you possess, or the position you hold in society.

The Roman Catholic churches are open in New York, Boston, Philadelphia, Baltimore, Washington, New Orleans, St. Louis, etc., at daybreak every morning to listen to the details of the domestic affairs and business intentions, of the more opulent classes of society, while they are asleep!

Often facts or conversations begun in one place, are fully confirmed in another. The most clever of Rome's police visit from house to house, to collect what can be gathered of interest in this way. Thus are obtained the most minute secrets of society. Then, as at the Caraveta in Rome, the church of the Inquisition has its nightly oratories, for the élite of the cities in the United States, which are a fashionable resort. Besides, there are its courses of spiritual exercises, always well attended; the conferences for the scrupulous, where everything of a secret nature is drawn from them; and friendly visitations, which are fruitful in supplying information: and this is practised all over the land.

This army of the Pope are courteous and zealous in serving their friends; they ask places for them under the government, and, of course, obtain them.

Without even knowing a family personally, or being admitted into their house, these Jesuits are so familiar with their history as to know where they reside, what is the topic of their conversation, what their intentions, and even the names and ages of the parties. In this way the church of Rome is supported by the Inquisition, which in its turn is sustained by the Jesuits. After ten years' experience of a Jesuit in serving the Inquisition and the court of Rome; his occupation as a teacher of American youth, is the most important post he can fill to aid the apostate church!

When the pope fled from Rome in 1849, he left the inquisition under strict injunctions that every officer should remain at his post, and the prisoners in the holy office to be kept as closely guarded as before. It was a fortnight after the new government under the Roman Republic was assumed before this was discovered. The government then took possession of all it contained, and ordered the holy office to be made the abode for poor families; and its doors, which for three centuries had been closed, were for the first time opened to the view of the people! What a scene was there, as the people crowded in to behold the prisoners and subterraneous passages which had held so many victims, who had sealed their faith with their blood! The most terrible oaths and imprecations were made against the priests; and sometimes the spectators would be intimidated and look behind, fearing even then some father inquisitor might be near to lay hold upon them.

It was in this building that war was made against the printing-press, the censorship was organized, a holy act was pronounced treason, and every possible invention of cruelty was exerted to enchain the human mind. Here were thrown together the monarch and the peasant; here the wife was transformed into the accuser of her husband, the son into the betrayer of his father.

This edifice was erected in the middle of the 16th century, and its walls rest upon a prison of Nero. It had originally two stories and two galleries, but in the 17th century the lower galleries were shut in to make prisons. Since then another story has been added, and is at present the part in use.

The officials of the holy office reside in another part of the building. A high wall extends across it, to exclude from human view the horrid crimes and mysteries, which, for three centuries, have been practised there.

The government, in 1849, appropriated that part of the inquisition, under the closed gallery of the second court, for the stables of the national artillery. The father inquisitor, a Dominican, was then residing in it, but all his resistance was in the shape of a protest, which was disregarded. A space was opened in the walls to make a stable for the horses, and in doing so the workmen saw an aperture. They at once removed the rubbish, and descended into a small subterranean place, damp and dark as possible, with no passage out, and with no floor, but a black oily earth resembling a cemetery. Here and there were scattered various pieces of garments, of former fashions, the clothes of the victims who had been thrown down from above, and died of wounds, fear, or hunger.

A penny of Pius VIIth was picked up, indicating the probable time that this prison was walled up. The men then began to explore further, and on removing the soil, human bones were uncovered, and in some places very long tresses of hair, which had undoubtedly once ornamented female heads. Martyrs of ignorance and superstition who were first decoyed into a cloister, and then into such a dungeon! Oh, women! what was your alleged crime? Had you expressed your abhorrence of a life of sin with your confessor? Did you die for your integrity? Who will answer these questions? Many spectators carried away some of this human hair, pieces of which are in possession of friends of the author in the city of New York.

The "trap-door" inclosed numerous victims, of whom it was deemed important to destroy all traces. It is immediately under the judgment hall, the second story of the first edifice, and under the vestibule of the "Second Father Companion," adjacent to the hall of the tribunal.

In each of the prisons are small cells, each capable of holding but one person, and these arranged like convent cells, being only reached by an extremely narrow corridor. The walls of this passage is lined with pictures, to represent the horrid character of the institution, and to show no forgiveness to heretics. Christ is painted at every step and near every door, not as the meek, forgiving Saviour, but as threatening vengeance from the cross. All the passages of scripture and mottos are but to prove the eternal flames are ready for hardened sinners.

In every cell there is a passage of scripture in large letters. "In my prison," says a writer, who obtained his liberation on the opening of the Inquisition, in 1849, was the 6th verse of the 109th Psalm: 'Set thou a wicked man over him, and let Satan stand at his right hand.' In another was the 17th verse of the same Psalm: 'As he loved cursing, so let it come unto him; as he delighted not in blessing, so let it be far from him.' And in another the 19th verse of the 28th of Deuteronomy: 'Cursed shalt thou be when thou comest in, and cursed shalt thou be when thou goest out.'

"It still remained for us to visit the ancient torture chamber. This is in one of the subterranean dungeons, and you descend by a narrow stone staircase. You see plainly, in a stone imbedded in the wall, the iron ring intended to receive the axle of the wheel; in the middle you perceive the square stone on which the beam was secured for the torture of the cord. Iron rings attached to the vault showed the place for administering other tortures. A great chimney in one corner pointed out the spot for the torture by fire; but this chamber was now only used as a cellar for storing the bottles of the Reverend Father Inquisitors."

Near the cellar the Republican Government had broken through a wall, which, although of recent structure, had been tinted over with gray earth, to simulate age; though on examination of the stones and cement, it was found to be but just completed! This aperture conducted to a hall, in which were two large ovens, of considerable height, filled with calcined human bones. *When the inquisition could no longer burn its victims publicly, it burned them privately in its own furnaces!*

"It was about sunset, on the 27th of March, 1849, I was apprised," says a distinguished prisoner, "that something extraordinary was taking place; and as I expected it would prove to be something dreadful, I fell on my knees, betook myself to prayer, and commended my soul to God. While thus employed my door was violently opened. The first person who entered was a man of short stature, who, with great impetuosity, threw himself on my neck, embracing, kissing, and bathing me with the tears, which all the time fell from beneath his green spectacles. This was the Minister Sterbini, the author of the decree which abolished the holy office, and those who followed him, having embraced me in their turn, he left two of them with me, saying, 'You are free!—I must go and liberate others!'

"I found myself laboring under extreme weakness of the limbs, the effect of my long confinement. It was with great difficulty that I could walk a few steps. The two, therefore, supported me in their arms, and conducted me in triumph to the midst of a crowd assembled in the court-yard, who, as soon as they saw me, began to shout for joy and clap their hands, exclaiming, 'Liberty of conscience for ever!' I was now taken to an apartment with the other liberated prisoners, where the kind-hearted Roman people, so different from their priests, were eagerly providing broth, wine, and cordials, to recruit our feeble powers. Meanwhile fresh arrivals from the prisons continually took place, till we reached the number of about thirty, on which Sterbini, now quite worn out with exertion, asked each one, separately, where he would like to be conducted. I replied, 'That for my part, being a foreigner, I had no settled home, but that if he would be kind enough to send me to the parish priest of the Magdalene, he would be benevolent enough to receive me.' 'The priest of the Magdelene, for whom you inquire,' replied Sterbini, 'knew what the priests were before we did. He quitted Rome a long time ago, and with Rome he also abandoned the Romish religion.'

There, where the French government put the correctional prisoners, the monks and friars had prisons in the holy office. These cells had beds, but the greatest filth imaginable prevailed everywhere. Old chairs, worn-out cushions, coverlets, tables, old clothes of prisoners who had died in the cells years ago.

" In a certain very small cell were things which indicated horrible secrets: a piece of a woman's handkerchief, or large size, and an old bonnet of a girl about ten years old. Poor little child! What offence, perhaps unknown to you, could it have been, which threw you into this place and destroyed the innocent peace of your infantile years; which taught you to weep in the season of smiles, and thus deprived you of your dear and early life? In another cell were found your sandals, and several nuns' cords, a little spindle, caskets containing needles, crucifixes, and unfinished stockings, with the knitting-needles still well pointed, etc.

"And so, in almost every one of the prison-rooms were to be seen clothes, ornaments, and other relics of their former occupants; and, as every thing was wrapt in deep and mournful mystery, the imaginations of the people recalled ancient tragical stories, and they wept over the misfortunes of persons of whose names they were ignorant.

"The walls of all the cells were covered with inscriptions, some of which expressed despairing grief, but most of them resignation, even in that abode, and under the sufferings inflicted there, so well fitted to becloud the mind, to terrify the boldest heart, and to bend the most iron-will.

"Under the two courts, subterranean apartments abounded, communicating with each other. A few only were solitary; and to those there was only one way of access, viz., a trap-door, which denoted *death!* Some of them were prisons at first, and afterwards converted into store-rooms. To their ceilings were still fastened iron rings, which formerly served to give to the *Question*, (torture!) and afterwards to suspend provisions. In one cell on the ground-floor, in the second building, a square piece of marble was observed in the floor, which looked like the cover of a hole. It was raised, and beneath was a vault, which proved to be a *Vade in pace*, (go in peace —that is, a place of silent death.) Not a ray of light ever could have entered, except when that funereal marble was lifted for a moment, and then it soon again fell, over the head of the condemned person, who was left to die of hunger, in the cold and darkness, and amidst a stillness unbroken unless by his own cries or prayers.

"A portion of those subterraneous apartments were closed in the present century, or near the close of the last, as was plainly discovered by a careful examination of the walls, that had shut them in, which had been artificially colored with a grayish hue, to make them *look old*. This artifice was accidentally discovered.

"The rubbish having been removed in one place, indications of a stone staircase were observed, which was cleared, and persons went down thirty steps. At the bottom was found a small chamber, filled up with a mixture of earth and lime, and which proved to be but the first of many others like it. The prisons of Pope Pius V. were now at last discovered. Along the walls were recesses, hollowed out, so formed and arranged as to bring to mind the ancient Columbari, or dovecotes. There, it appeared, from what was observed, the condemned were buried alive, being immersed in a kind of mortar up to their shoulders. In some instances it was evident, they had died slowly and of hunger. This was inferred from the position of the bodies, and marks were seen in the earth of movements made, in the convulsive agonies of the last moments, to free themselves from the tenacious mortar, while it was closing round their limbs. The bodies were very numerous, and were placed in lines, opposite each other. The skulls were all gone; but these were afterwards found in another place.*

"Of those victims of religious fury we know nothing.

* The French legation in Rome was pleased to circulate the report, that the government of the Republic had had the bodies transported thither, to defame the Inquisition and the government of the priests. That report does not greatly honor the ingenuity of the French legation, for the bodies form large deposits, in layers, which are under walls then built over them.

"The rest of the edifice has nothing remarkable. The hall of the dreaded tribunal, over which presided the Dominican Commissary of the Holy Inquisition, was in the interior of the first fabric. This was very simple, having a colossal figure of Pius V. at the end.

"Above the seat of the Father Inquisitor was a crucifix, with the image of the church beneath it, trampling upon heresy; and near by was the terrible Dominican Gusman. On the sides opened two doors. That on the right led into the room of the first Father Companion, and that on the left to the room of the second Father Companion. These two magistrates of ancient times assisted the High Procurator of the Inquisition, in discovering offences, and in converting the condemned offenders; to which latter office they devoted themselves in the following manner. When a trial was finished, and it was important to the Holy Office, to dispose of a condemned person without giving a public spectacle, he came in, conducted by the first Father Companion, who exhorted him to repent, to consign every thing to the hands of divine compassion, which punished him on earth to glorify, and purify him in heaven; he pressed him with insidious interrogations, in order to discover more of his offences, and to find traces of other offenders; and, finally, blessing him, if he confessed and was contrite, he *pretended* to send him to the second Father Companion. The guard, who awaited him on the occasion, well knowing the arrangements, conducted him towards the apartment on the other side, opened the door, and stopped short without passing it. As soon as the miserable prisoner touched the spot near the threshold, the floor gave way, and he fell through the trap-door into his tomb.

"These words are still written over that door: '*Chamber of the second Father Companion.*'

"This edifice is almost entirely the work of the Pontiff Ghislieri, called by the court of Rome 'Pius V.', and by Italy, (covered with blushes,) 'Brother Michael of the Inquisition'—('Fra Michele dell' Inquisizione.' Rome knows him, and so do Calabria, Tuscany, Venice, Spain, and Flanders. We will briefly trace this character in another place: for the Catholic world remembers the blood which the canonization of Pius V. cost, and on what foundation the papal throne is erected. This '*Saint*,' is the author of the bull (entitled '*Supra gregem dominicum*,') which forbids a physician to visit a patient a third time, unless he has confessed, and has a certificate of the fact.

"We have hitherto examined the parts of the buildings devoted to trials and tortures, following the astonished and indignant multitude; but another part remains to be visited, of a less terrible aspect, although yet formidable enough. I speak of the *Archives*, which contain the *Martyrology of the Human Race*, and the revelation of the barbarous jurisprudence of the Inquisition.

"The Inquisition was founded in 1204, by Innocent III., to combat the Albigenses, to devastate one of the most flourishing provinces of Europe, and to butcher more than half a million of men. *It is nothing else than a conspiracy established into a system*, against the moral and intellectual development of mankind. With such an institution the Popes so managed, that Christianity and Mahomedanism went hand in hand in murder, as the Caliphs and the Popes wished to persuade the world to be converted by the same logic—fire and sword. The Mussulman said: 'Believe or I will cut off your head.'

The Roman Court has always said: 'Believe, or I will burn you!' The difference is not great.

"The supreme tribunal, composed of cardinals, and presided over by the Pope, resided, and still resides, at the Minerva, where it has always met once a week, to judge, in the last instance, the important cases drawn up in the Holy Office by the Father Inquisitor, the acting captain of the Catholic Inquisition. The Assessor of this belongs to the high prelacy. The informers and agents, primates, priests, monks and laymen, indifferently, had, and have the name of Assistants; and they exist now. We have, among our notes, the names of many, which we may, when we please, give up to the just animadversion of the world. Certain of those assistants were honorary: others received pay; and whether honorary or paid the body was strong, especially in late years, as it turned out in Spain: for the honorary ones enjoyed many privileges. Among the honorary were numbered, and still are numbered several princes of Rome, of the ecclesiastical state, and a number of French legitimists. Such officials of the army of the Inquisition, therefore, were taken from the bosom of Sanfedism. The Familiars are only the executioners, the gensdarmes, of the Holy Office.

"The Inquisition tries heresy, suspicion of heresy, protection given to heresy, every kind of evil doing, sacrilege and enchantment, blasphemy, both heretical and non-heretical, insults offered to the Inquisition, whether by resisting its orders, offending its members or officers, either in person, or character, or property, or in any thing whatever belonging to them. The jurisdiction of the Inquisition extends over Jews, Mahomedans, and all *infidels, of whatever kind, comprehending all who teach anything contrary to the sentiments of the Court of*

Rome, concerning the Sovereign and unlimited power of the Popes, their superiority in councils, even general councils, and the divine arbitrament which they may exercise over the acts of governments and princes of *all countries.* Aside from all this, it is sufficient to fall under the jurisdiction of the Holy Office, that one refrains from confessing for a year, eats meats on prohibited days, or breaks any one of the precepts of the Church. The words *guilty* and *accused* are synonymous in the dictionary of the Inquisition, because the Church cannot be mistaken: therefore, whoever is accused must be guilty. And it is not only not permitted to save any person who falls under the jurisdiction of the Inquisition: but he must be accused, even though a father or a brother.

"The *Inquisition has supreme power over all particular Inquisitions;* and, because the Inquisitions of the *various provinces* are independent of each other, it terminates the differences which may arise between them. It regulates the procedure, prescribes the forms of trials at will, and they make it the judge of all graver religious and political business which relates to the Roman Court and the Papacy. Although the Inquisition is abolished in France, Spain, Germany, at Milan, Venice, and in England, the *primitive ordinance arrangement has not been broken on this account, but they are supplied with secret Inquisitors and with periodical information by the agents,* Jesuits, Sanfedists, friars and priests of all kinds, bishops and nuncios. This, to the Church of Rome, is the *Mirror of the World,* the true Council, the grand supporter, the universal police. In the states of the Pope, is the *Censorship of Books.* This seasons the food of the intellect, for the whole Catholic world, by means of *The Index.*

"The Inquisition, like the Papacy, is unchangeable. The Inquisition, which remains still the undegenerate daughter of Saint Dominic, who merited Paradise and the honor of altars, by shedding the blood of the Albigenses, *has not changed its objects nor its sentence, but only its means.* It has wanted, for a century, the omnipotence of the physical arm: yet it still condemns, though it dissimulates, and conceals its sentence, not, being able to kindle fires for victims, which it calls "Acts of faith," (*Auto da fe.*) It is not now able to conduct Catholics, at its will, to "a good death," except in the Roman States, where it is again in power, thanks to the Austrian, French and Spanish arms! However, it yet dares not immolate in public a human victim to Jesus Christ, but *remains free*, even *now*, to *use the ban*, *the dungeon*, *fetters* and *secret torture.*

"We have mentioned these facts, because they assist in comprehending the importance of the *Archives of the Holy Office.* These are the registers of all the trials and sufferings incurred by men of intellect, for efforts made against every kind of tyranny, established in the name of men, or in the name of God: the history of that contest which has been carried on for three centuries. We believe that the documents anterior to the sixteenth century exist somewhere else. The archives existing are very extensive indeed, and every page contains some malediction against freedom of thought, or a record of sufferings and tortures. Every one is impregnated with tears or blood.

"They are divided into three parts.

"The first consists of *the Library*: the most precious and unique of its kind. This contains all works relating to the Inquisition, written in the Catholic spirit; with the jurisprudence and apologies for the Holy Office, published in every part of Europe. It is thus a complete collection of works presented and registered in the Index: that is, the documents relating to all the crimes committed by Catholic intolerance against the highest displays of the human intellect. There is seen a collection of the original editions of all works written by Italian reformers, the greater part of whom died either in exile, in prison, under torture, or in the flames. Numbers of those works are unknown to bibliopolists themselves, even the most diligent and the most devoted collectors of rare books; and are the only, or almost the only copies in existence of some of the works. We need but reflect upon the history of the fifteenth and sixteenth centuries, to have an idea of this insatiable bitterness with which the Inquisition not only hunted and tortured the authors, but devoted itself to destroying the books, even to buying up whole editions and committing them to the flames, at the same time notifying every person possessing a copy to resign it immediately. The typographic art, although in a flourishing state in the former half of the sixteenth century, must have been nearly destroyed by the laws of Paul IV. and Pius V. and the Council of Trent. Consequently, in the second half of that century the great printing-offices disappeared, and the printers either failed or ceased their labors and went into exile. The Giunti of Florence were reduced to printing *breviaries*. The art remained nowhere unless at Venice, where the learned Monsignor della Casa published the first Index, after the cruel Orfano had received many victims, at the command of the Father Inquisitor, the Venetian Signori having chosen to substitute water for fire against the remains of the Italian spirit.

"In that library abound the codices and manuscripts collected by the officers of the Censorship. When an author presents a work, to obtain permission to print it, it is the custom of the Holy Congregation of the Index, if it thinks it proper to deny the permission, to retain the manuscript, that it may not be published in other countries. We remember to have observed a geography of the Roman States, by a certain Cavalier Fontana, a work which did not touch on any point of religion: but as it revealed by statistical data, things not proving the infallible goodness of the government, it was sequestered.

"This is a library of heresy and the more admirable, because it comprehends the great enterprizes of intelligence, the greatest combats for the truth, the most holy aspirations; and, as a thinking mind could not act without falling into heresy, it is the *library of liberty*, hidden and sealed with every kind of anathema and with blood.

"The first section contains the strongest exhibitions of the efforts of the intellect, panting to break the impediments which prevent the improvement of human nature; the second registers the penalties imposed upon its champions, and narrates the martyrdom of many a modern Prometheus. There stand, in beautiful order, the processes proposed and carried through by Ghislieri, as Inquisitor and as Pope—as 'Brother Michele' and as 'Pius V.' who said that clemency consisted in punishing heretics with the greatest severity, and instituted the custom of blessing medals, by washing them in Flemish blood. The inexorable disciple of Paul IV., adopted the dogmatical decrees of the Synod of Trent, to give activity to the Inquisition; and the disciplinary decrees, to supercede and absorb the jurisdiction of every lay government. Then, as now, the fear of punishment proved the best of remedies: torture, not the word of Christ, was the Roman Gospel. The princes seconded the iron-will of Ghislieri, both for a show of religion, for the fear of ecclesiastical intrigues, and from dread of the event in Germany and France. Brother Michael, it is true, was received by the Couraschi with a volley of stones, and the Venetian Signori drove him out of Bergamo, but, nevertheless, he knew how to substitute in Venice, the canal of Orfano for faggots to accomplish the death of Giuglio Ghirlanda, Antonio Ricetto, Francesco Sega, the priest Spinola, and the friar Lupetino. He procured the hunting out of the Protestants of Locarno: a work due in a great measure to the small cantons by which the flourishing town of Locarno lost her commerce. Ghislieri destroyed the reformed church of Lucca, co-operated in the slaughter of the poor Waldenses in Calabria, burned Giuglio Zanetti, Aenio Paleario and Pietro Carnesecchi. The last named would never bow his head, but went gravely and serenely to the stake, as if to victory, with the *Sanbenito** on his neck. These tragedies terrified the whole peninsula. A person accused of heresy died under the torture in Fænza; and the city rose in insurrection, assaulted the houses of the Inquisition, and killed a priest they found there.

"There were tumults in Mantua, Tuscany and Naples. The Index of Caraffa was put into vigorous execution; all the books issuing from certain offices which were held in fear were prohibited, to whatever subject they related; the inquisitors and their agents, like dogs long tied up, sprang into the printing-offices and bookstores, carrying away books without paying for them, and ruining the arts and trade. They foolishly wished to destroy *thinking.* There were fugitives from Sienna, Lucca, Pisa,

* Habit of Infamy.

Florence and all parts. The Italians carried their industry and wealth to France, Germany and Switzerland. Rome seemed like a great desert. The study halls of Pisa were empty; several students were imprisoned on suspicion; and their companions soon abandoned the inhospitable country. Many persons lost their senses from fear; five Siennese women were given over to the devil as mad; and, instead of the hospital, they were put into the flames!

"We mention these facts summarily, that the terrible importance of the trials of Pius V., may be understood (which are included in many of the documents of the reign of Paul IV.), and many of those relating to the war in Flanders and the slaughter of the Huguenots. Death prevented Ghislieri from publicly pronouncing his blessing on the festival of St. Bartholomew.

"The second section (of the library of the Inquisition) contains summary records of all the trials which have been held and decided by the supreme tribunal of the Minerva; all the resolutions by the Holy Office of cases of conscience, and all the objects taken from prisoners and delinquents: such as letters, books, manuscripts, pictures, ornaments, amulets, &c., a curious and very strange collection.

"The third part (of the library), formed under the chancelry, is the most important in our times, and reveals the vast organization of the Inquisition, and what kind of life, and how much life it still possesses. Here, more than anywhere else, politics and religion take each other by the hand, and are confounded in one; here is perceived the usefulness of *confession* and of the concentrated absolutism in the church; here politics control religious heresy, and the assiduous care of the priest is seen, who wishes to maintain himself as a prince; here are all the trials, all the revelations, all the design, all the secret intrigue of *modern* times.

"The Roman Church, after the German Reformation, endeavored to purify ecclesiastical practices: and if they did not succeed in this, it was owing to the essential defects of the internal constitution. To this department of the Inquisition belongs the '*Summary of solicitations*,' a record, of women who had been solicited to criminality by their own confessors in the pontifical state; and the summary is not brief.

"Although several book-cases were found empty, enough remained to allow us to comprehend the modern secret organization of the Holy office, and to discover the names of the officers and familiars of the tribunal. The names of these are in a register, *province by province*. Generally speaking all the prelates in mission, all the provincials and generals of the regular clergy, all the bishops, archbishops, and cardinals, not only of the pontifical state, but of christendom, all Sanfedists and exaggerated catholics, notable for rank and ambition, or genius and wealth, or for influence on public opinion and governments. Then the *Repertories of Correspondence* are numerous and exceedingly large. There is a Repertory of the correspondence of bishops, cardinals, and prelates, belonging to the pontifical state, which gives to the inquisitors information on religion, as well as politics; also that of the bishops, cardinals, prelates, priests, and friars of the *catholic world;* and that of the Apostolic Nuncios. From those documentary letters elaborate notes had been compiled and placed in orderly arrangement, forming the '*Catalogus Indicationum*,' which contains the names of all political and religious heretics from 1815 till 1847, tracing their moral portraits, recording their writings and actions, and treating of their sects, societies, ornaments, ramifications, agents, and friends.

"Such is the immense family of the Inquisition: touching every place, having its eye upon everything, from the confessional of the humble female, to the palace of great men and the royal residence of princes, it examines everything, studies and records everything. Liberty, in its estimation, is not only heresy, but reason itself is a kind of heresy; therefore the world is heretical, and therefore the Inquisition believes it to be its duty to observe everything, to comprehend, in its secret jurisdiction, the actions and thoughts of all men, and secretly utters its anathemas even against the governments which have lent them a musket. To it nothing is sacred, nothing respected: neither the sanctity of the *domestic hearth*, nor the religion of the *oath sworn to governments*, nor the *silence* of the confessional. All is scandalous treachery in those correspondences. There I found letters from Piedmontese bishops, who openly reasoned about rebelling against the government of Charles Albert, because he did not hold to the maxims of Count Solaro della Margherita. Elsewhere they lay before your eyes the relations made to a confessor, which bear on their face the violated words: '*Under secresy*,' which answer in the diplomatic vocabulary, to '*Confidential.*' Numbers of those relations came from abroad, and were collected by Nuncios. The timorous consciences of Catholics may be encouraged, for the sacrament of confession is good, and really something. And if the governments, if the multitudes knew to what offices the ambassadors of the court of Rome lend themselves, they would soon *renew* the English law. Any one who can write, might cover with infamy, by a single line, many illustrious men of France, Switzerland and Germany. Let us not do it, although we have the documents in our hands; let us not do it now from the vain stimulus of vengeance: but, if ever necessary to the cause of the people, it may then be done.

"This, then, is the true whispering gallery, of the police. It is the seat of the Cardinal Secretary of State, and the repertory of his letters; to him recurrence is had for information concerning all persons; for hints about men and things, or books to be allowed to be introduced into the state, etc., etc.

"The government of the Republic, being at war in defence of the national honor and the standard of the people, was not able to take possession of those documents; but an examination was allowed to a few persons. The Inquisition recovered the archives untouched, and now is revenging itself. But we have more solemn and obvious documents to prove the iniquity of the priest's government, in the disdain and the misery of the Roman people, in the hatred of all Italy, in the Gospel which they have torn in pieces, in the offended conscience of the human race."*

But men of all nations visited with the same exclamation of horror! Many Americans were there and saw it and wrote their impressions, which have not been given to the world. The most cultivated Italians who fled to the United States allude to this opening of the Inquisition as surpassing all sights ever imagined of popish

This description is translated from F. De Bonne's "L'Italia del Popolo," who was an eye-witness of what he describes.

tyranny. "The people roared with madness," said a priest when describing the popular outburst on entering the Inquisition. "The Roman women," said another Italian, "have heretofore been strong advocates for the priests; but they are no longer their partizans — they have seen the Inquisition." A foreign gentleman, like many other visitors, took notes while examining the Inquisition, in order to acquaint incredulous Americans of the real nature and practices of popery, adding, "that should he publish them and return to Italy, he should expect to be incarcerated in the same dungeons and by the same old jailers, who have been restored by French Republican arms."

The mysterious disappearance of certain persons was soon explained on beholding the numerous remains of human bodies in the cells of the Inquisition! Such mysteries have excited suspicion in the United States, as well as on the other side of the Atlantic. The intimate coöperation existing here by political diplomatists and the agents of the Inquisition, as proved by the documents in the Holy office, may remind the reader of persons from our midst who have been summoned by the pope to Rome, and were never afterwards seen or their destination known. Such *was* the case, of Bishop Reze, of Detroit, a Roman Catholic and an American citizen by birth. He was ordered to Rome for some offence against religion, and since that time not a word has been heard of him. He is doubtless in the Inquisition or has suffered a death penalty at its hands.

This subject is of the utmost importance to Americans, and the revelations given to them, should at once arouse them to action and induce them to legislate out of the country all convents and all similar institutions, which are secluded from the public eye.

This Inquisition, which now flourishes, with the pope of Rome at its head, has never ceased to be potential, except during the five months, in 1849, when the pope was deprived of his temporal power.

Twenty-five thousand persons, the tenth of the active population and the hundreth part of the whole, were either exiles or in the pope's dungeons, when Pius IX. ascended the papal throne in 1846.

It was difficult to find a family who had not some member in prison or exile. When it was supposed that Pius IX. would not coöperate with the Jesuits; as his predecessor had done, it was apprehended the Jesuits would poison him. The Romans at that time, believing the new pope a different man, from what he proved himself to be, would often shout, "Holy Father, beware what you eat! don't trust the Jesuits!" The centuroni, a band of robbers and vagabonds, who were organized as a secret society, headed by "Priests and Monks, in 1831, held the cardinal doctrine to kill a liberal, is the surest passport to heaven.

When the Dominican friars had to flee from their convent in 1849, they left in their hurry a document of great value, which disclosed their practices. It was a volume of autograph letters from various prelates and bishops, and common priests, addressed to the president of the Inquisition. The president is none other than the pope, who has the business transacted by the inquisitor general, who is a Dominican. In these letters it was found that almost every writer had *violated the secrets of the confessional*—secrets which they declared so inviolable that, one of their authors says, that "*God himself never knows what you say to your confessor!*" In all these letters, it is proper to remark, that the secrets revealed related to political state affairs, *no matter in what country.* Many of these letters were written by Irish and English Prelates, and clearly expose (what was well known before) that the confessional is nothing but an engine of the police.

These letters would have been published at that time, but no one anticipated the Pope would ever return. Now, the volume is concealed in Rome, with others of a similar character, and never can be had, until the papacy is destroyed. The letters, however, were seen by gentlemen of undoubted veracity, such as Sterbini, Marelli, Montecchi, and many others, who were exiled on the Pope's return, and resided in England or France, in 1851.

Antonelli, who is now the all-powerful minister and only influential counsellor of the pope, was, years ago, as prelate and governor of the province of Viterbo, sold to the Jesuits, soul and body. This debased wretch while there, obtained through an informer, the names of the principal young men of the town, who were accused of conspiracy. Antonelli had no proof whatever of their guilt, but he summoned the parents of each separately, and showed them a mock pardon, as coming from Rome, on condition that their sons should confess the crime and urged them to induce this, that he might show his mercy and forgiveness. The unfortunate young men, believing him, did confess to a crime of which they were ignorant! And the next night the whole forty-seven were arrested and thrown into the State dungeons.—*Nicolini.*

When this premier of the pope was at Marcerata as Delegato, he committed *adultery* and sent an assassin to take the life of the unyielding husband. This scandal caused his return to the court of Rome, and to punish him they made him treasurer, a situation which gives absolute right to a Cardinal's hat. It may be remarked here, that this is not unprecedented in the Roman Catholic church.

When the immoralities of a priest excite too much scandal, he is sent to another field of enlarged operations. This is the case in England, and in the United States of America, where the clergy are subject to the civil laws. But in Italy, where the priest is superior to all law, nothing can exceed their iniquities. In the small town of Senigallia, for example, with a population of but six thousand inhabitants, it has two hundred and fifty priests, beside two hundred monks and friars!

Rt. Hon. M. Gladstone, in two letters addressed to the Earl of Aberdeen, thus describes the chains of the persecuted in the Inquisition, under the Neopolitan Government.

"Each man wears a strong leather girt round him above the hips. To this are secured the upper ends of two chains. One chain of four long and heavy links descends to a kind of double ring fixed round the ankle. The second chain consists of eight links, each of the same weight and length with the four, and this unites the two prisoners together, so that they can stand about six feet apart. Neither of these chains is ever undone day or night. The dress of common felons, which, as well as the felon's cap, was there worn by the late Cabinet-Minister of King Ferdinand, of Naples, is composed of a rough and coarse red jacket, with trowsers of the same material. On his head he had a small cap, which makes up the suit; it is of the same material.

"The weight of their chains, I understand, is about eight rotoli, or between sixteen or seventeen pounds for the shorter one, which must be doubled when we give each prisoner his half of the longer one. The prisoners had a heavy limping movement, much as if one leg had been shorter than the other. But the refinement of suffering in this case arises from the circumstance that here we have men of education and high feeling chained incessantly together. For no purpose are these chains undone—and the meaning of these last words must be well considered—they are to be taken strictly."

It is common in Naples to arrest any person who may displease the police by a band of ruffians who are masters of life and property. One will go and denounce a man as a conspirator, to any of the tribunals; others will assume the secular dress and appear against him in evidence; others will assume the judges' robes, and sentence the poor victim to death or the dungeons. He has no redress, for the man who would dare to defend his innocence must join him in the dungeon. No newspaper dare make a single comment of pity! This Ferdinand is the king whom Pius IX. holds up as a model for the imitation of all Europe!

In Rome it is still worse, for there are really three tyrannies, actively potential. It is, and has always been the practice of the *sbirri*, who are pardoned assassins, to prowl the streets, enter houses, with or without pretext, and drag the innocent and unsuspecting to prison. The French soldiers, in 1849, lent their protection to this murderous band, who went to arrest the mothers and sisters, whose crime was, strewing flowers upon the grave of their sons and brothers who died fighting for the republic. Ten thousand captives, taken by the *sbirri* and French gend'armes, now fill the Roman prisons. In the dungeons of the Inquisition are numbers under sentence of death, many who since 1849 have never seen a friendly face, and do not know yet the crime for which they are imprisoned!

While thus heartlessly exulting over 15,000 captive subjects condemned, the pope boasts to the world of his paternal heart, and the unbounded love he has for his children!

Throughout Italy, we see the same tyrannical spirit. In Lombardy, women, aye ladies, have been publicly disgraced by flagellation; and this has been done to women, by Romish priests, more than once in these United States.*

In Lombardy, General Haynau's successor has imposed the Spanish Inquisition. He requires his agents and inspectors to give him an accurate account of what the suspected party thinks, nay, of what the informer supposes he would think in such and such given circumstances. This horrible atrocity would excite a smile, but for its awful reality.

Unbelievers and atheists, so long as as they are obe-

* Horsewhipping by the priests is quite an institution in Ireland, where women make no resistance and crouch like spaniels. We sometimes find similar chastisement practised by the popish priests in the United States. Joanna Conner was recently whipped unmercifully by a Roman Catholic priest, in Delaware co., Pa. Her crime was in marrying a Protestant, which constitutes a heinous offence to the church, even in this free country. The whip used on this occasion was made of twisted wire—one said to be used by him to punish refractory Catholics. He made the woman kneel, and whipped her with this horrid instrument of torture. She ran to the piazza, screaming; he brought her back, and again made her kneel, and lashed her; then directed her to bathe in salt and water! These facts have been duly attested, under oath. She stated in her affidavit that this priest had whipped other women in the place, and that it was his custom to chastise in this manner men, women, and children, who displeased him!

dient to the Pope, and outwardly reverential towards the church, are favorites rather than otherwise; and nothing stands between them and a cardinal's hat! "Had I," says Dr. Achilli, "believed nothing at all, I should have given offence to no one; if I had even adopted the language of Voltaire, I should have merely raised a laugh; but in speaking the language of the Bible, I attacked the priesthood, and incurred its hatred and persecution." For heretics (Protestants), Rome has an Inquisition always ready. On hearing that this horrible tribunal had laid hold of him, the monks of Naples began to chant their hymn of victory, "He who made war on us, is fallen; he who branded us with dishonor, is fallen to rise no more: the Inquisition will root out from the earth, the very memory of his name." "We ought to burn this heretic alive," said the Ancaiene, the general of the office.

Twice was this distinguished "heretic" incarcerated in the Inquisition in Rome. In 1849, during the few months in which the republic existed, Dr. Achilli devoted himself to the dissemination of the Word of God; and it was for this, that he was seized while Rome was in the hands of the French soldiery, and dragged to a dark, humid cell of the Inquisition. By superhuman power, he made his escape after six months, and fled to London, where he was persecuted by the Jesuits, in their usual way; especially towards one who had held such elevated positions in the church, and might have, in time, been Pope himself, being in the regular line of promotion to a cardinalate. From London, where he demanded a trial, and obtained a glorious vindication from his renowned reviler, Cardinal Wiseman, he came to the United States; and here the Jesuits pursued him, insinuating and influencing Protestants to disbelieve his statements, etc. This is precisely their course of action in all similar cases, which this volume records. But wherever his book is read, the reader must rise from its perusal, satisfied that no man would have done and suffered for the cause of the Saviour, what he has endured, unless sustained by the Christian's faith. He sacrificed himself, rejecting preferments in the Roman Catholic Church, for freedom to worship God.*

"When the Inquisitors determined to seize a victim, they send their officers commonly at midnight, in a coach. They knock at the door, and when some one inquires 'who is there?' 'The Holy Inquisition,' is the answer. The door is instantly opened—as the officers take the whole family if they do not find the accused. If the neighbors hear the noise of the coach, they dare not go to the windows, for it is well known that no other coach but that of the Inquisition is abroad at that time of night. Nay, they are afraid to inquire in the morning. If the accused be a daughter, son, or father, and some relative asks the cause of the tears and grief of the family, the only answer is, the girl was stolen away in the night; or the son, father, or mother did not come home the night before, and they suspect is murdered, etc. This is the only answer they can give without exposing themselves to the same danger.

"When the doors of all the prisons were opened in Spain, by the order of the secretary of Monsieur de Legal, the wickedness of the inquisitors was detected. Among the prisoners who obtained liberty that day, were sixty young women, well dressed, and of good appear-

* From Achilli's "Dealings with the Inquisition," the author is indebted for many important facts contained in this work.

ance, who were the seraglio of the inquisitors, as they owned afterwards. The archbishop went to Monsieur de Legal and desired these women to be sent to the palace of his grace, that he might take care of them and thus avoid scandal against the holy tribunal. The governor answered, he would do all that he could to aid the archbishop, but the French officers took them all away. One of these women afterwards married in France, and related to the author* what happened to herself in Zaragossa, and what she there saw. She was young (only thirteen), when her mother went one day to visit the Countess of Attarass, and there she met Don Francisco Torrejon, her confessor, and second inquisitor of the holy office. He paid her attention, asked her age, and many intricate questions about religion, and she kissed his hand reverently when they parted. My dear child, I shall remember you till next time, said the confessor. The night following he did remember her, for while asleep, she was aroused by a loud knocking at the door. The maid called out of the window, and was answered, 'the Holy Inquisition.' Her own father, like another Abraham, ran to the door and opened it, and to show his great obedience to the church, put in his child's mouth a bridle, while he was himself in tears. She was speedily carried away to an elegant apartment, was furnished with the most sumptuous repast, and a magnificent wardrobe. Here she met her confessor, Father Torrejon, and was made the victim of his iniquities, after which the role changed, and she was thrust into her narrow cell. This was the like experience of the whole number, which often amounted to seventy at a time. Every year some

* Gavin's Master-Key of Popery.

of the old ones would suddenly disappear, and new ones would come to take their places.

"'The next morning after I was there,' she continues, 'I was shown by the maid the pan and gradual fire: this was a dark room with a thick iron door, and within an oven and a large brass pan upon it, with a cover of the same, and a lock, the oven was burning at that time. Then I was shewn a wheel covered on both sides, and opening a little window in the centre, and shewing me, by the light of the candle, the inside, which was set with sharp razors. After that, I was shown a pit of toads and frogs. 'Now,' said my guide, 'I will tell you the use of these three things. The dry-pan and gradual fire are for heretics; and those who oppose the holy father's will and pleasure, they are put alive in the pan, and the cover being locked, the executioner begins to put a small fire in the oven, and by degrees increasing it until the body is reduced to ashes. The wheel is for them who speak against the pope and the holy fathers; the person is put inside, and the little door is locked, and the executioner turns the wheel until the victim is dead. The pit of toads and frogs is designed for all who show contempt for images, or disrespect for ecclesiastical persons; the victims are thrown into the pit and become their food! This was shown to me that I might, by the fear of instant death, willingly obey the wishes of the father inquisitor. The three colors of our clothes were the distinguishing tokens of the three father inquisitors. They used to give these colors, the three first days, to these women they brought for their use. Leonora, my companion in misery, said she had been over six years in the Inquisition, having been taken from her father's house at the age of fourteen, and our constant lament is to think that the holy fathers will put us to death as soon as they are tired of us, and with great reason, for they will never run the hazard of being detected by sending out of the house any of our companions. After I had been eighteen months in that place, the maid came one night and ordered us to follow her into the coach, which conveyed us to another house, where we were kept for two months; after which we were again removed to another house, where we were miraculously delivered by the French officers."*

* For valuable additional facts affecting immediately the interests of the people of this country, see Supplemental Chapter.

CHAPTER V.

THE SOCIETY OF JESUS.

How the Constitutions were made known—The result in France—The Means taken to avoid Detection—The different editions of this Mysterious Work—The Boy Trained by Jesuits—The Probationer—Colleges—Public Schools—Studies—Blind Obedience—Blasphemous Oath—Jesuit Mission from the Pope to our Country—They are above our Civil Laws—The General of the Order—His Power—How Elected—The Jesuits Expelled—The Jesuits Restored—Popery sustained by them—Pius IX—Protestants Duped by their Deceit—The American College at Rome—Spies of the Inquisition.

THE "Constitutions" of the "Society of Jesus" were first publicly promulgated in the celebrated suit of M. Lionci and Father La Valette. This civil prosecution was brought to recover from the Society certain monies lost to them by the Jesuits' Mercantile Missions in Martinico.

The Jesuits were constrained to bring the mysterious volume into court, and conscious of the just indignation which its publication would excite, they obliged all the members of the order to maintain a profound secresy respecting it.*

All France was aroused to the most intense indignation. The parliament issued their decree abolishing and banishing the "Society of Jesus" from the nation; and in that national act assigned these reasons: "The consequences of their doctrines *destroy the law of nature: they break all the bonds of civil society by authorizing theft, lying, perjury, the utmost licentiousness, murder, criminal pas-*

* Regulæ Communes, § 38. Cited Monarchie des Solipses, p. 120.

sions, and all manner of sins. These doctrines, moreover, root out all sentiments of humanity: they overthrow all governments, excite rebellion, and uproot the foundation and practice of religion. And further, they substitute all sorts of superstitions, irreligion, blasphemy, and idolatry.

The mysterious policy of these constitutions was never discovered to the *ordinary*, nor even all the *professed*, Jesuits. To the novices are communicated only the apostolical letters of Julius III., the abridgment of the constitution and the common rules. Nor have the other Jesuits access to any additional information concerning the nature of their institutes, but such as relates to the charge with which they are immediately intrusted.*

The still further precaution was adopted by the general of the order using *cyphers* in his correspondence, and it was directed that immediately on the death of any person who had in his possession letters from the general, the assistants, or the provincial of the order, such letters should instantly be burned, without being read.

NOTE.—When a history of the Jesuits was published in this country by Pitral, the Very Rev. Mr. De Blieck, President of St. Xavier Roman Catholic College, at Cincinnati, said, in a speech, that "It was a tissue of lies, and if a single charge therein contained was true, I would leave the order." Mr. Pitral replied by publicly challenging him to a public discussion to prove his assertion, and furnished further proof to confirm what he stated in his book.

The President Jesuit, bishop, of course, backed out, and Mr. Pitral addressed him thus: "Rev. Father, my position as a Roman priest has been such that I know whereof I affirm, and you knew that I knew, hence the Jesuitism displayed in letting me alone." So we say to the whole Romish Hierarchy of this country, you know by the authorities we produce, that we know what we state is true, and you may deny it if you dare.

* Monarchie des Solipses. Declar. in Exam. Hist. Gen. des. Jes. III., 239.

Many edicts which possess the force of laws among the Jesuits, it is believed, have never been printed;* and even the constitutions they have seldom committed to the press but in the colleges of the order. Whenever they ventured to print this work elsewhere, they always took precautions to secure the whole impression. It was, however, clearly impossible that these precautions should be universally successful. The order has at all times had too many enemies to be able for any long period to retain the exclusive possession of a volume of which numerous copies were printed, though not published, and which all the activity of malice was exerted to procure. Hospinian, in the "Historia Jesuitica," published, in 1619, gives a complete abstract of the constitutions. They are quoted, with accurate knowledge, in the "Catechisme des Jesuites," of Pasquier, who died in 1615. They are also in the "Historia Jesuitica" of M. Ludovicus Lucius, Basle, 1627. M. Bernard, who wrote the "Historie de la Compagnie de Jesus," printed at Utrecht in 1741, refers to the edition of Lyons, in 1607, and mention has been elsewhere made of an edition in 1599.

The extracts from the Constitutions of the Jesuits which are found in the "Mercure Jesuite," are taken from an edition printed at Rome, 1583. There is a volume of the "Constitutiones," in small 8vo, in the British Museum, Rome, 1570. The copy produced on the trial of La Valette, was the edition of Prague, in 2 vols. folio, 1757, and contained 91 pages, "and although it is clear to me," says Mr. Penrose,† "that numerous additions have incontestibly been made to the original Constitutiones, yet no alteration in the letter of the statute has taken place, and there is no reason to apprehend that the text of the *Constitutiones Societatis Jesu, Romæ*, 1570, has at any

* Chalotais, p. 20.

† Rev. John Penrose, M.A., Corpus Christi College, Oxford.

time been violated. This, also, I believe, was a re-impression from a preceding edition, in 1550." (1558.)

It was in 1558, that the volume of Constitutiones, translated from the Spanish of Loyala, by father John Polancus, was originally committed to the press by the college of the society in Rome. A copy of this edition has supplied the text from which the *first English edition* has been faithfully and accurately reprinted. This Roman copy of 1558 has been subjected to a scrutiny with that printed at Antwerp in 1702, which has the sanction of the Society, and they are precisely similar in all particulars. It is from this edition, in which every consideration is made subordinate to undeviating fidelity to the original, we are able to give the American reader an exact sense of Jesuit-legislation.

The Romish hierarchy declares to the people of the United States the following determination, through its chief organ in our country: "The Church is a kingdom and a power, and as such must have a supreme chief (pope), and *this authority is to be exercised over States as well as individuals. If the pope directed the Roman Catholics of this country to overthrow the Constitution (and put down the American flag), sell the nationality of the country, and annex it as a dependent province to Napoleon the Little (a papist sovereign), they would be bound to obey. It is the intention of the pope to possess this country.*"*

That every protestant, foreign and native, may understand the means by which the work of "possessing this country" is to be accomplished (which is now being attempted), we commend to their attention the disclosures made from the "*Constitutions of the Society of Jesus,*" and the "*Secret Instructions*" of the Jesuits, which are unknown to the great majority of the people.

* Brownson's Review.

The Freeman's Journal, the organ of the Archbishop of New York, has the following significant and suggestive article, on the Atlantic cable: "How are we to regard this new triumph of mind over matter? Is it a good or an evil? Unquestionably for a long time the principal messages that will go backward and forward will be those that relate to finance, and items of news that, on the other side of the water, we might live very comfortably without. But the sole reason for such use of the telegraph will be that financiers and newsmongers choose to employ it and pay for it. It will be as free to others as to them. *The Church* will find occasion to use the telegraph; and many a time hereafter the thought at Rome will be flashed in a moment of time across land and sea to New York, to the valley of the Mississippi, and to the Pacific coast of the United States.

"Rome insists on hearing *every case* and *every side of every case*, before it renders judgment. But if questions can be asked and answered in an instant, how many delays in matters of importance may hereafter be avoided!

"We need not comment on how much of personal anxiety may be relieved, and how much private convenience may be served by this power of instant communication. But we will go farther. The ultimate extent of these developments of intelligence will render it extremely difficult for errors of fact to exist. As time progresses, facilities for freer communication will be multiplied. Intelligent and *free combination and cooperation among Catholics* can, for the cause of truth, do all, and more than all, that combinations of men who have in view objects not thus eternally true, can effect. When the Catholic Press rises to its true level, it will find in this grand system of telegraphs a wonderful aid.

"We will suggest but one other thought in this connection. The laying down of this telegraph has given to *Ireland* a most remarkable position."

What does all this Jesuitism mean? What sort of co-operation and combination among Roman Catholics for the cause of the truth? These are deep and solemn questions;

"After the age of fourteen, the boy enters on probation in the 'Society of Jesus.' He is received as a guest, in his usual dress, unless the Superior otherwise determine. The following day, it is declared how he shall conduct himself. He is told that he is in no way to hold intercourse within or without those walls, by word or by writing, except with such as are designated by the superior for that purpose. This is done, that he may weigh well with himself and with God, his calling, and resolution of serving the divine and *Supreme Majesty* in this society.

"Two or three days after he enters the house, a more accurate examination is made, as is set forth in the duty of the examiner, and a written examination is left with him to consider *alone*. Then the Apostolic diploma may be shown to him, and the constitutions and the rules to be observed in the house he has entered. If he has been cultivated, persons are appointed by the superior to ascertain how far, and what is the *nature* of his talents. During this first probation, the novice makes a general confession to the confessor who shall be designated by the superior to receive it. After this, his promise of obedience and a register of all he brought to the house is entered in his handwriting; he obtains absolution, receives the holy Eucharist, and enters the general community of novices; and here begins his second probation. If the probationer cannot settle himself in a life of obedience to be regulated by the society, or if he cannot subject his own opinions and judgment, it will be deemed expedient to dismiss him from the society.

"We come now to the third part, which relates to the advancement of those who remain in probation. The novice never leaves the house except at such time, and with such companions as the superior allows, and must persevere in never speaking or writing a word, except by authority of the superior. He is told the *soul*, the soul must be his care, and he must read some pious book from which all may profit, rather than a difficult one. For the sake of *holy poverty*, he is told he must use nothing as his own, but it is not necessary to give up the entire possession of his property while on probation, unless at the bidding of his superior, who may deem it a hinderance to his *spiritual* progress. He is then taught that to dispense his property or a part for the benefit of the society on his entrance accomplishes a work of great perfection. The superior appoints his confessor, who *knows* what cases should be reserved for his ruler. These boys are now drilled into a thorough disclosure to the confessor. They are told, they must *take pleasure in thoroughly manifesting their whole soul to them*, disclosing their penances, mortifications, defects, and desiring to be guided and directed, if they have deviated from rectitude, and not wishing to be led by their own judgment, except it agrees with those who are to them, *instead of Jesus Christ our Lord!*

"If the novice should, through his confession, manifest a disposition to pride, he must immediately be put to more abject occupations, to humble him, and the modes of penance and subjection are left to the *prudent* charity of the superior. A censor superintends both house and church, and reports constantly to the superior every thing relating to external decorum and decency." Observe this language! "Let all think, let all speak, as far as possible, the same thing, according to the Apostle. Let no contradictory doctrines, therefore, be allowed, either by word of mouth, or public sermons, or in written books, which last shall not be published without approbation and consent of the general (who shall submit them to the censure of three, at least, of learning and clear judgment in that department).

"On certain days in every week let the catechism be taught and the method of confessing rightly also, of communicating, of hearing the mass, and ministering it; of praying, meditating, reading according to the talent of each; and let it be seen that they practice what they learn; let all employ their time in spiritual concerns, and persist in acquiring habits of devotion; to which it will greatly contribute to assign certain or even all spiritual exercises to such as have not before employed themselves in them." "It is especially conducive to advancement, nay, even necessary, that all yield themselves to perfect obedience regarding the superior" (be he who he may) as Christ the Lord; "and submitting to him with inward reverence and affection; let them obey not only in the outward performance of what he enjoins, entirely, promptly, resolutely, and with all due humility, without excuses or murmurs, even though he order things hard to be done and repugnant to their own senses; but let them also strive to acquire perfect resignation and denial of their own will and judgment, in all things conforming their will and judgment to that which the superior wills and judges (where sin is not perceived), the will and judgment of the superior being set before them as the will of their will and judgment."

We next find the novice enjoined on "the virtue of obedience." He is not only to obey the superior, but all his subordinates, for his, the superior's sake, *who is Christ the Lord.* Then they are told to love poverty as their mother, and are made to try some of its results at proper periods. At the end of the first year, they must distribute their temporal goods, as the superior enjoins, under the regulations. There must be no *literary* studies, we are told, unless a dispensation should appear necessary for peculiar reasons. "For colleges provide for the study of literature, and houses for the practice of what they have learnt. After living in the *eternal* performance of the rules, we find that all the novices are enjoined to petition the superior several times a year, *to order them a penance for having neglected their observance.*"

In a chapter on the superintendence of the body, we find that "whatever is needful to its sustenance, is applied for to the superior, verbally or in writing, but not until the novice has had recourse to prayer. After this, if he still desires, he may make his petition, which refused or granted, he alike feels right. Eating, sleeping, rising, etc., are all upon rules of rigid self-denial. The castigation of the body, fastings, penances and labors, are disclosed to the confessor, and he reports to the superior.

After the novice, by his probation, has become a mere machine in the superior's hands, he is turned over to literature! So, in the fourth part of the constitutions, we discover a chapter *of the commemoration of founders and benefactors of colleges.* First: in every college of our society let masses be celebrated once a week, forever, for its founder and benefactors, whether living or dead." At the beginning of every month, all the priests who are in the college, ought to offer the same sacrifice for them, *forever.* Once a year a solemn mass must be said for the founder, and a wax candle, with the arms of the founder, or emblems of devotion, is presented to him if living; if not, to his nearest relative. As soon as the society gets possession of a college, the general communicates the fact to the whole society, everywhere, that every priest may thrice say mass for the living founder! Upon the death of the founder, the general of the order has three masses said for his soul throughout the society *everywhere*, and as often as mass is said by the priests, all who are not priests in the college, are bound in gratitude to take part. The founders and benefactors of colleges are made partakers of all good works which are done by the *grace of God*, not only in colleges, but in the whole society.

What relates to the admission and relinquishing of colleges and her temporal concerns is next discussed. Should the founder of a college exact any conditions contrary to the order of the society, the *general* decides whether to admit them or not; so the general can dismiss a college or house already admitted.

No scholar can be admitted into college who is *unquiet* and offensive to others in word or act; none who cannot settle himself in a life of obedience; none that will not subject his own judgments and opinions to his superiors, *as to God.* They shall only be admitted among the approved scholars who have spent two years under such probation, as we have seen, and have taken vows to enter the society.

The scholars, besides mass and confession, every week, must hear mass daily, take one hour in reciting the office of the Virgin Mary, examining their consciences twice a day, with other prayers, to fill up the hour. Others, who have not learned to read, beside mass, must take an hour in reciting their rosary, or crown of the blessed Virgin.

On their way to the public schools, (they must go nowhere else,) much is said about external and internal modesty: they must renew their simple vows twice a year.

The studies of each pupil are left with the superiors; but the acquisition of divers languages, logic, natural and moral philosophy, metaphysics, theology, scholastic and positive, and the sacred scriptures, which *assist* that object; and as the services of any endowed with good natural abilities, will be *useful* in proportion to his attainments in solid learning; let him be instructed in those branches. Let a thorough foundation be laid in the Latin language, rather than the liberal arts, then the study of the languages in which the sacred scriptures were originally written, is, we find, done "to defend *their version*" of the scriptures.

Latin is the tongue spoken in the colleges by the "students in humanity;" composition, public and private extemporaneous speaking, lectures, etc.,—all these have their place, but they are enjoined to avoid every *appearance* of ambition, and other inordinate passions.

"Let public schools be opened, at least for polite learning, when it can be done, and let care be taken that all the scholars attend the sacrament of *confession* once a month, and let them be well instructed in *Christian learning!*

"The correction with the external scholars should never be withheld, only let it be administered by some one who is not of our society. It is peculiar to our society that we receive no *temporal* remuneration for spiritual services, etc.

Chapter VIII. is devoted to directions to the scholars in what relates to their fellow-creatures. Here they are told to employ *all means* to win others to the service which engages them. "The methods the society pursues (which must be engaged over the various quarters of the world, and with such different classes of men,) in preventing the inconveniences which may arise, and in securing the emoluments which contribute to the greater glory of God, by employing all the means which can possibly be employed; and although that unction of the Holy Ghost, and that wisdom which God is wont to communicate to those who confide in his Divine Majesty, can only teach this, a *way* may still be opened by which the scholar may use his lessons to the furtherance of the society to the glory of God!

The whole power, and administration, and superintendence of the colleges is in the general of the order, who appoints the rectors, etc.

Observe, now, the subordination inculcated, requiring that they should "Revere and venerate their rector, as one who holds the place of *Christ our Lord;* leaving to him the free disposition of themselves and their concerns, with unfeigned obedience; keeping nothing concealed from him, not even their *consciences*, which they should disclose to him—as is set forth in the Examen—at the appointed seasons, and oftener if any cause require it; not opposing, not contradicting, not showing an opinion in any case opposed to *his* opinion.' *They should pay obedience to their superiors in the place of Christ.*

Regularity is so enjoined, that when the signal for a stated duty is given, the pupil must obey, not stopping to complete a single letter!

Of the books which should be studied in the universities of the society, they insist on the more solid and more *safe* in doctrine, like St. Thomas,* Dens' Class Book of Maynooth College, Escobar, Liguori, Sanchez, etc., etc.; nor are any entered on, whose doctrine or authors are *suspected.*

We find much badinage on the subject of not receiving money, saying, "the Lord Christ is *alone* to be their reward!"

We come now to the mode by which the society admits to *profession:* At the time appointed, the general, or some one empowered by him, offers the sacrifice of mass in the church, in the presence of the inmates of the house and others; when the person receives the Eucharist, and with a loud voice pronounces his written vow, in these words: "I, N., make profession and promise Almighty God, before his Virgin Mother, and before all the heavenly host, and before all bystanders, and you reverend father, general of the society, *holding the place of God*, and your successors; or you, reverend father vice-general of the Society of Jesus, and of his successors, *holding the place of God*, perpetual poverty, chastity and obedience, and therein, *peculiar care in the education of boys*, according to the form of living contained in the apostolic letters of the Society of Jesus, and in its constitutions. Moreover, I promise special obedience to the Pope, *in missions*, as is contained in the same apostolic letters and constitutions. Then the name of the country, the day, month, year and church is added,

* St. Thomas Aquinas is commanded in their constitutions but is not at present a text-book in their colleges, because they have invented other doctrines in opposition: as, for example, upon the doctrine of the grace of God and free will of men. Concerning the grace of God, they hold the famous doctrine the "Gracia versatilis," *the grace accommodating itself to the will of men!*

with the name of the person to whom he made the vow. "Then he partakes of the most *holy body* of Christ and the services conclude as before. He leaving all things to his superior, *who doubtless holds the place of Christ our Lord.*"

Those who are admitted as *scholars*, after their first probation, vow in this manner: "Almighty, Everlasting God, I, N., albeit every way most unworthy in thy holy sight, yet relying on thy infinite pity and compassion, and impelled by the desire of serving thee, in the presence of the most holy Virgin Mary, and before all thine heavenly host, vow to thy Divine Majesty, perpetual poverty, chastity and obedience, in the Society of Jesus, and promise that I will enter the same society to live in it perpetually, *understanding all things according to the constitution of the society.* Of thy boundless goodness and mercy, through the blood of Jesus Christ, I humbly pray that thou wilt deign to accept *this sacrifice* in the odor of sweetness, and as thou hast granted thine abundant grace to desire and offer, so thou wilt enable me to *fulfill the same.*

The *sixth* part, of this extraordinary work, instructs as to the persons of those who have been adopted into the society. Holy Obedience is so strenuously enjoined, that they are bound to obey where there appears the *slightest indication of the superior's pleasure, without any express command.* They are told to attend to his voice, *just as if it proceeded from Christ our Lord,* (for as much as we pay obedience to *His place,*) persuading ourselves that everything is *just; suppressing every repugnant thought and judgment of our own* in a certain obedience, and that moreover in all things which are determined by the *superior.* Thus obedient, he should *execute anything* on which the superior chooses to employ him in the service of the society; and altogether believe that he will answer the divine will better, than by following his own will and differing judgment. "They are commanded," (even in the inner man), "to reverence their superiors *as Jesus Christ in them.*" Let every one persuade himself, that they who live under obedience should permit themselves to be moved and directed under divine providence by their superiors, just *as if they were a corpse*, which allows itself to be moved and handled in any way; or as the staff of an old man, which serves him wherever and in whatever thing, he who holds it in his hand pleases to use it!!!

Poverty, they preach as the highest virtue. Let us look at their crafty instructions on this subject. When the pope or superior orders them, (in the United States, for example,) they must present themselves freely, for the glory of God! They are to wear a becoming dress accommodated to the custom of the place, but one, that does not contradict their profession of poverty. They are forbidden to allow trifles to be given to the great, which they say is to get something more valuable in return, and are not to frequent the society of the *leading men*, except when the love of pious works, or their intimacy with them, makes it appear a duty!

They are told, to abstain as far as possible from secular affairs.* "No one, of the professed coadjutors, or even scholars of the Society of Jesus, may allow himself to be examined without the license of the superior in civil or criminal causes, and the superior will never grant permission, except in causes, which relate to the *Roman Catholic Religion.*"†

* Reader, watch these Jesuits, who control the Roman Catholic Church in the United States, whose minions boast, through their presses, in open day, that they aim to control the destinies of our country!

† P. 62, Constitution of the Society of Jesus.

We turn to chapter V. in the sixth part, which has this astounding heading: "That the constitutions involve *no obligation* to commit sin." "It seems good to us in the Lord, that excepting the express vow by which the society is bound to the pope for the time being, and the three other essential vows of Poverty, Chastity and Obedience, no Constitutions, declarations, or any order of living, can involve an obligation to sin mortal or venial; *unless the superior command them in the name of our Lord Jesus Christ, or in virtue of holy obedience; which shall be done in those cases or persons, wherein it shall be judged that it will greatly conduce to the particular good of each, or to the general advantage; and instead of the fear of offence, let the love and desire of all perfection succeed that the greater glory and praise of Christ our Creator and Lord may follow!*"

The seventh part of the constitution treats of the Pope's missions throughout the vineyard of the Lord. The vow, to the vicar of Christ, puts them at his disposal and binds them without any excuse to go into whatever part of the world, he shall send them, whether amongst believers or unbelievers. "Since the society has engaged every thought and will of its own to Christ our Lord and his vicar, neither the general of the society for himself nor any subordinate member for himself, may directly or indirectly treat with the pope or his ministers to remain or be sent into any part, rather than another; but inferior members shall leave all considerations of this kind to the vicar of Christ and their superior; while the superior shall leave whatever relates to his person to the pope and the society of the Lord. Let him yield himself freely when appointed by his holiness to do whatever service is most acceptable to the Apostolic See."

If the pope designates no individual, the superior determines who is best adapted to the mission. It is proper that the whole mission be fully disclosed to the party sent, and the object of the pope's intention; and if possible in writing, that what is enjoined be more exactly accomplished.

"If the time he is to remain in a place be not specified by the pope, he may remain there months more or less; or in short, as it shall be conducive to the general benefit. All of which shall be conducted at the superior's determination, who shall regard the pope's sacred intention for the service.

"Beside the business enjoined on him, he should consider in what other way he may employ his efforts, without detriment to his mission, as said before.

"The General of the society, may also send out members wherever he shall judge most expedient, but who, nevertheless, are prepared to obey the Apostolic See. And it is the duty of those sent to yield full and free obedience to the Superior, as one who governs him in the place of Christ. Wherefore, the superior who sends any, (should generally instruct in writing,) is to be informed by frequent letters, how the mission goes on.

Speaking of a willing mission in any direction; the constitution says: "when its members are dispatched to an extensive region, (like India, or the United States for example,) larger liberty must be allowed, that they may go from place to place; if, not repugnant to the pope; that God may dispose all men to receive his grace, by means of their society.

"Whoever is endowed with the talent of writing books conducive to the common good, and shall compose such; nevertheless, shall not publish them except the general shall previously see them, and subject them to the judgment and censure of others; that if they shall seem good for edification they may come before the public and not otherwise."*

The eighth part of the "Constitutions of the Society of Jesus," treats of the *mutual union* among its members dispersed over the globe with their superior, and among themselves.

This union, we discover, is indispensable to the aim they have in view, and for this reason only their select men are admitted to profession, and are coadjutors or scholars After dwelling at length upon union, and obedience to the shining lights of the order near them; it claims "a frequent intercourse between inferiors and superiors and immediate intelligence of one another; and the knowledge of all that is communicated from various places for edification, and of all that happens, will greatly assist also; such arrangements being made, that in every place whatever tends to mutual consolation and edification in the Lord, may be known from the others. Chap. I., part 8, p. 73. Thus it is that the confessional drills this papal militia—the body-guard of the pope in the United States, and makes the pope of Rome and the jesuit generals and superiors throughout the world, as familiar with every political religious movement in our country, as though they dwelt in the White House, at Washington.

Chapter II. of part eighth, informs us that on very

* Here we see the authority with which Dens, Bailey, etc., wrote their theologies, Sanchez and Le Grand their "Mysteries of Marriage," and here is the source of all the polluted and obscene books which constitute the religious studies and works of the Jesuits, as seen in this volume.

special occasions, the Jesuits hold general congregations, but the system of tactics is so very complete, that there is seldom an occasion to render this necessary. We find when this congregation is called, it is not the whole Jesuit militia, but the professed of which they have comparatively few, and certain coadjutors.* Upon the death of the general, the vicar, whom he nominates before death, for the duty, informs all the rest of his professed brethren, who assemble to elect a successor. The election is made in a similar way to that of the pope, each claiming *that the Holy Ghost impels to it!* The "Constitutions" further say: "And if by general inspiration, without awaiting the process of voting all should elect the same, he shall be General. For the Holy Ghost, who impels to such an election, easily supplies the want of every order and form of electing." When elected "all come forth to do him reverence, and on both their knees shall kiss his hand."

Chapter II. part 9, treats of "What sort of person the general should be," and says, "that he be most intimate and familiar with God and our Lord, as well in prayer, as in all his actions." In the following chapter, his power over the society is discussed. And here we see, that it belongs to him to see the Constitutions of the society observed everywhere. That he can grant dispensation in all cases where dispensation is necessary; and with the prudence which the Light external shall communicate. That he shall determine the study of literature, as he pleases, in all the houses, colleges, and other institutions of the society, over the *whole earth.* That in him is vested all authority over rectors, preceptors,

* The reader will remember, that the professed are under the last vow, and can never be anything else than a Jesuit.

and officials of colleges, and all other institutions of their order. That *every* Jesuit is subject to him, whether professed or not and he may resolve to send them to any part of the world for a period definite or indefinite, as he shall determine, *to do any action* of those which the society is wont to exercise for the succor of souls. He may recall missionaries, and proceed in all things as he shall think for the greater glory of God! In no wise, however, opposing these missions, which originate with the Apostolic See.

The general shall arrange the duties of confessors, preachers, and lecturers, according to the talent of each man for the station. He shall avail himself of the powers conferred on the society by the pope, and communicate so much of them to each inferior member, as he shall judge useful, etc. He shall employ corrections, and enjoin penances adequate to the satisfaction of all defects, regard being had to persons and circumstances. He generally appoints his provincials, rectors of colleges, etc., for three years, but even that period may be shortened and extended, when it shall seem to the greater glory of God and our Lord! He must take care the society derive advantage, and not detriment, in all things. He shall scrutinize, as far as possible, the consciences of those who are under his obedience, and especially to whom he entrusts duties of great importance.*

After such superhuman authority, as is vested in the general, we are surprised to find he, too, has a superintendent! Chapter IV. so instructs "that even perfect men have a soul to be cared for." So this office is to remind the general, with great modesty and humility, what he believes is required of him to the greater service

* *Provincials*, to whom he entrusts duties of *great* importance, and obedience and reverence should always be paid him as one who holds the place of Christ.

and glory of God. He is to be reminded, if he has committed "mortal sins, proceeding to external acts; used the revenues of the college for his own purposes, or alienated the real estate of the society," etc.

In chapter VI. part 9, the duty of the general is defined, and much stress is laid upon the character of the provincials and the local superiors, in the government of the society, and a man celebrated for learning and other gifts, must reside with the superior to inspect the concerns of India; another of Spain and Portugal; another of France and Germany; another of England; and another of the United States of America; and so of the rest, wherever the society is scattered, and every one of them ought to recommend to God the part specifically entrusted to him. Provincials, rectors of colleges, or superiors of houses, should have their assistants, to whom they shall communicate the more important occurrences; although after hearing their opinion, the power of determining is in themselves.

In the tenth part, we find the "society was not instituted by human means, but by grace of the Almighty God, and our Lord Jesus Christ; and to preserve it in its prosperous conditions great diligence must be used to remove ambition, the mother of all evils in every commonwealth and society; and let not the society be deprived of the men who are necessary to the end it has in view. Let every one consider by what means he can promote the salvation of souls, in humility and submission, to our profession; he shall at all times listen to the advice of the general, *or any one appointed by him.*"

Whatever tends to unite every member of the society with its *Head*, must be done; this is accomplished by uniting individuals to superiors, and these with one another, and with their provincials, and all with the general. Let them neither be, nor be shown any tendency of feelings for either side of any faction, which may perchance occur among christian princes or rulers; but a certain universal love, embracing all parties in the Lord, even though opposed to each other!"

The first approbation of the Society of Jesus, was made by Pope Paul III., in 1540. Its suppression by Pope Clement, took place 21st July, 1773. The pope hesitated on the subject four years before he signed the bull, aware, as he was, of the importance of this order to the church, and the scandal which would follow its suppression. But the propaganda, furnished him means of understanding the danger, as well as the benefit of the order, which were unknown to the rest of the world; and he deliberately pronounced it inherently wicked and mischievous, dangerous to the peace of the world and unworthy of longer toleration!

In the two centuries the Society had existed, at that time, it had so disturbed the peace of Europe, that thirty-seven states had suppressed it before the pope did so. But, in 1814, the Pope Pius declared "that the whole catholic world demanded with a unanimous voice, the re-establishment of the Society of Jesus, and that it would be a great *crime towards God*, to neglect the aid which the special providence of God had put at the disposal of the Roman Catholic church, and if placed in the bark of Peter, tossed and assailed by continual storms, we refused to employ *the vigorous and experienced rowers*, who volunteer their services, in order to break the waves of a sea, which threaten every moment shipwreck and death." He further declared in his bull, that all the concessions and powers granted to the Russian empire; and the two Sicilies, should henceforth extend to all his ecclesiastical states, and also *to all other states*, and he closed his edict forbidding any one to infringe, or by an audacious temerity to oppose all, or any part of this ordinance.

In entire consistency with this, every succeeding pope has coöperated with the Jesuits, to the present hour. Pius IX, is using these "*experienced rowers*" in the United States, with a success that seems incredible. Here, the *only* country from which they have never been expelled, and where they have fled, when the governments of Europe were reduced to the necessity of driving them out,—here they have already made *great progress* in undermining our civil and religious liberties.

Now, when the pope, the head of this order, declares that the religious orders hold the first place in our Republic, and that the Romish Church owes its lustre and support to these orders, and has endowed them with many exemptions, privileges and faculties, we ask the judgment of our Protestant fellow-citizens, upon the propriety of an *immediate legal expulsion of the Jesuits from our country.*

In the design for acquiring accessions to the church of the pope, we find "American catholic libraries," for the avowed purpose of obtaining proselytes, by lending gratuitously, books treating of religious controversies and piety, "especially to their Protestant countrymen." When under the influence of admiration for the pageant of the ceremonies, the delicious music, etc., Protestants, ill-grounded in their own principles, and favorably impressed by their influence and polite attentions, are easily interested and taken captive.

These Jesuits have found their way into colleges, theological institutions of Protestants at this day, in England and the United States. They pretend to be converted, and enter Protestant churches. They were found in the Reformed church in France and Holland, and caused grievous and fatal divisions by false doctrine. They were in the ranks of the old English Puritans. This was discovered by a letter from the Jesuit confessor of the king of England, to the Jesuit confessor of Louis XIV. "How admirably our people imitate the Puritan preachers," said he, in this intercepted letter.

An American college at Rome, for the education of the sons of America, according to the Romish organs in our country, is now being built! That is a fresh step to advance the subtle power of Romanism. The pope ordered the funds for this purpose, (one hundred thousand dollars) to be raised in the United States. Did Protestants contribute?

"The English college" at Rome, has been eminently useful in helping Romanism in England.

In October, 1827, the pope for the first time in several centuries, visited their summer retreat, fourteen miles from Rome. A student then present, described the affability and condescension of the pope, in a very graphic manner. He allowed the pupils to kiss his foot and his hand; blessing their heads; dining at their table; and conferring on them, as they knelt before him, the very significant appellation, "the hope of the church." He went home to the Vatican, and sent a present of a beautiful young calf, ornamented with flowers; and directing his masters of ceremonies, that in the procession of the Corpus Christi, the students of the English college should carry the hangings which are borne over the pope, as he carries the holy sacrament.*

Maynooth College, in Ireland, from whence most of the Jesuit priests of our country emigrate, was at first founded for ecclesiastical scholars alone, but a lay department was afterwards added by the Jesuits, to secure their system of education to *secular* men.

We see now that the Jesuits have neither heart, soul nor conscience. They are sent to our country to do *any* deed they are ordered, no matter how bloody. They come under sealed orders, and ask for the education of the children, according to their own maxim: "Give us the education of the children of this day, and the next generation will be ours—ours in maxims, in morals and religion." They are now doing with education in the United States exactly what they have done in every European kingdom. They affect all the learning of the world; they establish their academies, and their professional honors to win the young into their embrace. The Jesuit nuns are pursuing the same course in concert with the aspiring and licentious priests, in deluding young girls. These "Sisters of Charity," "Sisters of the Sacred Heart," etc., invade the sanctity of families, and ensnare the souls

* In this manner attentions are lavished on Americans by the pope's hierarchy among us; for America, like England, is the hope of the church! Other orders, encouraged by the example of the Society of Jesus, are directing all their energies to extend and perpetuate the dominion of the Holy See among us. The Jesuits, we should understand, do not limit their education to ecclesiastics; but their object is, through their peculiar system of instruction, to obtain influence, not over the clergy alone, but over the minds of all ranks and professions, especially those who might rise to eminence in political and secular pursuits.

of the innocent and confiding. Their zeal is more fervent for the cause of the pope in the United States, than in any other country in the world.

When Pope Clement XIV. abolished the Society of Jesus in 1773, as being too diabolical to be endured by humanity; he said, "It will cost me my life, but I must abolish the dangerous order." It did cost him his life. A notice was placarded on his gate a few days after his bull appeared, stating that, "the See would soon be vacated by the death of the pope." He died of poison a few days after that announcement. On his dying bed the pope said to those around him, "I am going to eternity, and I know for what!"*

Reader, remember that in the mission of the Jesuits now in the United States, they are entirely dependent upon the Roman Catholic bishops. They must communicate, for example, with them upon every thing relating to the advancement of the papal church. The bishops are appointed as Apostolic Legates, to oversee and superintend the Jesuits, and to counsel, assist and direct them in every possible manner that will further the cause of popery among us.

Every bishop in the United States is the head of the interests of the Roman Catholic church in his own diocese. He is responsible for every thing that is done, and must secretly give account to the Holy See of the different operations of the missions in his diocese. This correspondence Archbishop Hughes and the rest of the bishops must hold directly with the Inquisition, and by means of the Inquisition, he receives all his instructions.

The spirit of the Inquisition is the spirit of every

*Brewster's Encyclo., vol. xi., p. 171.

Roman Catholic bishop. The doctrine of the Jesuits must be received by every bishop. He is threatened with canonical penalties in case of non-performance of these obligations. By this is meant a suspension from his office, and a fine to be paid to the Holy See, if he does not exactly fulfil these duties to the Jesuits.

Every bishop, on being consecrated, receives these instructions, which are so many laws of which he must well inform himself, and scrupulously obey. Amongst the many oaths which he is obliged to take, is one which is regarded of the highest importance, by which he promises "to obey all the laws of the *Holy Inquisition*," and to give every kind of assistance to advance the interests of the Holy Mother Roman Church in his diocese.*

The semi-centennial celebration of the Jesuit college of Mount St. Marys, at Emmittsburg, Maryland, occurred the present month (October, 1858). The event is said to have been regarded "by the entire Catholic community of the United States with extraordinary interest." The Pope of Rome was toasted, with this Jesuitical remark by the president of the college: "It is not because he is a sovereign, but because, whether in adversity or prosperity, he is *the friend of man, of liberty, and liberal principles!*"

Archbishop Hughes responded in these words: "There never was a Sovereign Pontiff who showed more kindness to the United States than Pio Nono has done!" "He delights to learn there is more need of more mis-

* The archbishop of the diocese of New York has recently publicly declared himself a member of the "Society of Jesus." This he did when he laid the corner stone of the new St. Patrick's Cathedral, and put the motto of the Jesuits at the head of the stone. This, none but a Jesuit can do. The motto is A. M. D. G.—"Ad majorum Dei gloriam."

sions and more bishops—a paternal love of which *other nations have been jealous.* This has been exemplified by the origin of the idea that America should have a college near the centre of unity. (Applause.) It was not extraordinary, perhaps, that he was pleased with the idea of an American college at Rome; but it was hardly to be expected that he should appropriate, out of his own private purse, $42,000, as he had done! and I do not fear that we shall be failing, when the pope appeals to us in behalf of this institution. *It is natural he should wish to draw this country near to the eternal rock on which Christ built his church.* In accordance with the rules of the Society of Jesus, a solemn requiem mass was chanted for the souls of the dead founders of St. Mary's College, and the procession formed according to the constitutions of the Jesuits, while the bells tolled a solemn dirge."*

* N. Y. Herald.

CHAPTER VI.

THE PRINCIPLES OF JESUITISM.

Introductory--Philosophical Sin—Vincent Fillincius—John De Lugo—Anthony Escobar—Thomas Tamlusin—George de Rhodes—Isaac de Bruyn—Blasphemy—Casnedi—Profanation—Francis De Lugo—George Gobat—Trachala—Impiety—John of Sales—James Gordon—Imago—Escobar—Amadeus Guimenius—Jesuits of Caen—John Marin—Le Meyne—Francis Odin—Idolatry—Gabriel Vasquez—Perjury—Lying—False Witness—Sanchez—Leonard Lessins—Fillincius—Busenbaum and Lacroix—Theft and Secret Compensation—Emmanuel Sa—Reginald—Francis Amicus—Thomas Tamlusin—Stephen Baury—Homicide—Henry Henriquez—Reginald—Fagundez—Amicus—Airault—Parricide and Homicide—Gobat—Fagundez—Suicide and Homicide—Bridgewater—Robert Bellarmine—Frances Tolet—Marianna—John Ozorius—Andrew Endœmen—John—James Keller—Benedict Justinian—Leonard Lessins—John De Descastille—James Gretser—The Pope Absolves from all Civil Oaths—James Gretser—Paul Laymann—Busenbaum and Lacroix—Gregory of Valentia.

THE "principles" of the Jesuits are so intensely blasphemous and depraved, that much of them cannot be reproduced upon these pages. They write and publish only by the authority of their Society, consequently *their works are binding upon every member throughout the world.* Some extracts from a few of their most accredited works, will exhibit the teaching and practices of these disguised and subtle foes to civil and religious freedom—now so formidable in the United States—and we submit them, without further comment, to the American people:

PHILOSOPHICAL SIN, ETC.

VALERIUS REGINALD: *Praxis fori pœnitentialis.* Lugduni, 1620. (Coloniæ, 1622, Ed. Coll. Sion.) If a man does not *reflect* that it is not lawful to delight in a sin, and while his *will* is abhorrent from it, *he is evidently excused from sin, although he should think upon it with delight for a whole day*."—Lib. xi. cap. 5, sec. 3, n. 46.

The reason is, as long as the *understanding* does not reflect on the wickedness of that which is offered to the will. . . . *The consent of the will is not a sin, etc.* PAUL LAYMANN. *Theologia Moralis.* Lutetiæ Parisiorum, 1627. (Ed. Coll. Sion.) Saurez, Sanchez and Vosquez are right, who maintain that for an action to be imputed unto man for sin, *it is necessary that the agent reflect*, or should have reflected, *upon the sinfulness of the action or on the danger of the sin.*—Tract. 2, cap. 4, n. 6.

If the mind is so absorbed in what may be convenient or useful, that it either reflects not at all or very slightly upon the discredit of an action: *in which case it either will be no sin or only an imperfect or venial sin;* which I think happens *with those who are so completely absorbed in the excess of their sorrow, that they commit suicide.* —Ib. Tract. 3, cap. 5, n. 13.

VINCENT FILLINCIUS: (*Moralium Quœstionum de Christianis Officiis et Casibus Conscientiœ*, Tomus ii. Lugduni, 1633. (Ursellis, 1625. Ed. Coll. Sion.) *An action which is contrary to the natural aud divine law, will not be imputed unto us for sin, except in as far as we knew it to be sinful.*—Tract. xxi, cap. 4, de Consc. n. 116.

JOHN DE LUGO. *Disputationes Scholasticœ de Incarnatione Dominica.* (Lugduni, 1633. Lugduni, 1646. Ed. Bibl. Acad. Cant. (In the words of God to Adam, "*In the day that thou eatest thereof thou shalt surely die*"—"*if thou shalt eat it knowingly*" must be understood, for if he had eaten, *without reflecting on the offence to God, he had not sinned.* . . . As Christ said to Peter, "*If I wash thee not, thou hast no part with me*," so Paul said to the Corinthians, "*If ye are adulterers, ye shall not inherit the kingdom of God.*" But as Peter would not have incurred the penalty if he had not adverted to the command of Christ, so neither would the Corinthians, if they had not adverted to the divine offence; without which, *although it would have been a philosophical adultery* (if I may so express myself) *yet* it would *not have amounted to a theological adultery*, of which Paul was speaking, since he spoke of it, *in terms of a mortal sin.*—Disp. 5, Sect. 6, n. 101.

Anthony Escobar: *Liber Theologiæ Moralis Viginti quatuor Societatis Jesu Doctoribus reseratus.* Lugduni, 1656. (Lugduni, 1659. Ed. Mus. Brit.) *A confessor perceives that his penitent "is in invincible ignorance or at least in innocent ignorance, and he does not hope any benefit will be derived from his advice; but rather anxiety of mind, strife or scandal, should he dissemble?" Saurez* affirms that he ought, because, since his admonition will be fruitless, ignorance will excuse his penitent from sin. —Tr. vii. Sacram. Examen. iv. de Pœnitentiâ, c. 7, n. 155.

Thomas Tamburin. See *Methodus Expeditæ Confessionis.* Lugduni, 1659. Antverpiæ, 1656. Ed. Coll. Sion. Lib. ii, c. 3, sec. 3, n. 23. Although he who, through inveterate habit inadvertently swears a falsehood, may seem bound to *confess* the propensity, yet *he is commonly excused.*—Lib. ii, c. 3, § 3, n. 23. Since he is excused from the sin, he will be excused also, from confession.—Lib. ii, c. 3, § 3, n. 24.

Some maintain, *that the same must be said of blasphemy, heresy, and of the aforesaid* oath. . . . *and consequently that such things committed inadvertently are neither sins in themselves, nor the cause of sin, and there-*

fore need not necessarily be confessed.—Lib. ii, c. 3, § 3, n. 25.

George de Rhodes. *Disputationum Theologiæ Scholasticæ, Tomus Prior.* Lugduni, 1671. *Wherever there is no knowledge of wickedness, there is also, of necessity, no sin.* It is sufficient to have a *confused* knowledge of the heinousness of a sin, *without which knowledge there would never be a flagrant crime.* For instance, one man kills another, believing it to be nothing more than a trifling fault. Such a man does *not* greatly sin, because it is knowledge, only, which points out the wickedness. . . . Therefore *criminality* is only imputed according to the measure of knowledge.—(*De Actibus Humanis.* Disp. 2, Quæst. 2, sect. 1, § 2.) If a man commit adultery or homicide, reflecting, indeed, but still very imperfectly and superficially, upon the great sinfulness of these crimes, *however heinous may be the matter, he still sins but slightly. The reason is, that as a knowledge of the wickedness is necessary to constitute the sin, so is a full, clear knowledge and reflection necessary to constitute a heinous sin.*—*De Actibus Humanis.* Disp. 2, Quæst. 2, sect. 1, § 2.

And thus I reason with Vasquez: In order that a man may freely sin, it is necessary *to deliberate whether he sins or not. But he fails to deliberate upon the moral wickedness of it, if he does not reflect, at least by doubting, upon it, during the act. Therefore he does not sin, unless he reflects upon the wickedness of it.*—Disp. 1, Quæst. 3, sect. 2, § 3.

It is also certain that a full knowledge of such wickedness is required to constitute a *mortal* sin. *For it could be unworthy the goodness of God to exclude a man from glory, and to reject him forever, for a sin on which he had not fully deliberated: but if reflection upon the wickedness of it has only been partial, deliberation has not been complete, and therefore the sin is not a mortal sin.*—De Peccatis, Disp. 1, Quæst. 3, sect. 2, § 3.

Isaac De Bruyn: (*Theologia quam, Preside R. P. Is. de Bruyn, defendent, etc. . . . in Collegio Societatis Jesu.* Lovanii, 1687.) The existence of God is demonstrated. . . . yet as this is not known in itself, nor declared in express terms in reference to us, *there may exist, at least for a very short time, an invincible ignorance of it*, especially among the less instructed (Positio 2).

Charles Anthony Casnedi: *Crisis Theologica.* Ulissypone, 1711. So far from being false, I hold it to be most true, that a man sins not, when he does that which he *considers* to be right, without any *remorse or scruple* of conscience.—Tom. i, Disp. 7, sect. 3, § 2, n. 149.

It is the constant doctrine of the theologians, according to Father Maya and St. Thomas, that there is an *invincible* ignorance of some precepts, not only those which relate to mysteries of faith, but also of the precepts of the decalogue: as usury, lying, fornication, *which are not sins in reference to those who are thus invincibly ignorant.*—Tom. ii, Disp. 16, Sect. 2, § 1, n. 61.

Blasphemy: Charles Anthony Casnedi: *Crisis Theologica* Ulyssipone, 1711. . . . If through invincible error you believe lying or blasphemy to be commanded by God, *blaspheme.*—Tom. i, Disp. 6, Sect. 2, § 1, n. 59.

Omit the worship of God, if you invincibly believe it to be prohibited by God.—Ibid.

As often as you believe invincibly that a *lie* is commanded, lie.—Ibid. § 2, n. 78.

Let us suppose a Catholic to believe invincibly, that

the worship of images is forbidden: in such a case our Lord Jesus Christ will be obliged to say to him, *Depart from me, thou cursed, etc., because thou hast worshipped mine image. . . .* So, neither is there any absurdity (in supposing) that Christ may say, *Come, thou blessed, etc., because thou hast lied, believing invincibly that in such a case, I commanded the lie.*—Ibid. Sect. 5, § 1, n. 165.

PROFANATION: FRANCIS DE LUGO: (*Tractatus de Septem Ecclesiæ Sacramentis.* Venetiis, 1652.) *By what kind of communion is this precept fulfilled?* The question is, when the holy sacrament is voluntarily, but unworthily received. The law which commands an act, commands the substance, but not the manner of it. . . . Therefore the ecclesiastical law which enjoins communion, is only compulsory to the substance of the act, *which is sufficiently fulfilled even by a profane communion.*—Lib. iv. *de Eucharistiâ*, c. 10 ,Quæst. 3, n. 27 et 29.

Thus he who hears *mass* with an evil intent, he who receives baptism in a state of sin, or the priest who administers it in a state of sin, *all fulfil* the *command although by criminal acts.*—Lib. iv, c. 10, Quæsti 3, n. 29.

The divine, positive precept which enjoins the communion, ordains that it be received in a state of grace. *This I deny.* For this precept is fulfilled by an *unworthy* communion, as I have said and as Cardinal de Lugo teaches.—Ibid. n. 30.

GEORGE GOBAT in his *Operum Moralium*, Tom. i, et 11. Duaci 1700, 1701, says: the synod *advises* an inward reverence for Christ, but does not *command* it.—Tom. 1, Tr. 4, Cas. 3, n. 43 et 44.

TRACHALA: (*Lavacrum Conscientiæ Bambergæ*, 1759.) Says: The confessor should not be very strict in examining ordinary persons concerning the number of their enchantments, benedictions and vain observances, since, as Busenbaum observes, in those cases they sin but venially, in which *there is a tacit compact*, as Sanchez and others maintain; neither should he be very strict, about the *kind of superstition;* for there is no distinction made between them, as Diana, etc., maintain.

IMPIETY. JOHN OF SALAS: *In Primum Secundæ Divi Thomæ.* Barcinone, 1607; (Ed. Bibl. Archiep. Cant. Lamb.) An entire love of God is not due to him through justice, nor is even *any* due; though all love is due through a certain kind of *decency and credit.*—Tom. i, Quæst. 3, Tr. 2, Disp. 2, § 5, n. 40.

JAMES GORDON: *Theologia Moralis Universa*, Lutetiæ Parisiorum, 1634. (Ed. Bibl. Acad. Cant.) Speaking of the *love* of God says: I think the time in which this precept *is binding, cannot easily be defined.* It is a sure thing indeed, that it *is* binding, but at what precise time, *is sufficiently uncertain.*—Tom. ii, Lib. vi, Quæst. 13, c. 4, art 2, n. 8.

PETER ALAGONA: *S. Thomæ Aquinatis Summæ Theologiæ Compendium.* (Lutetiæ Parisiorum, 1620.) By command of God it is lawful to *kill an innocent person*, to steal, or to commit fornication; because he is the Lord of life and death and all things: *and it is due to him thus to fulfil his command.—Ex primâ Secundæ, Quæst.* 94.

IMAGO: *Primi Sæculi Societatis Jesu.* Antverpiæ, 1640, says: The Society of Jesus is not a human invention, *but it proceeded from him whose name it bears.* For Jesus himself described that rule of life which the Society follows, first by *his example*, and *afterwards by his words.*—Lib. i, c. 3, p. 64.

The Society *extends over the whole* world, and fulfils the prophecy of Malachi. (*A print representing the two continents, at the foot of which is written*) "From the rising of the sun unto the going down of the same, my name shall be great among the Gentiles: and in every place shall incense be offered unto my name, and a pure offering.—Malachi i. *Ibid*, p. 318.

ANTHONY ESCOBAR: *Universæ Theologiæ Moralis receptiores alsque lite sententiæ, nec non problematicæ disquisitiones*, Tomus i. Lugduni, 1652. (Ed. Bibl. Acad. Cant.) A man of a religious order, who for a short time lays aside his habit for a *sinful purpose*, is *free* from *heinous* sin, and does not incur the penalty of excommunication.—Lib. iii, Sect. 2, Probl. 44, n. 212.

I am of this opinion, and I extend that short time to the space of one hour. A man of a religious order, therefore, who puts off his habit, for this assigned space of time, *does not* incur the penalty of excommunication, *although he should lay it aside, not only for a sinful purpose, as to commit fornication, or to thieve, but even that he may enter unknown into a brothel.*—Probl. 44, n. 213.

The sins of blasphemy, perjury, and unfaithfulness, committed in a state of drunkenness, either are not or are to be imputed to sin.

I think it sufficient to follow the *former* opinion which is probable . . *to utter such things in time of drunkenness, is not sin, but the effect of sin.*—Lib. iv, Sect. 2, Probl. 30, n. 246.

AMADEUS GUIMENIUS: *Opusculum, Tractatus Fidei.* Lugduni, 1664. (. . . 1661, Ed. Coll. Sion.) *An explicit belief in the mysteries of the Incarnation and the Trinity, is not a necessary means of salvation.* This is the opinion of Sotus (and many others) and of John Lacroix. Whence it is evident that he thinks with his associates that a declared belief in the mysteries of the Incarnation and Trinity are not necessary. And indeed justly, for otherwise as Serra has well observed with Laymann, salvation would be impossible to those who were born deaf, when once they were corrupted by mortal sin; since the mysteries of the Incarnation and Trinity could not be explicably propounded to them.—Prop. 1, n. 2, 3 et 4.

Jesuits of Caen: Thesis propaquata in regio, Soc. Jes. Collegio, Celelenimæ Academiæ Codomensis, die Veneris, 30 Jan. 1693. Cadomi, 1693. Neither is an avowed belief in Jesus Christ, in the Trinity, in all the Articles of Faith, and in the Decalogue, necessary to Christians.—Position 8.

John Marin: *Theologiæ Speculativæ et Moralis*, Tomus ii. Venetiis, 1720. God can speak *equivocally* for a righteous purpose, and a righteous purpose is *often* found.—Tom. ii, Tr. 14, de Fide Divinâ, Disp. 5, Sect. 1, n. 9.

Le Moyne: *Propositions, extraites des cashiers dictés au Collège d'Auxene, par le Frere Le Moyne, Jésuite, et censurées dans l' Ordonnance et Instruction Pastorale de M. l'Evêque d' Auxene du* 18 *Septembre*, 1725. A Christian acting *deliberately* may act precisely as a man, and lay aside the character of the Christian man, *in actions* which are not properly those of a Christian.—Le Moyne, Lib. ii, de Act. Hum. c. 1, Sect 2, Art. 1, Obj. 1.

Francis Odin: *Epistola Beati Pauli Apostoli ad Romanos explicata per Franciscum Odinum, Societas Jesu Presbyterum.* Parisiis, 1743. *If God did not will that the Jews should come to the faith, and through faith unto salvation, he indeed played his mimic part skilfully and splendidly.—Ep. ad Rom. C. x. V.* 21, *in notis.*

Busenbaum and Lacroix: *Theologia Moralis, nunc pluribus partibus aucta à.* R. P. Claudio Lacroix, Societatis Jesu. Coloniæ, 1757. Coloniæ Aggrippinæ, 1733. (Ed. Mus. Brit.) When and how often is the love of God binding, remains uncertain. . . .—Tom. i, Pars. ii, Lib. ii, de Fide, Tr. 3, c. 1, Quæst. 37, § 2, n. Sotus, Angelus and others say, that it is binding on every festival . . . on the other hand, Castro Palao and others commonly deny it, and with greater probability.—Ibid, § 3, n. 133.

Sotus and Valentia say it is binding when an adult is about to be baptized. But it is objected, that it is not necessary on account of baptism, because for that sacrament attrition* is sufficient.—Ibid, § 4, n. 134.

Idolatry. Gabriel Vasquez: *De Cultu Adorationis. Libri Tres.* Moguntiæ, 1614. . . . Without regarding in any way the dignity of the thing created, *to direct our thoughts to God alone, while we give to the creature the sign and mark of submission by a kiss or prostration, is neither vain nor superstitious, but an act of the purest religion.*—Ibid.

Perjury, Lying, False-Witness. Thomas Sanchez: Opus Morale in Præcepta Decalogi. Venetiis, 1614. (Antverpiæ, 1624. Ed. Coll. Sion.) He who may conceal goods which he requires for the sustenance of life, lest they should be seized by his creditors and himself reduced to beggary, may swear, when he is examined by the judge, that he has no concealed goods. *And they who are privy to it may swear the same thing.*—In Præcept. Decal. Pars. ii, Lib. iii, c. 6, n. 31.

* Attrition, a regret for having offended God, induced by a fear of his punishment.

When a man has truly or feignedly promised marriage, is, for some reason, free from the obligation of fulfilling his promise, *he may swear*, when required, *that he did not promise understanding. . . .* Because, by adopting a probable opinion, *he may think he is not bound, with a safe conscience.*—In Precept. Decal. Pars ii, Lib. iii, c. 6, n. 32.

A man is *urged* to take a woman for his wife when he is not *compelled* to marry, may *swear* that he will take her, by *understanding* within himself, *If I am obliged*, or *if she should afterwards please me!*—Ibid, n. 39.

He would not sin mortally who, influenced by his reverence for an oath, and from scruple, *should feign to swear, so that the bystanders and the notary might think that he did swear.*—Ibid, c. 7, n. 2.

Leonard Lessius: *De Justiœ et Jure.* Parisiis, 1628. Antverpiæ, 1621. (Ed. Coll. Sion.) *The witness and the accused are not obliged to answer according to the meaning of the judge.*—Lib. ii, c. 31, dub. 3, n. 14.

Vincent Fillincius: Moralium Quæstionum de Christianis officiis et casibus conscientiæ, Tomus ii. Lugduni, 1633. Ursellis, 1625. (Ed. Coll. Sion.) With what precaution is equivocation to be used?—When we begin for instance, to say—"*I swear*," we must insert in a subdued tone the mental restriction "*that to-day*," and then continue aloud, "*that I have not eaten such a thing*," or "*I swear*," then insert, "*I say*," then conclude in the same loud voice, "*that I have not done this or that thing:*" for thus the whole speech is very true.—Tom. ii, Tr. 25, c. 11. de Juramento, n. 328.

John Baptist Taberna: Synopsis Theologiæ Practicæ. Coloniæ, 1736. Qu. 5. Is a judge bound to restore the bribe which he has received for passing sentence?

. . . *If he has received the bribe for passing an unjust sentence, it is probable he may keep it. . . . This opinion is maintained and defended by fifty-eight doctors.*—Pars. ii, Tr. 2, c. 31.

Busenbaum and Lacroix: *Theologia Moralis, nunc pluribus partibus aucta a.* R. P. Claudio Lacroix, Societatis Jesu. Coloniæ, 1757. (Coloniæ Aggrippinæ, 1733. Ed. Mus. Brit.) "*Is a judge bound to restore the bribe which he has received for passing judgment?* Answer. If he has received it for a just sentence he is bound to restore it, because it was otherwise due to the pleader, and he has therefore received no benefit for his money. If the judge has received it for an *unjust* sentence, *he is not bound to make restitution*, as Bannez, Sanchez, etc., teach. . . . *Now, the exposure to such danger in the service of another may be valued at a price.*—Tom. iv, Lib. iv, de Judice, c. 3, Dub. 2, Art. 4, Quæst. 268, n. 1498.

Theft and Secret Compensation. Emmanuel Sa: *Aphorismi Confessariorum.* Coloniæ, 1590. (Coloniæ, 1615. Ed. Coll. Sion.) It is not a mortal sin *to take secretly. . . . And it is not necessary to restore.*

Valerius Reginald: Praxis Fori Pænientialis. Lugduni, 1620. (Tom. i. Coloniæ, 1622. Ed. Coll. Sion.) Servants may not take the property of their masters secretly by way of compensation, *unless it should in reality appear to be the case in the opinion of an experienced man.*—Tom. i. Praxis, Lib. x, c. 18, n. 258.

Servants are excused both from sin and restitution if they only take in *equitable* compensation. . . . Among the conditions of a lawful compensation this is the chief, *that the debt cannot be obtained by any other means.*—Lib. xxv, c. 44, n. 555. (Tom. ii. Moguntiæ, 1622. Ed. Coll. Sion.)

Francis Amicus: *Cursus Thoelogica.* Tomus v. Duaci, 1642. He who has stolen to a considerable amount, *is not obliged under pain of mortal sin to restore the whole.*—Disp. 38, Sect. 4, n. 47.

Thomas Tamburin: Explicatio Decalogi. Lugduni, 1659. (Lugduni, 1665. Ed. Coll. Sion.) That a number of small thefts may constitute a mortal sin, it is necessary they should be committed *continuously.* . . . If *four years* elapse between the commission of one theft and another, it is accounted by *Rebel* to be a considerable interval . . . *one year* by Sanchez . . . *six months* by some, and *fifteen days* by others.—Lib. viii, Tr. 2, c. 3, § 1, n. 3.

Stephen Banny: *Sommes des Péchés qui se commettent en tous Etats.* Rouen, 1653. . . . These trifling thefts, committed on different days, and at different opportunities, against one man or against many, *however great may be the amount which has been stolen, will never become mortal sins.*—Des Larcius, c. 10.

Homicide. Henry Henriquez: *Summæ Theologiæ Moralis,* Tomus i. Venitiis, 1600. (Ed. Coll. Sion.) If an adulterer, even though he should be an ecclesiastic, reflecting upon the danger, has entered the house of an adulteress, and being attacked by her husband, kills his aggressor in the necessary defence of his life, or his limbs, *he is not considered irregular.*—Lib. xiv, *de Irregularitate,* c. 10, § 3.

Valerius Reginald: *Praxis Fori Pœnitentialis.* Lugduni, 1620. (Tom. ii. Moguntiæ, 1622. Ed. Coll. Sion.) If you are preparing to give false evidence against me, . . . *it is lawful for me to kill you, since I should otherwise be killed myself.*—Tom. ii, Lib. xxi, c. 5, n. 57.

Stephen Fagundez: *In Præcepta Decalogi.* Lugduni, 1640. (Ed. Coll. Sion.) Christian and Catholic sons may accuse their fathers of the *crime of heresy* if they wish to turn them from the faith, although they may know that their parents will be burned with fire and *put to death*, as Tolet teaches. . . . And not only may they refuse them *food* if they attempt to turn them from the *Catholic faith*, *but they may also justly kill them*, observing the moderation of a *blameless* defence, if they forcibly compel their children to abandon the faith.—Tom. i, Lib. iv, c. 2, n. 7, 8.

If a judge had been unjust, and had proceeded (in trial) without adhering to the course of the law, then certainly, the accused might defend himself, *by assaulting and even by killing the judge.*—Tom. ii, Lib. viii, c. 32, n. 5.

Francis Amicus: *Cursus Theologici.* Tomus v. Duaci, 1642. It will be lawful for an ecclesiastic, or one of a religious order, *to kill a calumniator* who threatens to spread atrocious *accusations against his religion.*—Ibid, n. 118.

Airault: *Propositions dictees* au Collége de Clermont á Paris, par N. Airault, de la Société de ceux qui se disent Jésuites. Collation fait á la requête de l'Université de Paris, 1643, 1644. Paris, 1720. If you endeavor to ruin my reputation. . . . And I cannot by any means avert this injury of character, *unless I kill you secretly*, may I lawfully do it? Bannez asserts *that I may.* Still the calumniator should first be warned that he desist from his slander; *and if he will not, he should be killed, not openly, on account of the scandal, but secretly.*—Cens. pp. 319, 320.

Parricide and Homicide. Anthony Escobar: *Theologia Moralis.* Tom. iv. Lugduni, 1663. *A son either is obliged or is not obliged to support an infidel father who is in extreme necessity, if he endeavors to turn him from the faith* . . . . I conceive the latter opinion must be certainly maintained. They might also refuse them sustenance, although they should perish for want of food. Fagundez adds, that they might even kill them with the moderation of a blameless defence.—(Tom. iv, Lib. xxxi, Sect. 2, *de Precept*, iv. Probl. 5, n. 55, 56, 57.)

Since by the civil law a father and a husband is permitted to kill his daughter or his wife taken in adultery, the death either may, or may not, be intrusted to others with impunity. The husband and father may certainly intrust it to their children or their servants, and also to strangers.—(Tom iv, Lib. xxxii, sec. 2, de Prec. v, Probl. 35, n. 169, 170, 171.)

George Gobat: *Operum Moralium.* (Tom. ii, Duaci, 1700.) Father Fagundez, in Decal. lib. ix, thus expresses himself: *It is lawful for a son to rejoice at the murder of his parent committed by himself in a state of drunkenness on account of the great riches thence acquired by inheritance!*

It is sometimes lawful to desire a blameless drunkenness, by which the greater benefit would be produced.—(See Caramnel, in Theologiâ Regulari.)—Ibid. n. 57.

Suicide and Homicide. Paul Layman: Theol. Moralis, Wircelurgi, 1748. (Lutetiæ Parisiorum, 1627. Ed. Coll. Sion.) Although the doctrine of St. Augustine may be true, that it is not in any case lawful for a man to kill himself, unless God commanded it; yet it is plainly evident that learned men may not fail to perceive it.—(Lib. iii, sec. 5, Tr. 3, Pars. 3, c. 1, n. 3.)

High Treason and Regicide. Emmanuel Sa: *Aphorismi Confessariorum.* Coloniæ, 1590. (Coloniæ, 1615.

Ed. Coll. Sion.) The rebellion of an ecclesiastic is not a crime of high treason, because he is not subject to the king. *Aphorismi*, verbo *Clericus*. Ed. Coloniæ, 1590.

When sentence has been passed, every man may become executor of it; and he may be deposed by the people, even although perpetual obedience were sworn to him, if, after the admonition given, he will not be corrected.—(*Aphorismi*, verbo *Tyrannus*, n. 2. Coloniæ, 1615. Ed. Coll. Sion.)

John Bridgewater: *Concertatio Ecclesiœ Catholicœ* in *Anglia Calvino Papistas*, *Augustœ Treviorum*, 1494. The people are not only permitted, but they are required, and their duty demands, that at the mandate of the vicar of Christ, who is the sovereign pastor over all the nations of the earth, the faith which they had previously made with such princes, should not be kept.—(Ibid, fol. 348.)

Robert Bellarmine: *Desputationes de Controversiis Christianœ Fidei, adversùs hujus temporis Hœrticos*, tom 1. Ingolstadii, 1596. (Paris, 1608. Ed. Mus. Brit.) It is therefore for the pontiff to determine whether the king must be deposed, or not.—(Ibid, c. vii, p. 891.)

Francis Tolet. (*Commentarii et Annotationes in Epist. B. Pauli Apost. ad Romanos.* Lugduni, 1603. Moguntiæ, 1603. Ed. Coll. Sion.) All men should be subject to the higher powers, but not to the secular powers.—(*Annot.* 2, in cap. xiii. *Espad. Rom.*)

John Mariana:—*De Rege et Regis Institutione. Libri Tres.* Moguntiæ, 1605. (. . . . 1640. Ed. Mus. Brit.) I shall never consider that man to have done wrong, who, favoring the public wishes, should attempt to kill him, who may deservedly be considered as a tyrant. To put them to death, is not only lawful, but a laudable and a glorious action.—(Lib. 1, c. 6, p. 61.) The life of a tyrant is evidently wretched which, held upon the tenure, that he who should kill him would be highly esteemed, both in favor and in praise. It is a glorious thing to exterminate the pestilent and mischievous race from the community of men. For putrescent members are cut off, lest they infect the rest of the body. So should the cruelty of that beast, in the form of man, be removed from the state as from a body, and be severed from it with the sword.—(Lib. 1, c. 7, p. 64.) There is a doubt whether it is lawful to kill a tyrant and public enemy (the same decision will apply to both) with *poison* and *deadly herbs* . . . *for we know that it is frequently done* . . . . In my opinion, deleterious drugs should not be given to an enemy, neither should poison be mixed with his food or in his cup, with a view to cause his death . . . . Yet, *it will indeed be lawful to use this method in the case in question; not to constrain the person who is to be killed, to take of himself the poison which, inwardly received, would deprive him of life, but to cause it to be outwardly applied by another*, without his intervention: as, when there is so much strength in the poison, that if spread upon a seat or on the clothes it would be sufficiently powerful to cause death!—(Lib. 1, c. 7, p. 67.) It was thus that Squire attempted the life of Queen Elizabeth, at the instigation of the Jesuit Walpole.—(Pasquier, Catéchisme des Jésuits, 1677, p. 350, etc.; and Rapin, fol. Lond. 1733, vol. ii, book xvii, p. 148.)

JOHN OZORIUS: *Concionum Joannis Ozorii Societas Jesu, de Sanctis.*—(Tom. iii. Parisiis, 1607.) The power of the keys is delivered to Peter and his successors; in which power many things are included. First, to rule the universal church and to appoint bishops in different places; to preach the gospel throughout the world; to give, to resume, or to moderate all power; to establish kings, and to deprive them of their kingdoms again, if they abandon or oppose the preaching of the faith.—(Tom. iii, Conc. in Cathedrâ S. Petri, p. 64.)

When it is expedient for the spiritual welfare, the pope can remove rulers, kings, and emperors, and can take away their dominions from the wicked and disobedient kings who impede the promulgation of *the gospel*.—(Tom. iii, Conc. in Cath. S. Petri, p. 70.)

ANDREW ENDÆMON JOHN: *Apologia pro mon Henrico Garneto.* Coloniæ, Agrip. 1610. The Jesuit, Hammond, is accused of having absolved all the conspirators in the house of Robert Winter, on Thursday after the conspiracy (the powder plot), when the rebels had already taken arms in their defence.—Apol. c. x., art. 2, p. 272. Since he does not sin who thinks with probability that what he does is lawful, the confessor has not any *just* cause for refusing *absolution*. . . . It is very certain, moreover, that the conspirators who would otherwise have had a clear conscience, had for a long time meditated upon their purpose; they had *weighed* every reason by which they might persuade themselves, that there was nothing in their design contrary to the commandments of God, and as they *possessed the ability* they found many arguments by which to justify themselves in their design. Be it, then, as Coke would have it, that Hammond did absolve the conspirators after they had taken up arms in their defence. I answer that Hammond believed those reasons to be probable, which they produced in favor of the design, and he could not in justice refuse them absolution." . . . What fault will Coke find with this?—(Cap. x., art. 2, p. 274, et seq.)

As to what the Earl of Salisbury alleged, that when Garnet prayed for the failure of the plot, he added this reservation, "*unless it should greatly promote the cause of the Catholics.*" I do not see what it proves. He might abhor the cruelty of the crime; and still, because he was ignorant whether by these means God would choose to consult the good of England, might use that reservation. When Christ, in the agony of his bloody sweat, prayed that the cup might pass from him, he did not dissemble, although he chose that his Father's will should be done in preference to his own. Why then should not Garnet, although he might have abhored such a carnage in the State, conceive himself bound to endure it, if it were ultimately to prove extremely beneficial to the Church?—(Cap. xii., art. 1, p. 319.)

James Keller: *Tyrannicidium, seu Scitum Catholicorum de Tyranni internecione.* Monachii, 1611. (Ed. Mus. Brit.) "The Jesuits, you will say, should have remembered the apostolic rule, not to do evil that good may come. What do I hear of the word of God? Where does it entirely forbid killing? In the fifth commandment, you will say. Well! but what if I should tell you on the other hand, that the fifth commandment is encompassed with formidable difficulties, that no one can keep it. What would become of him who should violate it? You would not inflict any punishment upon him? If you did you would become a tyrant, and would punish a fault which an unfortunate could not avoid." —*Tyrannicidium, Quœst.* 2, p. 20, *et seq.*

Benedict Justinian: *In omnes B. Pauli Epistolas Explanationum, Tomus I.* Lugduni, 1612. "Except the ecclesiastical power, *there is no other power among men* which has received its strength and authority direct from God, and which can affirm with truth, that it may lawfully act with divine authority."—*In Epist. ad Rom.*, c. xiii., v. 2.

John Lorin: *Commentariorum in Librum Psalmorum*, Tomus iii. Lugduni, 1617. (Coloniæ Aggripinæ, 1619. Ed. Coll. Sion.) "Since Peter had more zeal than the rest of the Apostles. . . . when he struck the servant of the high priest, it is for *this reason*, among others, we may *conceive* that the sovereign priesthood was committed to him by Christ, and we may affirm that Ignatius was chosen to be the general of our order, because he would kill a Moor that had blasphemed."—In Psalm 105, v. 31.

Leonard Lessius: *De Justitia et Jure, cæterisque virtutibus cardinalibus.* Parisiis, 1628. (Antverpiæ, 1621. Ed. Coll. Sion.) "The sovereign Pontiff, as the vicar of Christ and the superior of Christendom, can directly annul and remit every obligation contracted with another upon the *faith of an oath*, when there is sufficient cause for it; which remission is *as valid* as if the person, in whose behalf the oath had been sworn, *himself had made it.*—Lib. ii., *de Jurem*, c. 42, *dub.* 12, n. 64.

John De Dicastille: *De Justitia et Jure, cæterisque virtutibus cardinalibus.* Antverpiæ, 1641. "The clergy are exempt from lay power, even in temporal things, is thus proved. No man is directly subject unto one, who has not any jurisdiction over him. . . . but the lay prince (or president) has no jurisdiction over the clergy or ecclesiastics. . . . But a secular prince cannot punish the clergy, therefore ecclesiastics are not subject to lay princes."—Lib. ii., Tr. 1, Disp. 4, Dub. 8, *de Judicio prout Actus Justitiæ*, n. 126.

"The clergy are exempt from lay power, not only by *human*, *civil* and *canonical* law, but also by *divine* law." —Ibid, n. 128.

JAMES GRETSER: *Opera Omnia.* Tom. xi. *Defensio Societatis Jesu.* "It is a question in the schools, whether it is lawful *to kill an innocent person?* What harm, I pray you, is there in these questions? Or what do they contain contrary to the public peace and tranquility? Certainly if the question, 'Is it not lawful to kill a tyrant?' be seditious, the question, 'Is it lawful to kill an innocent person?' will be much more seditious. The question is neither an affirmation nor negative, but a simple inquiry. And to put a question has nothing to do with sedition. The preacher adds that the Jesuits, in this question, incline to the affirmative rather than the negative, as their writings will sufficiently show. We do not *only incline*, but most willingly adhere to the part which has been chosen by St. Thomas and others, who reply to the question by distinction. In conformity with their doctrine, a Jesuit of great celebrity (Gregory of Valentia, Tom. iii., Disp. 5, Qu. 8,) has thus written. . . (A prince) is either a tyrant, not because he has unjustly usurped his throne, but because he makes a bad use of his otherwise legitimate authority, in the administration of the government; or else he is a tyrant through the power which he has forcibly usurped. . . . If he were a tyrant of the latter kind, any man might kill him."

Lest you should be anxious about the death of *John Guiqard*, know that it must be ascribed to *the times, and not to his guilt.* You will never be hanged if you continue *as innocent* as he was.—(Tom. xi, *Append. ad Apol.* p. 317, A.)

We are not so *timid* and *faint-hearted* that we fear to

affirm *openly*, that the Roman pontiff can, if occasion require, *absolve* Catholic subjects from *their oath, of allegiance*. . . . And we add, moreover, that if it be done discreetly and circumspectly by the pontiff, it is a meritorious work.—Vespertilio Hæreticus, p. 882.

Mariana: De Regis Instructione, Lib. i, cap. 6, argues: It is chiefly concerning tyrants of the latter that there is much discussion. . . . Say then, scribbler, Is every prince who *refuses to obey the Roman pontiff* a tyrant of the latter kind? Do the Jesuits determine this? This is what Marian requires that a tyrant of the latter kind may be killed by a private person; or that at least, that if such a judicial sentence cannot be pronounced, the common voice of the people may, with the consent and approval of learned men, proclaim this or that prince to be a tyrant.—Ibid, p. 883. B. C. D. E.

The more common opinion is, that it is never lawful to attack a prince, who has become a tyrant of the second kind, before a public and judicial sentence has been pronounced, by which he is solemnly declared an enemy of the State, and therefore, before he can be deprived of the power which he possessed by those who have the right of taking it away.—Ibid.

James Gretser: *Opera Omnia.* Tom. vii. *Defensio Romanorum Pontificum.* Ratisbonæ, 1736. The first (proposition) is, that secular princes have no power over the clergy who dwelling in their dominions, either by divine or human right.

We deny that *any* example can be produced from the Old Testament which proves that the Levites were subjects to laymen.—Lib. ii, Consid. 3, p. 467. D.

The clergy ought indeed to be subject to higher powers; *but to their own* and to those which are suited to their state, that is, to the ecclesiastical powers.—Ibid. H.

The clergy should also be obedient to the laws of princes, which they enact with the assent and *concurrence of the ecclesiastical magistrate.*—Ibid, p. 468, C and D.

But the clergy do not belong to the king's jurisdiction.

It will not be found in any Catholic author that a pope can be deposed by an emperor; but emperors may be deposed by the pope, will be found in many.—Ibid, p. 484, B.

Paul Laymann: *Theologia Moralis.* Wirceburgi 1748. (Lutetiæ Parisiorum, 1627. Ed. Coll. Sion.) As the body is subordinate to the soul . . . and things temporal to things eternal, so should the civil power be subordinate to the ecclesiastical power. . . . Whence Boniface VIII. concludes, in *Extrav. Unam Sanctam.* . . . It is necessary that the sword should be subject to the sword, and the temporal authority to the spiritual power; since the apostle says, "There is no power but of God:" yet the things which proceed from God must be regulated with order unless the sword were subject to the sword, and were reduced as an inferior to the highest power.—Lib. i, Tr. 4, c. 6, de Legibus, n. 2.

The clergy do not incur the penalty awarded by civil laws, neither can they be punished by the civil magistrate. . . .—Ibid, n. 4. *Corollary.*—The civil laws which invalidate a will, or which render persons incapable of making a contract or a will, in punishment of some crime committed by themselves or their ancestors, do not extend to the clergy, as Navarre and Saurez remark after the common opinion. The reason is evident. For such a law is penal, and comprises a coactive force, *which cannot extend to ecclesiastical persons.*—Ibid, n. 5.

That the clergy are not directly and specially bound by the civil laws, either by virtue of the laws themselves or by the civil legislative power; for they are entirely exempt from such authority by every kind of right. This is the opinion of Azor and Saurez, of Bellarmine in his apology against the king of England and of Adam Sauner.—Ibid, n. 6.

Busenbaum and Lacroix: *Theologia Moralis, nunc pluribus partibus aucta à R. P. Claudio Lacroix, Societas Jesu.* Coloniæ, 1757. (Coloniæ Agrippinæ, 1733. Ed. Mus. Brit.) To strike one of the clergy, or to bring him before a secular tribunal, is personal profanation.—Tom. ii, Lib. iii, Pars. 1, Tr. 1, c. 2, Bub. n. 48, Resol. 1.

A man who has been banished by the pope, may be killed anywhere, as Fillincius, Escobar and Diana teach; because the pope has at least an indirect jurisdiction over the whole world, even in *temporal things*, as far as may be necessary for the administration of spiritual affairs, as all the Catholics maintain, and as Saurez proves against the king of England.—Tom. ii, Lib. iii, Pars. 1, Tr. 4, c. 1, Dub. 2, Quæst. 178, § 4, n. 795.

Gregory of Valentia: *Commentariorum Theologicorum.* Tomus iii. Lutetiæ Parisiorum, 1609. (Lut. Par., 1660. Ed. Coll. Sion.) Without respect of person, may a judge, in order to favor a friend, decide according to any probable opinion, while the question of *right* remains undecided? . . . For the sake of his friend, he may *lawfully* pronounce sentence according to the opinion which is more favorable to the *interest* of that friend. He may, moreover, with the intent to serve his friend, at one time judge according to one opinion, and at another time according to a contrary opinion, provided only that no scandal results from the decision.

Can an adulterer, who is questioned by a woman's husband, deny that he committed adultery with his wife? I answer: *he can*, by equivocally asserting that he did not break the matrimonial tie, which, in fact, is true. And if he has sacramentally confessed the adultery, he can answer, *I am innocent of this crime*, because by confession it has been pardoned and removed.—Moral Theology of Ligouri, Lib. iii, n. 152. This work was "more than *twenty* times examined by the fathers and declared to be sound and according to God."—*Sana ac Secundum Deum.*

Can the human mind conceive such blasphemy, such deep stained pollution, as the Romish authors have declared their principles to be *as set forth by their own writers?* Read them, people of the United States. Read how the enemies of your country train the papal army to enchain your posterity, if not yourselves. Here is *their* revelation of the great conspiracy against human freedom cloaked under the garb of religion.

What should be thought of the patriot who remained peaceable and tranquil if the British or French army held any portion of our people or territory in subjection? Yet, a foreign foe at our doors, training papal millions in these principles, is not only allowed to live, but permitted to reign among us!

NOTE.—The original latin of this chapter is embodied in the manuscript, but omitted in print to reduce the size of the volume. These authorities are for the first time published in an English translation.

CHAPTER VII.

SECRET INSTRUCTIONS TO THE JESUITS.

How these Instructions were found—The Jesuits' denial—Their unquestioned Authenticity—Real Estate—Marriage Arrangements—Women, how won—The nearest Relative sacrificed at their beck—The way to get Public Offices—Decoying Widows—Daughters—Sons—The danger of Families who are under Romish Influence—Borrowing Money to defraud—How to secure Wealth and Talent—Modern Jesuits—What they do—Who associates with them—Politicians—Teachers—Preachers—Protestant—Holy Inquisition—The Rules and Maxims of Popery—The Oath to the Pope.

THIS code of Jesuit-laws is not to be made known to every class of Jesuits. They have bold, daring, infamous men, ready for desperate deeds, by steel, bullets or poisoned chalice. These know what others do not. They have disguised agents in mask. These know something peculiar to their work. They have crafty, shrewd, courteous, polished men, who associated with the distinguished and powerful; they have instructions, unknown to others. They have decent, serious, moral men, sent out to ensnare the moral, serious and unsuspecting. These teach that their vow is one of poverty, that they have nothing to do with politics or wealth; their sole object being to put down heretics! Hence, all classes swear, that they know no "secret instructions."

When these rules were discovered, however, every one saw and recognized the Jesuit-platform in their atrocious code and conspiracies against the rights of man and the cause of God.

In 1624, the University of Paris charged the Jesuits with being governed by "secret instructions." In the

History of the Jesuits, vol. i., p. 326, we find a Roman Catholic bishop of Angelopolis asserts the same thing. A work is in the British Museum, called "Formulæ Provisionum diversarum: a G. Passarello, summo studio in unum collectœ," printed at Venice in 1596. There is a copy of these "*Secret Instructions*" in manuscript, and at the end of it is this significant mandate: "Let them be denied to be the rules of the Society of Jesus, if ever, they shall be imputed to us." When the Duke of Brunswick took Paderborn, Westphalia, he seized the Jesuit college, and gave their library and papers to the capuchins; and these monks being no friends of the Jesuits, brought them before the public. At the end of this copy, the same characteristic injunction is found: "If these rules fall into the hands of strangers, they must be positively denied to be the rules of the society."*

Mr. McGavin, in the Glasgow Protestant, (vol. ii,) says: "John Schipper, a bookseller of Amsterdam, bought a copy of the *The Secret Instructions*, and afterwards reprinted it. The Jesuits hearing he had bought the book, demanded it back from him, but he had sent it to Holland. The edition Schipper printed was then purchased by the reverend fathers, some few copies excepted. From one of these a reprint was made, and the account prefixed, which is said to be taken from two Roman Catholic men "of credit." In 1669, the learned Dr. Compton, Bishop of London, published in England a translation of the *Secret Instructions*. His arguments on their authority, and his character as a scholar and a divine, are a sufficient guarantee that his name and influence would never have been given to sustain a work of dubious authority, or one calculated to mislead the public. The edition before

* See London Christian Observer, vol. xiv., p. 169.

us was published in London, 1723, and dedicated to Sir Robert Walpole, who was prime minister of George I. and George II.

In chapter I, section v, they are told, in order to give a colorable gloss to their poverty, the purchases of real estate, adjacent to the place where the college is founded, must be assigned by the provincial to distant colleges, that the government of the country can never attain a certain knowledge of the amount of their revenues. Let no place but opulent cities be pitched upon for founding colleges. Let the greatest sums be always extorted from widows. . . . . . In every province let none but the principal be fully apprised of the real value of our revenues, and let what is contained in the treasury of Rome be always kept an inviolable secret. Let it be publicly and privately demonstrated, that the only end of their coming there was for the instruction of youth, and the good and welfare of the inhabitants; that they do all this without the least reward, and do not encumber the people like other religious societies."

Chapter II treats of the way to become familiar with the great in any country. They are told to manage to get the ear of those in authority, and then secure their hearts, by which way all persons will become our creatures, and none will dare to give the society disquiet. The priests are to wink at the vices of the powerful, and to encourage their inclinations, whatever they may be; but this is to be done with generals always avoiding particulars." Section 4. "It will further us in gaining favor, if our members artfully worm themselves by the interests of others into honorable embassies to foreign courts in their behalf, but especially to the pope and great monarchs. Further, great care must be taken to curry favor

10*

with the minions of the great, who, by small presents and many offices of piety, we may find means to get faithful intelligence of the master's inclinations and humors, and thus be better qualified to chime their tempers."

"How much the society has benefited from their engagements in marriage treaties, the houses of Austria, Bourbon, Poland, and other kingdoms, are experimental evidences. Wherefore, let such matches be with prudence picked out, whose parents are our friends, and firmly attached to our interests." . . . "Ladies of quality are easily gained by the influence of the women of their bed-chamber. By all means pay attention to these, for thereby there will be no secrets in the family but what we shall have disclosed to us . . . " "In directing the consciences of great men, our confessors are to allow the greater latitude that the penitents may be allured with the prospect of such freedom, and will depend upon our direction and counsel. Princes, prelates, and all who are capable of being of signal service must be so favored, as to be made partakers of all the merits of the society." "Let it be cunningly instilled into the people, that this society is entrusted with a far greater power in absolving, in dispensing fasts, with paying and demanding debts, with impediments in matrimony, than any other. They will then have recourse to us, and thereby lay themselves under the strictest obligations. It will be very proper to give them handsome entertainments, to address them in a complaisant manner, to invite them to hear orations, sermons," etc. "Let proper methods be used to get knowledge of the animosities that arise amongst great men, that we may have a finger in reconciling them; and gradually become acquainted with their secret affairs," etc. "But should a discovery be made, that any person serves either king or prince, who is not well affected towards our society, no stone must be left unturned, by our members, or which is most proper, some other, to induce him by promises, favors or preferments, to entertain a friendship for and familiarity with us. Finally, let all with such artfulness gain the ascendant over princes, noblemen, and the magistrates of every place, that they may be ready at our beck, *even to sacrifice their nearest relations and most intimate friends, when we say it is for our interests and advantage!!!*"

Chapter III. These secret instructions direct "how those at the head of affairs should be treated, and others, who, though not rich, have the capacity of being otherwise serviceable." The directions are: "to court their authority for obtaining several offices to be discharged by us; if their secrecy and faith may be depended on, we may privately use their names in amassing temporal goods. They must be calming the minds of the meaner sort of people and wheedling the aversions of the populace into an affection for our society." "In prosecuting the same end, we must engage such prelates to make use of, both for confessors and counsellors; and if they at any time aim at a higher preferment from the see of Rome, their pretensions must be backed with such strong interest in our friends in *every* place, as we shall be almost sure not to meet with a disappointment." "Due care must be taken that the society have the power of presenting vicars, for the cure of souls, to all the colleges they found, to the end that we grasp the government of the church, and its parishioners by that means become such vassals to us, that we can ask nothing of them that they will dare deny us."

"Whenever the heretics oppose us, we must endeavor

by the prelates to secure the principal pulpits. If it happens that a nobleman or prelate is employed in an embassy, and pass through a province where we have colleges, let them be received with due honor and esteem, and as handsomely entertained as religious decency can admit to prevent their opposing our society, etc. 'In confessing noblemen, seem to have nothing in view but God's glory; but by degrees, and sensibly to be directed towards political or secular dominion, but in a solemn manner affirm, that the administration of public affairs is, what we with reluctance interfere with. Care should be taken to lay before them the virtues persons should be furnished with, who are to be admitted into public employ, not forgetting slyly to recommend to them such as are sincere friends of our order; but this must be done in such a manner, (unless the prince or bishop enjoin it,) for it may be done better by such as are their favorites or familiars.'"

"Wherefore, let the confessors and preachers be informed, by our friends, of persons proper for every office, and above all, of such as are our benefactors, and whose names let them carefully keep by them, that when proper opportunities occur, they may be palmed upon the prince or government, by the dexterity of our members or agents."

Reader, you plainly discover here how Protestants and Jesuits co-operate in the United States, and why leading political men, bend and fall before their supremacy at the ballot box! "Let confessors and preachers soothe the rulers, never giving the least offence in their sermons or private conversations, with a winning, complaisant address, to dismiss from their minds all imaginary doubts, etc. 'Upon the death of any person in power, take timely care to get a friend of our society, in his room; but this must be cloaked with such cunning and management, as to avoid giving suspicion of our intending to usurp the prince's authority."

In chapter V. we are told, that "resistance must be made" against those who attempt setting up schools for the education of youth in places where our members do so with honor and advantage. In such cases, princes and magistrates must be told, that different methods of instruction must necessarily imbibe different principles and we must persuade them that no society but ours is qualified for an office of so great importance! Let our members be mindful to give some public signals of their virtue and learning, by directing their pupils in the presence of the gentry, magistrates, and populace in their several studies, or engaging them in some other scholastic exercises, for gaining public applause!"

So we find at their annual college commencements in all parts of our land, the Roman Catholic prelates are seen exciting public applause; while those enemies to our liberties bring one boy forward to speak on "Patriotism," and another on the "Life and character of Daniel O'Connell," who hated our free institutions, and loved the pope so dearly, that he left him his heart, which was embalmed after his death, and sent to his holiness at Rome! These Secret Instructions devote much attention to the means of decoying rich widows. They say: "the confessor must so manage her that she will not do the least thing without his advice; that she must resort to frequent sacraments, because in that she freely makes the discovery of her most secret thoughts and every temptation." "Discourse must be made her concerning the advantages of widowhood, and the inconveniences of wedlock, etc. . . . It will be proper now and then to propose some match to her, that she is known to have an aversion for, and when she has been made disposed to live in widowhood, let her be led to make a vow of chastity for two or three years at least, that all tendencies to a second marriage, and all conversations with men, even her nearest relatives and kinsfolks, must be forbidden under pretence of closer union with God." "Let them renew their vow of chastity, twice a year; they must be visited and treated with not too much severity in confession; allow them whatever pleasures they have an inclination to. Let women that are young and descended of noble parents, be placed with those widows under vows, that they become accustomed to our directions; and let some woman be chosen by the family confessor, as governess over them," etc. They are then taught by these disgusting rules "to yield their whole estates to the colleges and works of sacred charity, such as buying ornaments for churches, wax-tapers, wine, etc., for the services and sacrifices." Mothers are instructed, in chapter VIII., "to practice chastisement severely on the young in their cradles, and when their daughters are nearly grown up, let them be denied the common dress and ornaments of their sex, and promising them a plentiful portion, on condition they become nuns, let them lament their own misfortune, in not having lived a single life."

"Let our members converse freely with their sons, and occasionally introduce them into our colleges, and let everything be shown in the best face, so as to invite them to enter themselves into the order. Let them see our gardens, villas, hear of our travels over the world, familiarity with princes, etc. Entertain them with pleasant stories, and shew them the preëminence of our order above all others. Be careful to provide for these youths tutors, firmly attached to our own interests."

Chapter IX. treats of increasing the resources of their colleges. It says: "When a confessor has got a rich penitent, let him immediately inform the rectors, and try all winning artifices to secure him. But the whole success of our affairs turns on this point, viz: that all our members, by studying a compliance with every one's humor, work themselves into the good graces of their penitents and others with whom they converse; to which end, where places are inhabited by the rich and noble, let the provincials take care to send a considerable number: what a plentiful harvest is like to crown their endeavors!"

"If it happen that rich married people, who are friends, have daughters, let these be persuaded, by our members, to make choice of a religious life. But should there be an only son, let no means be omitted to bring him over to the society, and freeing him from the fear of his parents; show him how acceptable to God, should he desert his parents, without their knowledge or consent; and if this be effected, let him enter the noviciate in a remote college having first given information to the general!"

"Let widows, or other devotees, be brought to give up all they have to the society, and be contented to live on such allowances from time to time, as we shall think they have occasion for," etc. "The better to convince the world of our poverty, let the superiors borrow money on bond, of some rich persons who are our friends, and when it is due, defer the payment thereof. Afterwords let the person who lent the money, be visited (especially in time of dangerous sickness), and by all methods wrought upon to deliver up the land. We shall thus gain handsomely without incurring the ill-will of the heirs. It will be proper to borrow money also at some yearly interest, and dispose of it at a higher rate, our friends compassionating the necessities of the society, when they find us engaged in erecting colleges and building churches, may forgive us the interest and may be the principal, and make us a donation in their wills."

"The society may also traffic advantageously, under the borrowed name of some rich merchants, our friends, and this may be done even to the Indies, which have furnished us not only with souls, but plenteously supplied our coffers with wealth." In section 14, they "insist that the physician of their friends be in the interest of their society, so that among other reasons he may give notice of the danger of the patient, who by the terrors of purgatory, his money may be extorted, to expiate it." "Women, too, (section 16,) are directed to withdraw, secretly, sums from their husbands, to the same pious end!"

Chapter XII. In discoursing on those to be favored in the society, it dwells upon "the necessity of securing those who are of distinguished families, or have wealth, or talents. And this attention must not wholly cease until they are under vows, fearing the result would operate against them." "If any are to be dismissed treat them with the utmost severity, hurry them from one duty to another, and though they do whatever you task them, always find fault, and under this pretense remove them." "For the slightest offence subject them to a heavy punishment, in public constantly abash them, till they are able no longer to bear it, and then turn them out," etc.

Chapter XV. treats of conduct to nuns and female devotees. "Manage to curry favor with the principal monasteries, and by degrees get an acquaintance, and work yourselves into the friendship of almost the whole city."

"Il Gesuita Moderno" is the title of a work concerning modern Jesuits, published in Italy about seven years ago, by the eminent writer Vicengo Gioberti, a professor and Romish priest, elevated by the late king of Piedmont, Charles Albert, to the rank of his prime minister.

Such a truthful and unimpeachable history of what Jesuits are to-day, should be read by every intelligent man and woman in our land. Here we see what Jesuits are this moment, not in Italy or France, but even in the United States. Their thoughts, their feelings, their pursuits, are opposed to liberty, under their appearance of being themselves liberal! They disguise their name, dress, manners, language, profession, etc.

From the Jesuits began the extinction of liberty in the present day in Spain, Portugal, France, Italy, upon the continent of Europe, in Mexico, and elsewhere upon the American continent! By whom, but the Jesuits, was Louis Napoleon put upon the throne of France and the pope himself restored to the Vatican? By whom, but the Jesuits, did Santa Anna attempt again to succeed in Mexico, and who but they keep it prostrate at the feet of the pope!

Who are allies of the crafty Jesuits in our own land? The ignorant and superstitious Romanists merely? No, the too-trusting and unsuspecting Protestants, whose love of toleration lead them to regard all sects of religionists as equally good.

To these, we add the dishonest and corrupt politicians of all political parties, who would sell their country for a railroad grant, or the liberties of the people forever, provided they could but get control of the government for the term of four years! !

The Society of Jesus, we have seen is avowedly instituted to oppose freedom of conscience, and to persecute, disperse and destroy heretics (protestants). Then, is it singular, that despotism, with every kind of civil and religious oppression, have ever reigned, where the Jesuits have prevailed. This is plainly to be discovered with regard to England, where their influence is enlarging every day, and it is no less visible in the United States at this present time! It is the Jesuits who are now fulfilling the mission of the pope in our country, in meddling and entangling protestant sects, struggling against, depreciating, ridiculing and libelling them by every means in their power. It is to undermine and destroy our national liberty, that the religious liberty of our country is attacked; our Bible thrust from the public schools of the country; and the very foundation of civil and social liberty disturbed, by the educational system they are forcing upon the people!

The "Archbishop" of New York calls the American schools, in which the Bible is read, "godless," "a universal deterioration of your youth," and declares that they are "responsible for the awful crimes which blacken our courts of justice," and that "no Catholic shall darken the doors of these schools." "The Bible," says St. Augustine, "explains the Bible!"

The Freeman's Journal republished in January, 1858, the following from the *London Rambler*, concerning the increase of Romish power in the United States: "Churches, schools, seminaries, colleges, religious communities, bishoprics and archbishoprics are rising as if by enchantment, in all parts of the republic. In the archiepiscopal province of New York, at the present time (1858), there are over eight hundred churches, and nearly one million of Catholic souls! The city of New York, which, twenty years ago, could number but seven, can now boast of over thirty places dedicated to Catholic worship within its precincts."

A few days ago a gentleman from abroad, visiting one of the public schools of this city, was called upon to make some remarks to the pupils. He complied with the request, and in the course of his address had occasion to refer to one of the parables in the gospel; turning to the principal, he asked for a Bible to read the passage. The teacher had not one at hand, and called upon the scholars to hand him a Bible. There was not one in the room! He then sent to the other apartments, and diligent search was made in vain through all the rooms of the building, in a school of probably more than a thousand scholars, and not a copy of the Bible was to be found!!!

"There are thirteen public schools in the city of New York from which the Bible is officially expelled. We are informed that some of the school officers, charged with the examination and selection of teachers, cannot write their own names."*

It is decreed by the Romish church that whoever shall read the Bible, without the permission of a priest, shall "be incapable of receiving remission of sins, and incur a temporal punishment."

Every man defends truth, when he attacks error; and against these insidious traitors and imposters, who are

* New York Observer, October, 1858.

here to compass this nation's downfall, no neutrality can be permitted. He who is not against them is with them, and, so recognized by them. If, for the sake of their influence, voters and time-serving politicians, preachers and teachers, remain inactive as they now are, the day may come when there may come *a massacre of Americans*, which will exceed that of St. Bartholomew's with the Huguenots of France, or the slaughter of the Waldenses in Calabria and Piedmont!

The very name of the "Holy Roman Apostolic Inquisition," is enough to excite alarm, when we know the pope has it established, through these agents covertly, even already among us. These agents are called the "Inquisitors of the heretical pravity," and are chosen from cardinals, bishops, prelates, priests, monks and friars. Their office is to try, judge, and condemn heretics according to their laws in the "Black Book," of which we have given an account in a previous chapter on the Inquisition. The Jesuits are here in the United States, to defend this "Holy Inquisition," and support the faith of the Romish Church, when despised. This Society of Jesuits has alarmed all Europe—enlightened, liberal Europe! The best sons of France, of Spain, of Germany and Italy, have declared they are associated with the crowned oppressors of the people, to strangle national liberty, both religious and civil.

The following is a part of the Jesuit's oath to the pope:

"I do denounce and disown any allegiance as due to any heretical king, prince, or state, named protestant; or obedience to any of their inferior magistrates or officers. I do further declare the doctrines of the Church of England, of the Calvinists, Huguenots, and other protestants, to be damnable, and those to be damned who will not forsake the same. I do further declare, that I will help, assist, and advise all, or any, of his Holiness' agents in any place wherever I shall be; and do my utmost to extirpate the heretical protestant doctrine, and to destroy all their pretended power, legal or otherwise. I do further promise and declare, that notwithstanding I am dispensed with, to assume any religion heretical, (that is, hypocritically I may become so,) for the propagation of the mother church's interest, to keep secret and private all her agents' counsels as they entrust me, and not divulge directly or indirectly, by word writing, or circumstance whatsoever, but execute all which shall be proposed, given in charge or discovered unto me, by you my ghostly father, or by any one of this convent. All which, I, A. B., do swear by the blessed Trinity and the blessed sacrament, which I am now to receive, to perform, and on my part, to keep inviolably; and do call all the heavenly and glorious host of hearers to witness my real intentions to keep this my oath. In testimony hereof, I take the most holy and blessed sacrament of the eucharist; and witness the same further with my hand and seal, to the face of this holy convent."

"Jesuitism formerly acted openly, like a conqueror; the modern system acts secretly, like an assassin. To belie what has been said of them, they have chosen another road, so as to govern in religion and society. If you should put the question to them, as to what they propose to attain, they would reply: 'The greatest glory of God!!' But if you question the facts, you will be forced to conclude, that it is an immoderate thirst for dominion, to render themselves necessary to the pope and to kings, in order to govern the pope and the whole Roman hierarchy. Thus Catholicism and Jesuitism and despotism, are one and the same thing."

Formerly there existed Jansenists and a Gallican church; but all this has disappeared, and no one can longer be a good Catholic, without being a Jesuit.*

Father De Smet has recently been appointed by the government as chaplain of the Oregon army! The Indians are said to be in such subjection to this Jesuit father, as to make him *a power* in the land, from the banks of the Rio Grande to the Columbia river. He, therefore, who is the sworn foe to our civil freedom, and laboring to destroy it, is deemed the most efficient agent to subjugate the Indians, to advance the policy of our institutions!!!

* De Sanctis.

CHAPTER VIII.

SAN FIDESTI SOCIETY, OR SOCIETY OF HOLY FAITH.

The Emblems of it—Awful Oath—Catechism—Established in the United States—Mode of Poisoning.

THESE subtle allies of absolute governments have a society of a secret character, called the "San Fidesti, or Society of Holy Faith," or "Brethren of the Catholic Apostolic Society of the San Fidesti." Its emblems are *destruction* and *death*. Hope is forever extinguished.* They are significant of *complete* annihilation. The inscriptions and mottoes are the summing-up of all the anathemas and excommunications, hurled by the church, against all who rebel against her laws. Here is their oath:

"I, N. N., in presence of Almighty God, the Father, Son and Holy Ghost, of the ever immaculate Virgin Mary, and of all the celestial court, etc.; of you, honored father, swear, that I will sooner cut off my right hand, and die of hunger, or under the greatest torments; and I pray the Lord God Almighty to condemn me to the endless pains of hell, than to betray or deceive one of the honored fathers and brethren of the Catholic Apostolical Society to which I subscribed at this time, or if I do not

* We have seen a card recently, having the American flag, and a hand grasping an instrument, aimed at it. This is one of the emblems of the San Fidesti, shown by one member to another in our presence, inadvertently.

scrupulously fulfil its laws, or give assistance to my brethren in want. I swear to defend myself in the cause which I have embraced, never to spare a single individual belonging to the infamous combination of the Liberals, *whatever may be his birth, parentage, or fortune*, and to have *no pity for the cries of children, nor of old men or women, and to shed the blood of the infamous Liberals, even to the last drop, without regard to age, sex, or rank.* Finally, I swear implacable hatred to all the enemies of our Holy Roman Catholic religion, one and true."

The catechism of the San Fidesti Society, secretly attested as genuine, by Signor Arduini, in "Italia del Popolo," of March, 1850, p. 96.

Domanda. Have we a fine day?

Resposta. To-morrow, I hope, will be better. *D.* That will be well! for the road is bad. *R.* It will soon be improved. *D.* In what manner? *R.* By the bones of the Liberals. *D.* What is your name? *R.* Light. *D.* Where does the light come from? *R.* From heaven. *D.* What do you intend to do to-day? *R.* To separate the grain from the wheat! *D.* What is your original name? *R.* * * * *D.* What is your profession of faith? *R.* The destruction of the enemies of the altar and the throne. *D.* How long is your staff? *R.* It is long enough to *strike* them. *D.* What plant produced it? *R.* One sown in *Palestine*, grown in the *Vatican*, and under whose leaves all the *faithful* are safe. *D.* Do you intend to travel? *R.* Yes. *D.* Where? *R.* To the contests of faithfulness and religion, on board the vessel of the "*Fisherman.*"

We have now, the catechism of the same society, for those initiated into a *higher* grade.

D. Hail! welcome. Tell me, for the second time, who

from the Jesuits, inquisitors, etc. Under the laws of *suspicion*, this society was active under the late Pope Gregory XVI., as it now is under Pope Pius IX. Exiles, executions, arbitrary imprisonments, the frequent examination of dwellings, with innumerable acts of oppression, are the work of this society. When the pope visited Ancona, in 1841, and was besought by wives and suffering friends, he coolly answered, "Don't speak to me of that set of men; I will have nothing to do with assassins." In another chapter of this work, we have shown, that the same atrocities of the Sanfedists, in executing the will of that tyrant, have been enacted under Pius IX.

There are two orders of this society, Padre Sanfidesti and Fratelle Sanfidesti. The latter class know no limits to the crime which they are bound by their oath to commit, as ordered, without any inquiry of any kind from their leaders, and know no secrets of the society, *further* than their orders.

Signor Gajani delivered a course of lectures in New Haven, under the auspices of Professor Silliman and other distinguished men, in 1853. In one of them, he stated, that the pope's nuncio, Bedini, came to the United States, among other purposes, to establish this Sanfidesti Society, and *did establish it* among us. He said, that by-and-by, we would see one distinguished Protestant dropping off, then another; that dissension and distrust would be created almost imperceptibly among friends. One means of taking off by poison he explained thus: "It is a subtle liquid, looking like water, and prepared with much extreme nicety, as to elude the most skillful medical examination. When it is deemed desirable for any individual or individuals in a family to be put aside, for political or other causes, this poison is given to you are? *R.* One of your brethren. *D.* Are you a man? *R.* Yes, indeed; and I consent that my hand and my throat be cut, to die of hunger, and in most terrible torments, if I deceive or betray a brother. *D.* How do you *know* a brother faithful to his God and his prince? *R.* By those three words: "Faith, hope, and *indissoluble union.*" *D.* Who admitted you among the Sanfedists? *R.* A venerable man with white hair. *D.* What did he do to admit you? *R.* He made me place one knee upon the *cross* and my right hand upon the holy *eucharist*, and armed me with the blessed sword. *D.* In what place did he receive you? *R.* On the banks of the *Jordan*, in a place not contaminated by the enemies of the holy religion and of princes, at the hour when the Divine *Redeemer* was born. *D.* What are your colors? *R.* White, white and red I cover my head; and I cover my heart with white and yellow. *D.* Do you know how many we are? *R.* We are certainly *enough* to annihilate the enemies of the holy religion and monarchy. *D.* What is your duty? *R.* To hope in the name of God and of the only true Roman Catholic church. *D.* Where does the wind come from? *R.* From Palestine and the Vatican; and it will disperse all the enemies of God. *D.* What are the knots which bind you? *R.* The love of God, of the country, and of truth. *D.* How do you sleep? *R.* Always in peace with God, and in the hope of waking at *war* with the enemies of his holy name! *D.* How do you call your steps? *R.* First alpha, the second Noah's ark, the third the imperial eagle, and the fourth the keys of heaven. *D.* Courage, then, brother, and perseverance.

This society is composed chiefly of vagabonds and outcasts of society, but is directed by officers, high in authority in the Romish church, men of education, selected the cook or chamber-maid, who are told by their confessor to put it in the food or water, once in eight days, to save their employers' souls! The party eating or drinking will gradually be undermined in health, but will be *unable to discover the cause*—so will his physician—but the work goes slowly on, and after months of suffering—sometimes, on stronger constitutions, it may be longer—the party expires." It was supposed, to be the agents of this society, by whom the Lafarge House and Metropolitan Hall were burned down in 1854. When it was announced that Gavazzi would lecture in that hall, the threat was made. He lectured there on Friday night, and next day sailed for Europe; that night they were reduced to ashes.

CHAPTER IX.

THE BIBLE IN THE PUBLIC SCHOOLS.

The Pope demands the expulsion of the Bible from the public schools in the United States—The Archbishop of New York obeys—It is expelled—The reward—The school books of the country mutilated by Romish power—A secret conspiracy requires it—The Madeira Protestants—The blessing of Clubs in Philadelphia to elect a Roman Catholic Legislature—All opponents of popery—Protestants—Mortara—Roman Catholic Prayer Book introduced in Protestant famlies, by Servants—The fatal result—Archbishop Kenrick—On the Confessional—Cardinal Wiseman and the Breviary—The Bible the foundation of all our Civil and Religious Rights.

From the principles of the Jesuits, their constitutions and secret instructions, the American people, for the first time, have the palpable revelations of a secret oath-bound organization, in the United States, with the representative of the pope at its head, conspiring to put down our institutions, laws, and government, as shewn by their own writers. Its object is to advance the *civil* supremacy of *the* church, and its members are sworn to obey any orders which may emanate from and "by authority," at *whatever sacrifice of life and property may be necessary to secure the desired end.* It makes one shudder with irrepressible horror to *know* that an organized army is in our midst, at our doors, around our firesides, in our schools, who are bound by oaths and obligations to obey the behests of one man, no matter, if in doing so, this land be deluged in blood, and the very existence of our institutions forever destroyed were they possessed of that power. The blasphemous oaths, uttered by every member, binds him to regard those high officials who represent the Pope in this country as God, and our Lord Jesus Christ. They are sworn to obey them as their advisers and directors, in everything, appertaining to their *civil and political rights and actions*, and by their avowed principles and practices, are ready to make a willing sacrifice of life, health, honor, character, or property, to defend or advance *the* Church. They are sworn to labor for her welfare in the United States, and to obey her orders. They are sworn to use every faculty they possess, every pecuniary or political advantage they enjoy, every exertion they can make and every act they can perform, solely to further the ends of the Church, whose single aim is to fasten papal tyranny and despotism upon the American people. These men are sworn to *disregard our laws, sacrifice our lives, property and honor; tamper with our institutions, violate the sanctity of our halls of justice, and deluge our streets in blood, if the Church require it!* Yes, men of America, this Society of Jesus is constituted the bulwark of the Roman Catholic church in this land; its millions of enrolled members, from the archbishop to the last Jesuit priest, have taken the awful oaths, which obliges them to be trained, equipped, and drilled, for the execution of any act of treason or blood, the Pope or General of the Order shall command to be done among us! Every week something new, more meddling, more inquisitorial, than the previous, occurs, and who can longer wonder!

From this parent Society of Jesus have sprung numerous other secret organizations, for the advancement of the Roman Catholic church, all of which subserve the one grand aim of absolute destruction to human freedom!

Consider the peril in which we are momentarily placed, while men, sworn to respect no oath or obligation, and to consider all oaths or affirmations, conflicting with the interests of the Church, as of no moral binding effect, and therefore null and void, if the *Church* require it. Men, sworn, *never to testify* against any member of their society, to his injury, in *any court of justice*, and never to acknowledge under any pretense, or for any purpose, that a secret society exists among them. With such enemies surrounding us, under a promise of absolution for past, present and future deeds of infamy, if the Church require it, what life is secure, what character unassailable, what laws or institutions indestructible? Yet these men, who *reveal themselves* as conspirators against our government, and waiting only until powerful enough to strike the fatal blow, enjoy the greatest toleration of religious sentiment, and have their countless inquisitorial edifices to ruin virtue and destroy liberty, protected by our laws!

Instead of the Bible, the pillar upon which our Protestant and republican structure of government rests; these conspirators to our freedom, place the "Garden of the Soul" into the hands of the innocent young daughters of the nation, and the polluting Breviary which is found in this work, to be especially recommended by Cardinal Wiseman for the daily use of priests and women of England and the United States.

The "Garden of the Soul" is in the hands of almost every Roman Catholic, and by reference to pages 213, 214 and 216, the questions may be seen, which are put every day, in this country, to every young girl, from the age of twelve years, by her father confessor, preparatory to mass and receiving the wafer, God.

The Rev. Herman Norton, late Corresponding Secretary of the American Protestant Society, stated, that he was well acquainted with a Protestant gentleman, who was persuaded by a polite Jesuitical Sister of Charity, to send his two young daughters to a Popish school, whose minds had been previously corrupted, by the Archbishop's prayer book, the "Garden of the Soul" in the hands of a servant. After a term of two years in the school, these girls secretly joined the Romish Church. On returning home, they absolutely refused to hear the reading of the Holy Scriptures or to unite in the family worship of their Protestant parents. The agonized father implored them to kneel before the Lord around the family altar, but they remained inexorable, and preferred to kneel before the priest in the confessional, to the only living and true God. Of similar facts in the United States, there are thousands.

Our Bible tells us, that when the Evangelist, John, attempted to kneel before God Almighty's angel, who showed him things wonderful in heaven and earth, the angel cried out at once, forbidding such homage to any being but God! But the priests of Rome demand absolute prostration of the penitent at their feet, while they are questioning the innocent girl from a Roman Catholic prayer book, the "Garden of the Soul;" and are in the confessional, according to Archbishop Kenrick, with the authority of God to pardon, bind and loose on earth!

The Word of God is not only a prohibited book, in the Romish system, but the reading of it, or hearing it read, is made the worst of criminal offences, and punished by the Inquisition.

We come now to the war on God's Holy Word by its expulsion from the public and free schools of this country. In 1841, Bishop Hughes, in effect, offered the Roman Catholic vote for sale, at Carroll Hall, in the city of New

York, if the Bible would be excluded from the common schools! Of this movement, the New York *Herald* of June 20, 1854, says: "The operations of Bishop Hughes on the *School* question, caused the nomination of a Catholic ticket for the Senate and Assembly, and had the effect to cause divisions between Americans and adopted citizens, at Tammany Hall." Thus, the *Herald*, ascribes to Bishop Hughes the first church movement in the political affairs of our country; by introducing "religion" into the arena of politics, and nominating a Catholic ticket for the Senate and Assembly on the *School* question! Let every Protestant and patriot, remember this fact. Thirty-eight schools in the city of New York, alone, abolished the Bible and commissioners were appointed, to expunge from the pages of the school books, all facts of history which were displeasing to the Papal system. Books so mutilated and defaced with black, can now be seen at the Bible House, in that city. This Bible expulsion from the schools begun by the Archbishop in the New York Legislature, was followed by a similar effort in the McClintock bill in Pennsylvania. Nine States of the Union have made the attempt to expel the Bible from the schools, and in California, they have been successful.

Appropriations of money have been asked of the Pennsylvania Legislature, even to build convents and houses, for the "Sisters of Mercy," and actually passed one branch of it!

Pius IXth rewarded the Jesuit bishop of New York with an archbishop's mitre for his zeal and success in abolishing the Bible from thirty-eight public schools, in the city of New York, alone; nor was this all—but he procured a papal school committee, to examine every book in the hands of the children, and every passage of truth in their books of history which were offensive to the Pope, were blotted out. Even those books which praised the pilgrim fathers for their zeal for God's service; who were exiles for conscience sake, were blackened with ink—and these popish Jesuits teach in the confessional, and in their schools, that the Plymouth Rock pilgrims were a band of robbers and pirates, who fled from Europe to America on account of crimes committed against the government of papal England!

The past success on this subject and the rapid increase of numbers and influence in the United States; over Protestants, as well as their own subjects; has again renewed the war on the Bible and caused a fresh expulsion of this Holy Book of God, from twelve of the public schools, in the city of New York, in 1858. This will be a mighty move, if not at once arrested!

It is not a matter which affects merely the professed believer in the Lord Jesus Christ; nor even the moral class of men, but those also who unhappily never read the Bible at all! but who would fight for the *privilege* of religious and civil freedom, and die sooner than have their posterity a band of crouching slaves, subject to the absolute will of a single despot! If the Bible can be taken from some of the schools, it may be taken from all. Can anything be more natural than that a system of despotism, cloaked under the garb of religion, maintained by principles, which trample down every one of God's laws, should sedulously seek to expel the Bible from the sight of the people? The Jesuit system of education can be effectively enforced only in this way. Then the morals of the people would not be guarded, either by a divine or human code, for who that acknowledged the principles of their theological works would think of adhering to the constitution and laws of our land. Who of the Jesuit priests will affirm to the people of the United States, to-day, that they are not solemnly bound to inculcate, by all means, and at any cost, their system and principles, amongst the American people? The Church *now* requires the expulsion of your Bible. People of the United States! Fear this!

Pius IX., in his allocution to the cardinals in September, 1851, said, "That he has taken this principle for basis, that the Roman Catholic religion, *with all its rights*, ought to be exclusively dominant *in such sort*, that every other religion shall be banished and interdicted."

There is a society, in Europe, called the Christian League, organized for "the circulation of the Holy Scriptures; for the advocacy of human rights, and to give to *all* nations religious liberty." Against this society the present Pope, Pius IXth, issued a bull, a few years since, declaring that "all those who enrol themselves in such societies, or who presume to aid or abet them in any way, are guilty of a most grievous sin before God and the Church." "It is your duty to remove from the hands of the faithful (all) Bibles translated into the vulgar tongue. We especially reprobate the aforesaid Christian league, it being their determination to give to all nations religious liberty." Can this language of the Pope be misunderstood? Is there any thing of a doubtful character in the sentiments it expresses? Is it not the re-affirmation of the infallible system of popery, showing the *spirit* of the Papal See, is *now*, to all intents, one, with popery in the darkest ages of its existence? Here we have the express command of Pius IXth to every Romish priest in the United States, (as everywhere beside,) to remove from the hands of Catholics all Bibles printed in the language of the people. Here we see his open edict against religious and civil liberty, and the command of the Church is brought to bear in all its force, and *dares* to suppress and extirpate the Word of the Most High God in our own country.

A society, embracing nearly all the wealthy Roman Catholics of Europe, has been organized, with the express design of establishing Roman Catholic colonies in our Western States. London is its head-quarters, but it has branches in almost every capital in Europe.

The prospectus of this society proves clearly that its objects and designs are:

1st. To provide the means for colonizing the surplus Roman Catholic population of Europe in our Western States.

2d. To do this in such a manner as to create a large demand for articles of European manufacture; and,

3d. To make Romanism the predominant religion of the United States.

In connection with this pamphlet, the Society also published a map of North America, showing the proposed field of Papal occupancy and ultimate ascendancy; in which field is comprised the States of Illinois, Indiana, Ohio, Michigan and Wisconsin Territory, with Canada West. The part of the map colored blue indicates the section of American territory, and the red shows the relative and adjacent portion of Canada, which it is by this Society designed to occupy. Nor are we at liberty to doubt that occupancy will be but the precursor of disruption from the Federal compact and the foundation of a Catholic empire in North America.

This field of colonization embraces the entire range of our lakes and the whole of our beautiful and fertile West.

The West is rapidly being settled by a foreign Catholic population, acknowledging the Roman pontiff as their head. In a few years, the population of these Western States will probably equal the present population of the United States; and over that immense population the influence of the Church of Rome will be universal, and the interests of the papacy all-absorbing! When this is so, the dismemberment of the American union and the establishment of popish supremacy over the fairest portion of this republic will be inevitable. The hatred borne to our institutions influences the annual remittance of European gold to our country, to further the cause of the foreign hierarchy. The Leopold Society in Austria sends its yearly sums to be distributed in the West. *The Freeman's Journal*, the papal organ of the Archbishop of New York, gave the following, in 1854, as an appropriation of foreign capital, to spread Romanism in the United States:

	Francs.
For the Establishment of the Redemptionist, (Baltimore,)	54,120
Rt. Rev. Dr. Loras, Bishop of Dubuque, (Iowa territory,)	41,820
Lefeure, Coadjutor Bishop of Michigan,	10,600
Purcell, Bishop of Cincinnati, (Ohio,)	41,800
Fenwick, Boston,	19,894
Kenrick, Philadelphia,	19,680
Wheelen, Richmond, (Virginia,)	24,900
The congregation of the Fudites, in diocese of Vincennes, (Iowa,)	20,080
The Missions of the Fathers of Mercy,	24,600
Lazarists,	35,000
Jesuits in Missouri,	40,428
Jesuits in Kentucky,	15,000
Lazarists, designed for Texas,	25,000

Shall the Protestant Bible and freedom be saved in the

West? or shall it be reduced to the present condition of the South American States?

A few years since a nobleman bought an immense body of land in Pennsylvania, to colonize Roman Catholics, and a Western paper states, that "colonies are continually arriving among us, of the priesthood and laity, with the avowed purpose of carrying out the designs of founding a Roman Catholic empire on this soil. In one case it was said a colony was composed of twelve hundred families; in another, of an order of monks, who are reported to have just purchased, in the heart of one of the richest of our North-Western States, some sixteen hundred acres of land. From Pittsburg to New Orleans the land is covered with a population yielding the most implicit obedience to the Romish authority and dominion. At every prominent point in the entire west, bishops, priests, churches, convents,, etc., etc., are to be seen. These openly and clandestinely are inquiring into the affairs of Protestants, and by their urbanity, meekness, and assumed sanctity, are securing their *children*, and thus preparing for an easy triumph over our American heritage."

Here, then, is the grand movement, to establish a Roman Catholic empire on this soil! In a few years the West will have a population more than equal to the present population of the remaining States of this Union; it will elect our rulers and make our laws. Shall it be conceded to the Romish despot? Americans, there is but one way to arrest this movement, and your salvation and that of your posterity requires that you settle this question now—hereafter it will be too late! Resist the expulsion of your Bible from the schools, or the next generation will be Roman Catholic! Stop your children from learning Godless nonsense, by taking them away from Jesuit instruction. The Bible is the foundation of all education—it is the foundation of our institutions. The American people are not a Roman Catholic race; and in the adoption of laws which made our national existence, the question of their incompatibility with the Romish doctrine was never permitted to arise. Our fathers were not influenced by considerations favorable to Roman Catholics, and, even as colonies of the British government, they complained of Jesuit incursion, which then impeded their march to national freedom! It is the Word of God, our Creator and Preserver, that has made the nation free, by making the people fear his laws, and love, obey and serve Him who is the Lord of life and immortality! If the Bible is once surrendered to our Romish foes, Christian education, in all its glorious results will be destroyed, and the sun of freedom will have set forever.

The Roman Catholic Jesuits are sworn to educate this country into their principles and practices, in order to subjugate it. To this end, bishops, priests, monks and nuns all labor to destroy the Holy Bible.

The persecution of the Protestants of Madeira from 1843 to 1846, will further prove what the Roman Catholic spirit is at this day. The queen of Portugal allowed two Protestant congregations to worship on that island. In fact, it owed all its prosperity to the merchants of the United States and England. But no sooner had the English and American residents began to circulate the Bible and open Protestant schools, than the bishops and priests forbade the people from attending them, or worshipping God. They were commanded to adore the image, to attend mass in Latin, and the idolatrous confession of the priests. Those who refused to do this, for the sake of Christ, were thrown into dungeons and buried like dogs, when they died there. Some were whipped to death, others had their houses burned over their heads. The British minister, invited the English families, who were thus persecuted for loving God's Holy Word, to take refuge under his roof. Miss Rutherford, an English lady, invited forty of these Protestants to her home, and while there, engaged in praising God, a mob attacked the house with stones, clubs, and rocks, and broke up the meeting. The most respectable women were grossly insulted, and the most brutal outrages were perpetrated. The pope issued his bull of excommunication, which was immediately read from every popish pulpit on the island, in which he forbade the people to extend any humanity to their relatives or friends who were Bible Christians. Mothers were arrested and thrown into prison, and their helpless infants torn from them and left to die for want of nourishment, except, when taken into the Roman Catholic Church by *baptism*. Even goat's milk was prohibited to nourish the little innocent babes. This bull was issued in the name of the bishop of the island, Don Januario Vicente Camacho, and is before us. Through the aid of the American and English Protestants, these persecuted Bible worshippers fled to the Island of Trinidad, and from thence to the State of Illinois, in these United States.

Says Mr. Hogan.*

"While I was a Romish priest in Philadelphia, a consultation was held between the Popish priests in the

* Extract from Mr. Hogan's "Popery as it was and as it is." Mr. Hogan was pastor of St. Mary's Roman Catholic church, in Philadelphia, for twelve years.

diocese of Philadelphia, and it was secretly resolved by them that the best mode of checking *Hogan's heresy*, as they termed my advocating the reading of the Bible, was to take possession of the church in which I officiated in the name of the Pope. They accordingly wrote to his holiness, humbly praying this man-god to send them out a bishop, and to give him and his successors in office a lease of St. Mary's Church in Philadelphia, and all the appurtenances thereunto belonging. Accordingly, his royal holiness the Pope sent them a bishop, with the aforesaid lease. I was immediately ordered out of the church, and having refused to depart, unless the trustees thought proper to remove me, this emissary of the Pope, only a few days or weeks in this country, had me indicted for officiating in St. Mary's Church, although I had the full and undivided consent of the trustees.

"But the bishop's legal right was questioned; the case was brought before the Supreme Court of Pennsylvania, Chief Justice Tighlman, presiding. I was discharged from bail and custody, and the rights of the trustees sustained. But the priests and bishops were not content with this decision. They put their heads once more together, and fancied that they discovered another mode by which they could rob the people of their rights, and defeat the intention of the donors of St. Mary's church; and what was their plan, think you, fellow-citizens? The bishop called a meeting of all the priests and leading Roman Catholics in the diocese. Every lay member was ordered to bring with him a hickory-stick (or club). The meeting was held in the Church of St. Joseph; and at the hour of twelve, at night, the *Romish bishop of the diocese of Pennsylvania*, an Irishman, not more than a few months in the country, attended in his pontificals, told the multitude who were there assembled, to lay down their sticks in one pile, in order that he might *bless* them for their use. This was done as a matter of course. The bishop said mass, sprinkled holy water upon the sticks, blessed them; and this done, the whole party bound themselves by a solemn vow never to cease until they elected a legislature in Pennsylvania that would annul the charter of St. Mary's church; and, as an American citizen, I blush to state the fact, they succeeded. The charter was annulled by an act of the legislature, and property worth over a million of dollars would have passed into the hands of the Pope and his agents, were there not a provision in the constitution of that State, empowering the Supreme Court to decide upon the constitutionality of the acts of the legislature.

"We brought the question of the constitutionality of the act before the court, Justice Tighlman presiding. The court decided in favor of the trustees and myself. This, I believe, is the first attempt the Pope has made to establish his *temporal power* in this country. The priests have headed the papists as a body, and have resolved to carry, by the ballot-box, their schemes."

Whoever protests against popery is a *protestant*. No sect has suffered more from the persecution of the Romish church, than the Israelite, and in common with them, the whole protestant people of the United States, should be warned of by the case of young *Mortara*. We cannot better illustrate the hostility of Rome to the Bible, than by calling the reader's attention to this fact as extracted from *The Press*.

THE MORTARA CASE.

This case, which has created so profound a sensation abroad, and given rise to such violent controversy in the journals of the continent, has been hitherto so little noticed here, save in the foreign correspondence of our newspapers, that it may be desirable, before giving our own view of this last aggression of the papal church, to state shortly, for the information of our readers, the circumstances as they occurred. The son of some Jewish people at Bologna, aged six years, has been forcibly taken from his parents on the pretense that two years previously—that is, at the age of four—he had been subjected to the rite of lay baptism by his nurse. The child has been placed in an institution called the refuge of catechumens, and is still forcibly withheld from his parents under the express sanction of the pope, who has been appealed to, on the ground that by the canon law he has become a subject of the church into which he has been fraudulently baptized.

This monstrous outrage on all usage, on all fundamental principles of law, and upon those universal rights of man which it ought to be the first object of all law to establish and to uphold, has excited, we are glad to observe, the strongest and most unfeigned indignation among the greater portion even of the members of the Roman Church. The *Constitutionnel* the *Journal des Débats*, and the *Nord* have animadverted in the most earnest manner upon the scandalous conduct of the papal priesthood, and urgent appeals have been made to the French government to interfere in the matter. Of their right, of our right, of the right of every member of the family of European nations to use their influence by representation to have this grievous wrong redressed, there cannot, we apprehend, be the slightest doubt, if not in the mere interest of Mortara, a Jewish citizen in the papal states, at all events in the interests of humanity at large. Much as we pity and feel for the parents of this unfortunate little victim of papal greed and despotism the interests of the family are absorbed in the greater question of the interests of humanity, and of the necessity that all Europe should make a stand against this new attempt of the Inquisition to assert the immunity of their order and of their system from the control of natural and civil law.

The real issue that is raised by this act of the Inquisition, and upon which the *Univers* on its behalf, before it was aware of the strength and universality of the feeling against it in the first instance, took its stand, is the pre-eminence and supremacy of ecclesiastical law and ecclesiastical authority whenever the church and state are in presence together, and whenever civil and canon law are in antagonism. That is the issue which Rome is bent on trying now, and which she will continue to try with that continuity of policy and perseverance of action in which no other power, save Russia, has ever equalled her. She tried it here in England in 1851, when she parcelled out the dominion of Queen Victoria into territorial principalities. She tried it in Sardinia upon the question of marriage. She tried it in Austria upon the question raised by the concordat. She tried it in Ireland upon the occasion of the progress through the kingdom of one of her temporal princes, by proclaiming, through the marked and designed omission of the queen's health on a great public occasion, the supremacy of the pope and his authority, and she is trying it now in the face of

Europe by the violent abduction of this boy, and by the reëstablishment in Germany of those ecclesiastical councils which the Emperor Joseph II. so wisely abolished and interdicted. In the first attempts she has failed ignominiously. Her territorial bishops are myths, her cardinal-prince is a laughing-stock. In Austria alone she has met with success. It remains to be seen whether the emperor of the French, by the aid alone of whose soldiery the pope sits in the Chair of St. Peter, will permit all law, natural, human, and divine, to be set aside and overridden by an organization of despotic priests seeking irresponsible *temporal power*. We have italicized the last words because we desire especially to impress upon the minds of our readers the great and important fact that these aggressions have every one of them been as a temporal, not of a spiritual character, and that in every one of them the object has been the acquisition of purely temporal despotism, of undisputed and irresponsible control over the political ordinances, the social life, and the private property of all men in *all* countries.

The affair of the Jew boy Mortara, is assuming considerable gravity. The French government has represented, in very serious terms, to the pope that it is absolutely impossible that, in the middle of the nineteenth century, the Roman Catholic Church can be allowed to kidnap an Israelite child, baptize him, and shut him up in a convent away from his parents. But his holiness has answered the famous *Non Possumus*—"such is the law of the church, and I cannot, dare not, will not alter it!" The French government has been deeply hurt at this response, and is now pressing on the pope to reconsider it. In the meantime, the affair is creating a profound sensation in France. Public opinion pronounces decisively and indignantly against the conduct of the papal see. The ultra-montane party, however, defends that conduct with all its usual violence. As the matter stands, it is not easy to see what will be the issue. The pope cannot, evidently, give up the child without rendering the canon subservient to the civil law, and without in the eyes of fanatical Catholics, abandoning a soul to perdition; but the indignation of the French, and it may be added of all civilized Europe, will never let the little creature remain in the papal clutches. It is seriously recommended by many eminent personages that the French government shall make its troops at Rome rescue the child by force.

CHAPTER X.

CATHOLIC CONGREGATIONS.

Slander and Calumny—Their aim—Business—What they study—Association of Mechanics—Congregations influence Politics—They control Domestics—Daily Mass.

We find in the United States very frequent allusions to the "Catholic Congregations;" and Protestants suppose it merely means a community of Roman Catholic worshippers for that single object! This is not so. "They are an association of men, acting in view of temporally promoting their own welfare and that of the church. These associates are religious and worldly, pro fane and holy; mass and business are equally performed by them. They are the manufactories of slander and calumny. By them are forged the arrows directed against the enemies of the Romish church. In their assemblies are studied Loyola's Precept-book, Dens' Theology, Molina's Casuistry, and Liguori, who sums them up. There the pupil is taught that famous sentence: "It is necessary to be a hypocrite, in order to cut one's way through the world."

These "congregations" are established all over our country, as in France, where, says M. de Montlosier, (who had studied these institutions, and been a witness on the spot,) "every town has three congregations—of the gentry, of the professional students, and of the common people."

The inferior classes of society were in this respect treated as superior classes. By means of an association, called that of St. Joseph, all mechanics are at present enrolled and disciplined: there is in each district a sort of centurion, who is a bourgeois of consideration in the arrondissement. The general-in-chief is M. L'Abbé Leoven. Under the auspices of a great personage, he obtained the grant of the Grand Hall of Versailles. Here he proposed to organize eight or ten thousand mechanics from the departments. Enormous expenses were already incurred in preparing this edifice for the reception of the enrolled . . . A million will hardly suffice for all they have consented to do at the will of M. L'Abbé Leoven. "While the mechanics were disciplined, the wine merchants were not neglected, some of them have been ordered to supply them with wine at a cheaper rate. Even while they are getting drunk, they have formulas of pious meditations, or prayers, to recite. There is no situation, down to the appointment of domestics, of which they have not taken care to possess themselves. I have seen at Paris chambermaids and valets, who were said to have been recommended by the congregation."*

"The villagers of the country, officers of the court, the royal guard, have not been able to escape the 'congregation.' It is within my knowledge that a marshal of France, after for a long time, having solicited the place of sub-prefect for his son, could not at last obtain it but through a recommendation from the curate of his village to a chief of the congregation" . . . "The Chamber of

* Who doubts that such organizations exist in our country at this present time?

Deputies, in the month of April last, sometimes counted one hundred and thirty, sometimes one hundred and fifty members of the congregation. Such are the different soils to which the congregation is attached by strong roots. It possesses still stronger hold upon the consciences of men, from the religious sentiment which it professes, and in their opinions from the royalism of its doctrines. *Above all, it has the civil and political authorities almost entirely at its beck, for it has had the nominations of almost all.**

Now let Protestants see what the Catholic congregations are doing in the United States.

We will inform them from the Catholic organ, *The Freeman's Journal*, of August, 1858. It says: "The Missionary Company of the 'New Congregation of St. Paul the Apostle,' have just made a purchase of ground on 59th Street, New York city, comprising 32 lots, near 9th Avenue. They commence their labors with the special encouragement of Pope Pius IXth, and the personal as well as canonical approval of the most Reverend Archbishop of New York." The circular says: "The religious house we propose to establish is not a merely local institution, but is intended to be the centre of missions to be given in all parts of the country. A reference to the past history of our missionary band shows that missions have been given since April, 1831, in the dioceses of Baltimore, New York, Cincinnati, New Orleans, Philadelphia, Boston, Pittsburgh, Albany, Brooklyn, Louisville, Newark, Detroit, Charleston, Mobile, Richmond, Savannah, Buffalo, Wheeling, Cleveland, Erie, Burlington and Florida. Missions have been given in 17 of our cathedrals, and in

* La Religion la Sociétié et le Trône, by M. le Comte de Montlosier, (Paris,) 1826.

66 parish churches. The whole number of missions has been 88; and the whole number of communions 173,000.

"A new religious congregation, under the title of 'The Congregation of Missionary Priests of St. Paul the Apostle,' has been organized in this city under the auspices of Archbishop Hughes, with a view to the more vigorous prosecution of the missions and other works of the apostolic ministry, in which, as a body, they have been engaged for the last seven years. A very eligible site adapted to these purposes has been chosen in the suburbs of the city, on which it is intended to build a temporary church and so much of the convent as is required for immediate use. The sum required to purchase this lot and erect the necessary buildings is from $40,000 to $50,000, and Catholics of the United States are looked to for this sum."

Thus we see the practices put forth, under the cloak of religion, to obtain power and dominion over our country; and amidst the constant and incredible success which they fearlessly announce, has attended their diabolical efforts to destroy us; blind and tolerant Protestants, read of the prosperity of the "Catholic congregations" with extreme complacency!

"Pope Pius IXth entered on the thirteenth year of his pontificate on the 17th of June of the present year, 1858, Cardinal Mattei, on the occasion of this anniversary, went according to custom to congratulate his holiness in the name of the Sacred College. The pope, in a most gracious reply, after expressing his gratitude to Providence for having sent happy days to succeed those trying ones of the first years of his reign, congratulated himself on the prosperous situation of the church.

"The pope has published an encyclical letter, addressed

to all patriarchs, primates, archbishops and bishops, recommending them to exercise strict watch over all ecclesiastics having the charge of souls, that they be obliged to perform mass not only on Sundays and holy-days, but on every day in the year."

The above notices show the condition in which the pope regards his church in the United States, and accounts for the increased activity of his emissaries, who now celebrate mass every day in the year!

CHAPTER XI.

"THE GUILDS" OF IRELAND.

Rome has Changed its Policy in the U.S.—Henceforth Aggressive—the Design of Popery Here—To Make the Nation Papal—The Address—Rules of the Guilds.

WHILE the Romish Church was laying its ecclesiastical net-work in the United States, its policy was one of defense; now it is one of aggression. Protestants have allowed the priesthood to increase their organizations and accumulate their strength so rapidly, by the indifference with which they have regarded it, that the language now used by the prelates and priests in our country is as imperious and dogmatic as it would be in any papal country in Europe! In England and the United States openly avowed measures are being now taken to put Popery up, and bring Protestantism down!

They act in this country upon the axiom that the public sentiment of the next generation will depend upon the prejudices and instructions given to the youth of the present time. If the young in the United States can be prejudiced against Protestants and in favor of Romanists, they will in future give the ascendency to popery. Thus it is, that Romish influence is exerted to bring the largest number of youth into their houses of education, that young men and young women may be made papists.

There is an organization in Ireland called "the Guilds," designed to aid the interests of the Vatican. These secret associations, intimately affect the Protestant interests of our country. We will give the reader a few extracts from the address and rules of the Irish "Guilds:"

"In rendering the nation good Christians (*i. e.*, Roman Catholics,) and associating, by the power of their common Catholicity, in one great fraternity, we cannot be unconscious that great results can be legitimately expected. An aggregation of our guilds is a guarantee to perseverance.

"Every brother has the eye of hundreds pursuing him, besides the particular vigilance of his own body.

"The wardens of each guild are bound to make returns of the moral and material condition of those whom they have in charge; their attendance at confession, the oratory, etc., and thus every brother has a continual stimulant to edifying perseverance in grace. Men are by these means fenced round with sacred guardianship, placed in a position between which and the divine blessing, there is nothing to interpose. But we expect more, we expect, in time, a public opinion for truth and virtue an all-pervading, sound, indomitable (Roman) Catholic spirit."

"We believe that it is our duty to extend public opinion in favor of practical Catholicity (*i. e.*, Popery), and to adopt such means as men employ to forward merely material ends. We think our designs far more high, holy and important than any that can engage literary, political or agricultural improvers, and that they therefore should command as much solicitude, thoughtfulness, earnestness and labor. Nay, we really believe that we shall reach all the 'other things' by God's way much sooner than those who, as an American philosopher says, 'vote God out of the State,' and depend upon themselves.

"This 'public opinion,' in sustaining of true religious feeling, will have an extensive operation, and in almost every department of society. Individual Catholics and large classes, committees, juries and boards, corporations and legislatures, the whole state, social, political, commercial and literary, must feel the influence of our ever-working, never-sleeping spirit of Catholic (Popish) truth and feeling, which will have the right and power to be reflected in every movement of the State.

"If some unhappily constituted minds seem rather to be patrons than disciples of the doctrine of Christ; if they assume to themselves the right of judging when they are ignorant, of censuring when they are absurd, and of differing when they are ignorant, absurd and heretical; if there be a species of spurious respectability, pursued at the sacrifice of heaven, and earth and common decency; if a heretical hue of soul, conversation, reading and opinion, be weakly deemed by them intelligent, philosophical and progressive, it is not very frequently because they are malicious or infidel, but only because they are superficial and victims of their own shallowness, easily impressible and wrought upon by their associations. Before the tide of a noble Catholic opinion, all these lighter bodies, that occasionally produce such inconvenience, would be rapidly swept away, and, indeed, from their very lightness, would more effectively exhibit the direction and power of the current.

"A sound Catholic opinion—preaching Catholic principle, and inculcating and pursuing sound Catholic practice—would write the history of the Church in our hearts. We would glory in her great names, reverence her ministrations, study her privileges and her interests, and watch over her healthy vigor with jealous care. Knowing her mission of love and hope, and appreciating its importance to the present and future interests of society, we would vigilantly guard against every assault upon her liberty, and open every home and heart to her approach. Believing her to be the power of God, the mercy of God, the love of God, the will of God, God *embodied*, we would view and estimate all deeds, difficulties, observances and neglects—policy, diplomacy and law, just as they affected HER; approve as they sustained and discountenance as they opposed her reign, until we should have placed her in a position which revelation proclaims and history witnesses as her own—the position of the ever-living and ever-suffering Saviour of the world.

"Let us ask, then, can we overrate the importance of a great public opinion in favor of the Church? These countless influences to which we have adverted, and many others which we have not named, are daily and hourly pronouncing on the Church. In any form of social being, public opinion must mould the prejudices or principles of the great majority of such individuals. From its nature it will insensibly sway them. From their own interests it will rule them, where truth might be ineffectual. And hence to create, foster, extend and render such an opinion supreme in this Catholic country, is the guarantee of the practical freedom of religion, and that the public resources shall be the servants of goodness, and justice, and truth.

"In view of such a noble mission as that to which they have adverted, the Council need not remark that every feeling but that of Catholicity must be subdued. The affairs of the politician, the affairs of commerce, social and trade affairs have their own place, their own means, and their own objects; these may be very good or very bad, desirable or objectionable, but with them the 'Young Men's Society' has nothing to do. We seek to save men's souls and to create a large Catholic organization. A Catholic heart, a generous, self-sacrificing Catholic spirit is all we need and all we can seek. Therefore, let the postulant be a man, and determined to be a good one, and we can ask no further question, and demand no other qualification.

"Let every brother feel convinced that the most trivial infraction of discipline is an assault upon our existence, and as he loves the society let him avoid violation of rule, and prevent it."

The second rule provides that only such books are to be read "as shall be approved of by the spiritual director" (*i. e.* the priest), and the tenth provides, that without his consent, "no new rules can be adopted, and no act is validly performed which is performed against his consent," illustrating in the first place, the mental slavery which every member of these guilds must submit to, and, in the second place, the supreme prerogative asserted by the priest.

Of the special rules of the guilds, the first describes the mode in which the Church of Rome carries out this part of her scheme:

"Each brotherhood is divided into guilds of *fifty*, and when any of such guilds rises to one hundred members, it is sub-divided into two, the last fifty on the list being formed into a new guild. The guild that first rises to the number required for sub-division should have the first place in the 'Young Men's Societies' general meetings,—'Honor to whom honor is due!'—and every succeeding guild, also, as it manifests its energy, by enlisting the highest number (100) which a guild can contain, should have its place in regular order after the guild that has last been divided into two. The new guilds should keep their place according to the date of their formation. The punctuality with which this rule is observed will determine the success of the 'Young Men's Society.' "

The sixth and eighth describe the manner of getting new members and the raising of funds:

" Each guild shall appoint a standing committee of two, to assist the wardens and canvass for postulants, to be associated with the holy guilds."

"The wardens of the guilds shall collect the weekly contribution, mark the cards and hand the money to the secretary."

The general meetings, "for the reception of members, are held every Sabbath evening,"—strange Sabbath work!—when, among other things, a hymn is sung, of which the following is a stanza:

"Faith of our fathers! Mary's prayers
Shall win our country back to thee,
And through the truth that comes from God,
England shall then indeed be free!
Faith of our fathers! holy faith,
We will be true to thee till death!"

Charged with this instruction, the Irish come to America, ready to unite with ardor in any secret plot or association that the bishop or priest may direct for holy Mother Church.

CHAPTER XII.

THE WEALTH OF THE ROMISH CHURCH.

The means used to acquire Money—Church Property in England—How held in the United States—Secret Councils—Acts to set the Laws of the Country at Defiance—The practical Result—A Buffalo Laity—Switzerland injured by Jesuits—Enormous increase of the Papists in the U. S.—Their immense Wealth—Churchyards—Heretics denied a Burial—John Huss and Jerome—Wickliffe—Henry five years unburied—New York Schools of the Jesuits—Church Property in Mexico—How the Priests extort Money from the Dying—The Illinois Catholics and the Canada Priests—Cathedrals in America—Coronation of a Heathen Goddess—Indulgence granted—The Telegraph and the Pope—What it all means.

Public attention has within the past few years been called to the enormous accumulation of real estate by the Roman Catholic hierarchy in this country, and upon inquiry, it is found the same policy is practised here which has distinguished the Roman Catholic prelacy in England. Long before the government of the United States existed, the bishops and monks were acquiring a title to the landed estate of Great Britain. They used all means to procure a devise or grant from a person on a death-bed, "for the good of the church," and recourse was had to every other method for obtaining property. This wealth the priesthood retained for the holy see, the bishopric, or the monasteries. Thus absorbing the landed estate, they used their wealth to acquire temporal power and authority. The British people at that time were well disposed towards the Romish church, and belonged to it, but they began to see that the priestly influence was gaining an ascendancy which they felt was becoming dangerous to their interests. They, therefore, passed an act of parliament to prevent the Romish ecclesiastics from receiving grants and bequests of real estate. These Romish priests, true Jesuits, controlled the courts so far as to evade the law, by inventing the system of "uses" and "trusts," whereby one man held land for another man's benefit. Parliament passed new laws, but the artful priests managed to set them all at defiance, and went on, as usual, until the time of Henry VIII.—the dawn of the Reformation, when a statute was enacted, that effectually prevented any land grants in such manner for a period of more than twenty years, and since then England has had this evil reduced. There was no spirit of persecution in all this; but an essential movement of the people to prevent the priesthood from acquiring unjust temporal power. It was absolutely necessary to protect the lay members of the church, and securing to them the property for which they paid their money.

Now, in the United States, where the British law of Henry VIII. (prohibiting ecclesiastics from holding the property of the laymen) is also our common law, we find the Romish prelates the absolute owners of the whole church property, the real estate, buildings, burial grounds, etc., etc.; and claiming so to own and control, as to have the power to turn a congregation out of doors and shut up any church whenever they see fit to do so. The immense increase of wealth, by these means, alarmed England, even when Roman Catholic; how much greater should be the fears of Protestant America. When charters of incorporations are granted by the civil power, they have to be expressly authorised to hold real estate, and then the amount is limited by the legislature, in order to prevent the acquisition of a power thought to be dangerous to the welfare of the people. But the Roman Catholic bishops—the deadly foes to our principles and institutions, who are aiming by every possible means to betray us—are exempted from the wise and salutary laws which control the state! Why is this? The legislatures of some few of the states have been petitioned by the Catholic laymen for power to control the property of the church; and in New York and Connecticut, laws have been passed, placing Roman Catholic citizens upon an entire equality with every Protestant sect.

A very important feature in the Roman Catholic action in this country, is, their stated provincial councils, which are held in secret, whose transactions are in the Latin language, so that they may be kept from the people.

As far back as the year 1829, the hierarchy determined to pervert the system of allowing the trustees, chosen by the laity, to control the church property. In that year, the council of Bishops assembled in Baltimore, on the 1st of October, and passed the following ordinance: "Whereas lay trustees have frequently abused the right (jure) granted to them by the civil authority, to the great detriment of religion and scandal of the faithful, we most earnestly desire, that in future, no church be erected or consecrated, unless it be assigned by a written instrument to the bishop, in whose diocese it is to be erected for divine worship, and the use of the faithful, whenever this can be done." Approved by Gregory XVI., October 16, 1830.

This suggestion by the bishops did not meet the sanction of the laity at that time, and things went on as before. But in 1849, at the seventh provincial council, held in Baltimore, the college of bishops adopted this decree: "Art. 4. The Fathers ordain, that all churches and all other ecclesiastical property which have been acquired by donations or the offerings of the faithful, for religious or charitable use, belong to the bishop of the diocese; unless it shall be made to appear, and be confirmed by writings, that it was granted to some religious order of monks, or to some congregation of priests for their use."

Here is the bold declaration that the right of property in the Romish churches of the United States, is vested in the bishops. This decree, it was supposed, under the atmosphere of their sacred council, would bring the trustees of the several states to their feet; but the "civil authority" was too powerful! The council again assembled at Baltimore, in 1852, and passed a third ordinance in their council, which particularly affects the liberties of American citizens. Its 16th section reads thus:

"Whereas the things given to God for the use of divine worship and works of charity, come under control of the church, whose duty it is to see that the pious will of the donors be faithfully executed; and whereas the sacred canons have often defended them against the usurpations of laymen, we strictly forbid the interference of laymen, in the administration of those things, without the free consent of the bishops. Hence, not called to this by the bishop, they usurp them, convert them to their own use, or whatsoever manner they may be, frustrate or defraud the will of the donors, or if they try to wrest out of the bishop's hands, the things committed to his trust and care, even by means of the laws, we define and declare that they fall, *ipso facto*, under the punishment inflicted by the fathers in the Council of Trent (Sessions 22, chap. xi. De Reformatione,) on the usurpers of ecclesiastical property."

The punishment here threatened is no less than that of excommunication. It declares that the party "Shall be under an anathema, until he shall have wholly restored to the church or to the administrator or benefices thereof, the jurisdictions, property, effects, rights, fruits and revenues which he has seized, or in whatever way they have come to him, even by way of gift of a superstitious person, and until he shall have furthermore obtained absolution from the Roman pontiff."—(Council of Trent, p. 170.)

"Even by the means of the laws!" says this Baltimore ordinance of 1852, "Any person who should withhold from the bishops the property of the Church, even with the aid of the laws, shall suffer excommunication! The mere reading of this ordinance—which can be found only in Latin, in the Catholic book stores of the country—is enough, we should think, to satisfy the most sceptical that the Romish hierarchy claims supremacy over the civil laws of every country, and particularly of the United States, at this present time.

Thomas Aquinas, a favorite author of Romanists, says: "That it is necessary for salvation to submit to the Roman Pontiff;" "that the pope, as supreme king of all the world, may impose taxes on all Christians, and destroy cities and castles to preserve Christianity." He adds, "that the pope is the summit of both powers, and when any one is denounced as excommunicated for apostacy, his subjects are immediately freed from his dominion and their oath of allegiance to him."*

* Bell. v. 1-5. Thomas II. Secund. ques. 12, art. 2.

Bellarmine declares it to be the common opinion of Roman Catholics, "that the pope, by reason of his spiritual power, has, at least indirectly, a supreme power, even in temporal affairs." Baronius, the historian of the pontificate, says: "The civil principality is undoubtedly subjected to the sacerdotal, and that God has subjected the political government to the dominion of the Church," and "they are all branded as heretics who take from the Church of Rome and See of Peter, one of the two swords, and allow only the spiritual."*

The Council of Trent decreed thus: "The pope is prince over all nations, kingdoms, etc." Cardinal Zaba tells us: "The pope can do all things, and is empowered by God to do many things, which He (God) himself cannot possibly perform!"

The present pope follows the doctrine of the learned Bellarmine, and prefers, for the time, to defer the direct exercise of his temporal dominion in the United States, and to work indirectly and secretly, until he shall accomplish greater political results! In 1809, the pope issued his anathema against the emperor Napoleon, and virtually absolved all his subjects from their allegiance to the throne of France. In 1794, the Council of Pistoia approved the declaration of the French clergy, that the pope had no power to depose kings, or absolve subjects, thus clearly showing the pope claimed this power; and in 1851, the pope anathematized a book written to refute the doctrine that he (the pope) had a right over temporal things.

"In July of that year, 1851, Pius IX. excommunicated the king and parliament of Sardinia, and declared a law

* Bell. v. 1. Baronius, anno 57, § 23, 53. Ib. anno 1053, § 14. Haeresi, Politic, anno 1073, § 13.

null and void, which the government had passed to suppress monastic and religious communities, colleges and churches, etc., and placing the revenues and property in the hands of the civil power. In Spain, in the same month (July, 1851), the government passed a church property law, and forbade bishops to confer holy orders, which law the pope abrogated, and declared it null and void.*

These authorities are sufficient to prove the power which the Roman hierarchy claim at this day in the United States; but we will give one from the organ of the Archbishop of the province of New York. The Jesuit prelate is said to be the real, though not the ostensible editor of *The Freeman's Journal.* The following extract we find published in 1853: "The Pope of Rome has supreme authority over every diocese and over every square foot of surface on this globe. His rights are circumscribed only by the ends of the earth and the consummation of ages." Hence, the pope has partitioned our country into eight provinces, and placed over each a bishop, only requiring a cardinal to complete the most potent engine of evil that ever existed on the face of the earth!

Let us see, now, what has been the practical effect of the Romish ordinance on the church property question. The Catholic laity resisted it in New Orleans, in Buffalo, and in New York. It was to settle the latter case that the nuncio Bedini was ostensibly sent by the pope in 1854; but the trustees and laity remained firm, and they were excommunicated! The Catholics appealed to the New York Legislature, and prayed that Protestant assembly to relieve them from the oppression. They asked

* North American Review, for Jan., 1856.

that they might be confirmed in their right, to keep their own property out of the hands of the bishop and his successors. The result was the passage of the celebrated Church Tenure Bill, which reiterated the law of 1783, adding, that when a bishop held the property of a congregation, and died without passing it to the trustees, it became the property of the State, to be held in trust for the congregation, and returned to them the moment they elected trustees. In the debate on the bill, Hon. Erastus Brooks remarked, that Archbishop Hughes probably held property in his own right to the amount of $25,000,000 in the city of New York. The archbishop flatly denied the fact, and challenged Mr. Brooks to the proof! He said it was all "God's property!" Mr. Brooks went to the office of Registry, and copied the records, and published the statement of what he found, and thereby accomplished the most triumphant vindication of the truth he had asserted.

Switzerland, Protestant and republican Switzerland, could not escape the jealousy of surrounding despotisms in Europe. The Romish power stole into her boundaries, to subvert her liberal institutions. The Jesuits sneaked into citizenship and obtained the right to vote, created dissension and civil insurrection, and, in the name of "the Church," secured an ascendancy in the cantons, and held the Diet in awe, till they were finally driven out of the country, in 1847, at the point of the bayonet! The same course is persistently being pursued in our country by the Jesuits. Look for a moment at the increasing numerical extent of the Romish Church in the United States! Fifty years ago there was in this whole country one Roman Catholic diocese, two bishops, sixty-eight priests, eight churches, two ecclesiastical institutions, one college and two female academies. At that time the entire population of the country was less than seven millions. Had the Catholic Church only kept pace with the progress of the population, we should have had this day four dioceses, eight bishops, two hundred and seventy-two priests, three hundred and twenty churches, eight ecclesiastical institutions, four colleges and eight female academies. Instead of this, we find in the single diocese of New York they have more than doubled.

In the entire United States, instead of four dioceses (which a proportionate increase would have given) there are forty-one; instead of eight bishops, there are thirty-nine, and two apostolic vicars; instead of two hundred and seventy-two priests, there are eighteen hundred and seventy-two; instead of three hundred and twenty churches, there are two thousand and fifty-three, besides eight hundred and twenty-nine stations; instead of eight ecclesiastical institutions, there are thirty-five; instead of four colleges, there are twenty-nine; and instead of eight female academies, there are a hundred and thirty-four. In other words, taking the number of priests and of churches as a basis of computation, the Catholic church has increased within the last half century, seven times as fast as the population!

How is this progress to be explained? The pope of Rome says, "Freedom of conscience is an absurd and dangerous maxim," and "the liberty of the press is the fatal license of which we cannot entertain too great a horror." The Church holds the conscience of its subjects in the United States, and by its confessional, repels every sentiment of freedom, and exterminates it. In this way it seizes the right of suffrage; it annuls our statutes by its councils; it parcels our territory into provinces, and enforces its irrevocable decrees, through the agency of its secret spiritual police. It is the Roman Catholic church which has fomented discord among Protestants, and courted them through Jesuits, until they have controlled thousands, who are unconsciously in their snare. While the moment a member of the Roman Catholic church is suspected of entertaining freedom of opinion, he disappears, or is found to have died by some mysterious violence.

The pope of Rome is, to-day, the greatest millionaire in America! He wields a power over the temporal affairs of this Union, and grasps wealth far greater than belongs to our government.

He binds these millions in perpetual mortmain, to be held in obedience to his single will! The church of St. Louis, in their petition to the New York legislature, said, "For simply refusing to violate the trust law of our State, we have been subjected to the form of excommunication, and our names held up to infamy and reproach. To our members the holy rites of baptism and burial have been denied. The marriage sacrament refused. The priest is forbidden to minister at our altars. In sickness and at the hour of death the holy consolations of religion are withheld."

The increase of wealth has been in proportion to the increase of numbers, and the resources for its accumulation have no limit in the United States.

Three years ago, at a Roman convention held at Buffalo, it was stated that the wealth owned by the Roman Catholics in this country, and deposited in different Savings-Banks, amounted to the enormous sum of forty-eight millions of dollars! The property of the Jesuit-schools, nunneries, seminaries, colleges, etc., in the city of New York alone, according to their statistics published in one of the city journals, January, 1858, amounts to about two millions of dollars!

The "Calvary Cemetery," controlled by the archbishop, on Long Island, covers eighty acres; and at the bishop's rate of the prices for burying, will amount to one million two hundred thousand dollars.*

Rome has ever had large revenues from the grave-

* The avaricious character of the Roman Catholic hierarchy for wealth and power, is illustrated in the history of the Council of Trent, by Paulo Sarpi Veneto, published in 1620. Before the Council concluded its sitting, the pope was urged, by France, to grant the *cup* in communion. This subject, with the use of the vulgar tongue in the service of the church, and the marriage of the priests, were discussed in a Consistory held by the pope, A.D. 1561. Cardinal Pio di Carpi opposed all these measures, and urged that "to grant the cup, would open a gate to demand an abrogation of all positive constitutions by which, only the prerogative given by Christ to the church of Rome, is preserved for those which are "de jure divino," no profit doth accrue but that which is spiritual. For the use of the vulgar tongue in the service, the inconvenience would follow, that all would think themselves divine; the authority of prelates would be disesteemed, and all would be heretics. From the marriage of priests it would ensue, "that having house, wife, and children, they will not depend upon the pope, but on their prince; and the love of their children will make them yield to any prejudice of the church. They will seek to make their benefices hereditary, and so in short space the authority of the Apostolic See will be confined to Rome. Before single life was instituted, the See of Rome received no profit from other nations and cities, and by it, is made patron of many benefices, of which marriage would quickly deprive her." For these reasons the pope refused the request of France. This history also informs us, that the pope having, through the Jesuits and his legates and bishops, the control of the Council of Trent, and the sole power of originating measures, prevented the reform in the church in these and other particulars, and subsequently rewarded with rich benefices the bishops most useful to him, in the Council.

yard. It is, indeed, a vital portion of the papal imposture to make it ignominious to repose in any but the ground which the Catholics consecrate. The canon law of this church prohibits the burial of "heretics," at all! In this way spiritual obedience was enforced, and Europe governed, for several centuries before the Protestant Reformation. Just before the dawn of that glorious era in England, a man, named Tracy, was accused of having expressed heretical views in his will, he was found guilty and his body was immediately dug up by order of a commission issued for the purpose! 1 Burns Eccl. Law, 266.

Soon after the Norman conquests, the Roman See began the exercise of its power, in holding the exclusive possession of the dead, and in deciding who only should lie in their consecrated earth. At the same time denying to those excommunicated, the right of burial in any other earth. The formula of the tenth century gave these cast-off corpses "to the fowls of the air or beasts of the field."

John Huss, and Jerome of Prague were burned at the stake in the fifteenth century, by order of the Council of Constance, and their ashes were not allowed to mingle with earth, but were thrown into the Rhine. If by chance any suspected of heresy found a grave, they were instantly taken up and their ashes treated as those of heretics freshly burned.

Wickliffe, the first English translator of the Bible, had dared to question certain dogmas of the papal theology, but dying in his bed in 1384, he was buried in a churchyard in Leicestershire, and remained for forty-one years. But being afterwards judicially condemned for heresy, his bones were dug up and burnt, and his ashes cast into the river Avon, in the year 1425, of the Christian era. This practice of the Romish church was confined to no particular class of men.

Henry the fourth, Emperor of Germany, after being the victor of more than sixty battles, died under an excommunication of Hildebrand, Pope Gregory VII., and for five years his body was compelled to lie unburied in sight of the majestic Cathedral of Spires, which his own father commenced, and he had finished! From the year 1207 to 1213, Pope Innocent III., kept out of their lawful graves all the dead, from the channel of the Tweed. No funeral bell was allowed to toll; the corpses were thrown like hogs into ditches, and the marriage ceremony was obliged to be solemnized in the church-yard.

Look around over your cities and country towns, and the far West. Take for example the City of New York. Look at the statistics: sixty or seventy schools, seminaries, and colleges, with their three hundred and twenty Jesuits and Jesuitesses for teachers, with the vast sums of money amounting to *one million nine hundred and forty-eight thousand dollars*, according to statistics made, as we understand, under the supervision of the priests. But these are only their operations in New York. What then must be the whole amount of their machinery at work in our other large cities, inland towns, and districts of country, from the Atlantic to the Pacific?

In California, the Romish archbishop Alemany, has become sole possessor of all the landed property belonging to the church at the time of the treaty of Guadalupe Hidalgo, now valued at an enormous amount. All the church buildings, ranches, grave-yards, etc., are included!

"People often wonder where all the money comes from

employed by the Roman Catholics in building the splendid chapels, cathedrals, priests'-houses, colleges, nunneries, *et hoc genus omne*, while the occupants all plead poverty. The priests, for instance, whose usual answer to an appeal on the score of charity, is, "I live on charity myself." People are beginning to find the phenomena accounted for.

The great secret of Rome is this: Money to send out missionaries to all parts of the world, and missionaries to send back money. Where does it come from? Who maintains the Court of Rome, with all its cupidity, lust of power and crime? We tell you it comes from *foreign* parts. In return for this money and protection, what does Rome give? Her indulgences and quackeries! The Protestants as well as Romanists swell the coffers of the Popish Church in the United States. How willingly Americans are seduced to furnish the instruments of power which are surely to be ultimately used against themselves.

To build the splendid cathedrals in the United States, especially in Philadelphia, Cincinnati, Albany, Cleveland and Buffalo the people were fined. The Irish Catholic population of New York paid at the rate of one dollar per capita. Dr. Duff states, that the superintendent of the Erie Railroad assured him that throughout a tract of one hundred and twenty miles, the Irish Catholic laborers paid nearly *twenty-two thousand dollars* for this purpose, into the hands of their bishop.

The coronation of pictures and exposure of saints' bones, is becoming another fruitful source of raising money in our country! Who would have thought that such *heathenish* sights as the coronation of a pagan goddess would ever occur in our Protestant country, and that, too, on the Sabbath! This scenic performance occurred in June, 1858, at Hoboken, New Jersey, after being duly announced by Archbishop Hughes' organ. Two years before, in the same church, there was a similar Sunday entertainment for the "faithful," in enshrining the bones of their saint Quietus, which they pretended were sent from Rome. An important feature in the last exhibition of this sort was, that the pope granted his plenary indulgence to all who should attend that day! and the archbishop, as if to show still further contempt for the laws and institutions of our country, granted "forty days' indulgence to all persons who should visit that picture during the octave!"

A plenary indulgence in the Romish church means that an individual is thereby placed above the penalties of sin. The Romish doctrine is, that "indulgence is the remission of all sins, and that *God is not allowed to punish after they have granted an indulgence.*"

Such an exercise of absolutism as this, demands the serious and immediate consideration of the people of the United States. A bishop can grant indulgence for one hundred years—an archbishop for four hundred years! according to their rules.

A few weeks since, *one hundred and three thousand dollars* were subscribed for a grand cathedral to be erected in the city of New York—three thousand dollars more than was even asked! Two thousand of this sum was the donation of Protestants (heretics), "who wanted to see a Romish edifice erected on American soil to correspond with the architectural beauty of those in popish countries!" Deluded men, unsuspecting, tolerant Christians!

At the call of the archbishop, upwards of seventy

thousand Catholics, mostly *foreign Irish*, rallied by "societies" and "congregations," headed by their priests, to the spot where the corner-stone was laid. By the prelate's order, each of these had opportunity given to leave an offering of money on the stone.*

Pitrat, who challenged archbishop Hughes to deny his facts, says, "When a child is born the priests call for money. The children who are admitted for the first time to communion, bring us money; they marry, bring us money; they die, and their friends pay us for the passport which we deliver to them, and pay us for the right to weep for them. When "mass" is said for souls in purgatory, they pay us money. Without money, no prayers, no masses, no baptism. If a chapter is read over the head of your children, bring us money. Money to throw water on the cattle, sheep, goats, pigs; to bless the tables, chairs, and the articles of furniture, money; to bless carriages, wagons, cellars, stables, houses—bring us money. They say to us, 'Build us splendid and majestic churches, adorn our sanctuaries with fine marble and handsome carving, with statues, pictures, ciboriums. Purchase us sacerdotal ornaments, with silk tissued, silver and gold, shining with embroideries and pearls. Bring us money for all these purposes, and chiefly for our own use."

In England, excommunication had to be made penal, and the payment of Peter's-pence stopped, and the church property sequestrated, when, as Lord Hardwicke says, it had absorbed more than half of England. France, Spain and Sardinia had to take similar proceedings. In Mexico, not long since, when President Comon-

* We have heard of poor Irish servants who gave a month's wages to this work.

fort confiscated the property of the priesthood, they had *forty-one millions* on deposit.

We well know that science and progress are in hostility to the spirit and letter of the Roman Catholic system, and it is a subject to be well considered that Archbishop Hughes has become a stockholder in the ocean telegraph! In other words, the *Pope of Rome* is a stockholder in the telegraph! for Archbishop Hughes, like every Jesuit, has again and again declared, that he is not worth the bed on which he sleeps, and that all the Church's property is God's property, that means, the Pope's, who "is to him in the place of God!" Now, is it not a most remarkable fact that Pope Pius IX. should be holding stock in a company of heretics! It is no longer strange to us, since we see that the Romish Church thus obtains monied interest that she may augment her power the more effectually. A year ago, the organ of the Archbishop of New York intimated quite as much as we have shown.

It is true, numerically, Protestantism is yet far in the ascendant, but the Romish Church is found in every country and island of the habitable globe. Not only the priesthood, but the laity are equally at the command of the pope. He summons whom he pleases to Rome, and he is there! What could be more feasible than to form a combination throughout the Catholic world, and, like Napoleon I., concentrate upon any given point in the United States? With such oaths and such a discipline as belongs to the Jesuits—which we present in this volume—we have no guarantee against any concerted action or aggression, should any such outbreak be deemed expedient by our opponents; for we have no such secret associations as theirs.

CHAPTER XIII.

BEDINI'S MISSION TO THE UNITED STATES.

His object to establish the Inquisition—Right of Church Property—Letter of the Pope to this Government—Cardinal Antonelli—The Italian's Letter—Bassi's Death—Gajani's Lecture.

THE principal object of this mission was the question between the Trustees of the Church of St. Louis, in Buffalo, and their Bishop, respecting the administration of the revenues of that church. The Bishop claimed that the administration of that church, like that of all others in his diocese, should be in his hands, and entirely at his disposal, according to the canon-law of Rome. The Trustees claimed that the administration was only in their hands, according to the civil-laws of the State of New York. The Bishop had excommunicated the Trustees and interdicted the church; and the Trustees, in agreement with the principal members of the church, threatened to separate themselves from the Bishop's communion; therefore, a legate of the Pope was necessary to settle this question. It is a principle, vital to the Roman church, that the administration of the revenues of ecclesiastical property be in the hands of the Bishops, to be at the disposition of Rome; and they esteem it a great scandal that in the United States of America the secular laws interfere in that matter, and effect a diversion. On this occasion, the Nuncio Bedini was charged to treat with the authorities of the government at Washington to obtain favors for the holy see, beginning with the installation of an apostolical nunciature, on the same footing as that in the Low Countries, with the privilege of an ecclesiastical court for matrimonial cases, and other things, denominated "of mixed jurisdiction." That ecclesiastical court, which is usually mentioned in credential letters, and is to be acknowledged by the same authority which is acknowledging the accredited representative person, is announced as "a court of spiritual affairs," and it is nothing else, in plain terms, than the Inquisition itself. A nuncio, established in this manner, becomes head of the inquisition, which operates by means of the Jesuits, with all secrecy, and has for its object the promotion of the interests of the church—this is the meaning of the motto in the coat of arms of the Jesuits, "Ad majorem Dei Gloriam"—by persecuting in every possible manner the real enemies of Rome, and favoring, as far as possible, her real friends. Real enemies are understood to be those who really do and intend to do her harm; and real friends are those who are disposed to do her good. Some Catholics are sometimes considered enemies, and some Protestants *friends.* On Protestant friends favors are most largely bestowed, the favors received from them being paid a hundred-fold.

Bedini presented to *Protestants* precious rings, brooches and snuff-boxes with diamonds; while to Catholics he gave *indulgences* and *pontifical dispensations.*

Their friends, in particular ways, are introduced and highly recommended for any kind of employment, and very often, through their mighty exertions, accommodated with public offices; at the elections, the vote of the Roman Catholics, (especially the Irish,) which is in the hands of the Bishop, is given to those who in any manner have shown favor and inclination to the Roman Catholics.

The Nuncio corresponds with the inquisition.

If Bedini had found decided favor in Washington, as had been promised him by L. Cass, Jun., in Rome; and if the cry of the Italians had not been raised against him as the murderer of that eminent patriot, Ugo Bassi; in short, if his mission had had a successful issue, he, Bedini, would have been the first Apostolic Nuncio in the United States; and God knows what his intentions and aspirations were against the very palladium of liberty, our Bible, and our Constitution, he might have achieved against our civil and religious liberties. We do neither know what were his secret instructions, but his mission, as everybody knows, having ended badly, he so far compromised the interest of the holy see in this country, that, on his return to Rome, he was set aside with an office of no consideration, and without any hope of promotion to the cardinalate, at least, for the present.

We will now introduce the curious state documents from Rome, in connection with this Nuncio.

Note.—The priest of each parish in Rome, notes: "1st. The residence, street, number, and story, occupied by each parishioner. 2d. His name, family and baptismal, and place of birth. 3d. His rank, whether noble or not, tradesman, student, workman, &c. 4th. Whether married, bachelor or widower, &c. 5th. If a stranger, we must indicate how long a resident of Rome, and how long he has lived in the parish. 6th. Where he lived before coming here. 7th. What sacraments he has received, and if that is not sufficient, observe that there is a blank space to write down other observations." "The same is done with Protestants, except we indicate them especially as Protestants. Besides, every year we must denounce to the ecclesiastical board and to the police all Protestants living within our parish."—De Sanctis.

CARDINAL ANTONELLI TO MR. MARCY.

Excellency:—Monsignor Gastoni Bedini, Archbishop of Thebes, appointed by the Holy Father as Apostolic Nuncio to the Empire of Brazil, has been directed to repair to the United States, and under such circumstance to compliment the honorable President in the name of his Holiness. This prelate being endowed with the most brilliant qualities of heart and mind, was well deserving of this distinguished commission from the Holy Father, I beg, therefore, that your Excellency will be pleased to receive him in that kindness of spirit which is characteristic of your disposition, and to extend to him whatever assistance he may need. Your favor will be the more necessary to him to facilitate his being kindly received by the President, to whom he is to present a Pontifical letter. I venture to flatter myself that you will respond to my request, especially in consideration of the object in view; and with this hope I have the honor to tender you the assurance of my distinguished consideration,

Your Excellency's lantroveno,

(Signed) G. A. Antonelli.

Rome, March 31st, 1853.

To his Excellency the Minister of Foreign Relations, Washington.

Pius IX. *To the President of the United States.*

Pius IX. Pope.

Illustrious and Honored Sir.

Greeting:

As our venerable brother Caxelamus, Archbishop of Thebes, accredited as our Envoy in Ordinary and Nuncio of the Apostolic See near the Imperial Court of Brazil, has been directed by us to visit those *regions*, (the

United States,) we have at the same time especially charged him to present himself in our name before your Excellency, and to deliver into your hands these our letters, together with many salutations, and to express to you, in the warmest language, the sentiments we entertain towards you, which he will testify. We take it for granted that these friendly demonstrations on our part will be agreeable to you, and least of all do we doubt but that the aforesaid venerable brother, a man eminently distinguished for the sterling qualities of mind and heart which characterize him, will be kindly received by your Excellency; *and inasmuch as we have been entrusted by Divine commission with the care of the Lord's flock* THROUGHOUT THE WORLD, we cannot allow this opportunity to pass without earnestly entreating you to *extend* your *protection* to the *Catholics* inhabiting those REGIONS, and to shield them at all times with your power and authority. Feeling confident that your Excellency will very willingly accede to our wishes and grant our requests, we will not fail to offer up our humble supplications to Almighty God that he may bestow upon you, illustrious and honored sir, the gift of his heavenly grace, that he may shower upon you every kind of blessing, and unite us in the bonds of perfect charity.

Given at Rome, from the Vatican, March 31st, 1853, the seventh of our Pontificate.

(Signed) PIUS IX., Pope.

These are exact copies of the letters transmitted to the United States Senate, and on file, numbered (55) in the State department, bearing date 19th March, and received on the 18th April, 1854.

Mark this language of the Pope! "And inasmuch as

we have been entrusted with the Lord's flock throughout the world, 'extend' your protection to the Catholics inhabiting those REGIONS!" What a shame that the Lord's flock should be exposed by their residence in the heathenish REGIONS—(the United States of America)—should need that "protection" be extended over them, that they may be enabled to live among heretical Americans—stubborn republicans, who, not acknowledging a State church in papal Rome, have no power exerted to interfere between them and their Creator and Preserver. How studiously does the Pope protect American Protestant citizens at Rome, who cannot utter a sentiment of liberty, or be seen with a Bible, or allowed to have one in their possession, while their poor bodies are denied the rite of burial!

Bedini is represented in this correspondence with our government as "brilliant in heart and mind." Bedini! the famous assassin of more than 300 patriots at Bologna, and the cruel and infamous torturer of delicate women. Among the most atrocious and horrible executions of which this Nuncio was guilty, that of the patriot Ugo Bassi is prominent.

In 1844, the eloquent Bassi exclaimed in a moment of enthusiasm, "God gave all men as a great gift, the Holy Bible. Faith is the only means of safety." He was taken to Rome for this, and imprisoned. During the revolution in 1849, he was liberated, and entered the army as a chaplain. He was then seized by the Austrians while assisting a dying soldier, and sent to Bologna; being a monk, they did not kill him. Bedini was there, as the Pope's Extraordinary Commissioner, and immediately doomed Bassi to die. But he was a priest, and before butchering him, it was necessary, under the canon law of Rome to *unpriest* him. This ceremony is a very terrible one. The sufferer is brought into a church hung with black tapestry, the windows of which are darkened. Black candles are burning, and the prelate or inquisitor is also dressed in black. The priests proceed to tear from the victim the robes and priestly dress, pronouncing upon him the curses which are found in the Pope's ritual book. They then skin the palms, fore-fingers, and thumb, of both hands, and the top of the head! To this condition poor Bassi was reduced, and then pushed to the door of the church, and given into the hands of the ferocious executioner. These Austrian ruffians in three hours after, shot him, by the order of Bedini; who had thus divested him of his sacred character. When the priests standing around offered to confess him, Bassi replied:—"I will have only my God to assist me, you are imposters."

Two graves were dug in a deserted spot, outside of Bologna. An imposing military force kept off the horror-stricken citizens. A dead silence reigned. On a sudden it was broken by the sound of a distant coach, driven furiously, which entered the square formed by the soldiery. It was an awful moment. Bassi and his friend Laviraghi descended from the coach. Ugo was pale, but his countenance seemed lighted up by the glorious martyrdom which awaited him. He walked in composure to the side of his grave, and raising his dark, eloquent eyes to heaven, he exclaimed, "I die without remorse. I die for my God and my country. Viva Gesu! Viva 'It——" Six homicidal bullets prevented his uttering the whole name of his beloved Italy, as he expired.* He was but forty-two years of age.

* Nicolini on the Pontificate of Pius IX.

The mother of Bassi, on hearing the fact, exclaimed "Ugo! Ugo!" and fell dead on the ground.*

Signor Gajani, now a member of the New York bar, (1858) stated the following facts in a course of lectures, delivered in October, 1854.

"Bedini became a priest for the same reason that the present Pope Pius IX., did. He was fit for no other service. Even in this he fell into discredit, on account of his licentiousness and bad conduct. He entered the service of a prince in Rome, and his business as a servant was to announce visitors. I myself," says Gajani, "have seen him in this humble position. Soon after he was made train-bearer to his master's son, and followed him to Vienna. He gained the favor of this young Prince by base services, it would be improper to mention here. For some good reasons, I must omit the detail of other passages of his life." In 1843, he was sent as Internuncio to Brazil. He went with two servants, a secretary and a good cook; which last, a papal prelate never forgets. In Brazil, however, loud complaints were made, and he was disgracefully recalled by the pope, and an inferior position assigned him in Rome.† This is the papal representative from the Court of Rome to the United States, who found warm friends and admirers among Protestant citizens of our country, and of whose friendship *senators*

* The Brigadier of the Carbineers who had arrested him, has since met his own death on the very spot where he captured the noble Bassi.

† In the face of this fact, the pope, fearing the bold step he was taking to establish the Spiritual Court of the Inquisition in the United States would be found out, stated, Jesuitically, in his Letter, that Bedini "was on his way to Brazil! So when he, Pius IX., fled to Gaeta in 1849, he pretended to the French soldiery that it was a mistake, as he intended to have gone to France!!"—*Gajani.*

have even boasted! He had much better have been sent to the *penitentiary* than to the American government. Yet he was received and entertained graciously by fawning Protestants, and escorted under our national flag, upon an American steamer, in his tour to the lakes!

Seventy Italians, in New York, noble and true-hearted exiles from their country, addressed Bedini by a public letter, exposing his real character to the American people!

Such is briefly the history of the Pope's prelate, who was selected to establish the Spiritual Court of the Inquisition—the San-Fidesti Society—and to interfere with the Church property of the American people. Bassi's crime was for assisting wounded, dying soldiers. He had not been into battle. Bologna was his native place—all were anxious to save him—and even the Archbishop implored the suspension of the execution, till he might write to the Pope. But Bedini, composing his hypocritical face into a mocking smile, replied, that "he had a positive commission from the Pope, and the execution should go on." "You recollect how Bedini, when in New York, denied his participation in Bassi's death. Some will ask why the pope should choose such a prelate for this mission. I answer, firstly, that it is a very embarrassing thing to choose the least wicked among the Romish prelates. Secondly, Bedini is very cunning, and fit for everything that requires a sacrifice of honor and conscience. He can execute as a butcher, and can play the part of a good priest! Thirdly, the secret mission on which he was sent, was perfectly worthy of such an agent. He was sent here (among other things) to establish a secret Jesuitical Society, called San-Fidesti. This society was established when the Jesuits were suppressed by order of Clement XIV. Its first victim was that Pope himself. Bedini's object was to establish this society in America, and I know that he *succeeded.**

* Delivered in New Haven Oct. 17th, 1854, in presence of Professor Silliman and other distinguished citizens of the country.

CHAPTER XIV.

THE ROMAN REPUBLIC.

Death of Pope Gregory XIV.—Starved to Death and denied the Sacraments—Ceremonies over the Dead Pope—The election of Pius IX.—The Conclave—The Accident—The Amnesty—Appearance of the Prisoners when taken from the Dungeons—Family of Pius IX.—Immoralities—His Change and Promotion—Conspiracy—Jesuits expelled from Rome—Bennetti—Rossi—Jesuits expelled from France—Rossi murdered—Antonelli—Revolution—The Palace entered—The Pope submits—His Flight—Confessional—The election of the People—The Bible—The Pope deprived of temporal Power—Rome a Republic—Public Debt—The Pope prepares for War—France—England—Rome alone opposes the Pope—The first Roman Victory—French Treachery—Their Victory—The Pope's Joy—His Cruelty—Blasphemy—The Women—Incidents—Austrian cruelties in aid of the Pope—Foresti.

On the 29th of May, 1846, Pope Gregory XVI. was said to be dangerously sick. A strict watch was kept in every place, contradicting the report that he was in danger. The people, too, were afraid to betray their inward delight at the prospect of his death; as they had once before been severely punished by him for manifesting joy at the expectation of his decease.

This pope, the predecessor of the present pontiff, Pius IX., gloried in the acknowledgment, that he had never pardoned any one since he had the power, either in his convent or on the throne. The dean of the College of Cardinals, who had the sole right to assist the dying pope, repaired to the Vatican, but was denied admittance to the sick room by the premier of the Crown, who declared the pope was much better, and only wished his immediate servants around him. The papers announced that the pope was well, and would attend high mass next day, at the church of Santa Maria Novella. The gala coach was then drawn before the door of the Vatican, and the sick, old pope taken to it. He fainted in the act, was taken back to his bed, and thus hastened to a close his last hours. Still the truth was concealed, so far as an energetic police could do so, and the papers continued to deny that it was the pope's illness which prevented his attendance that day. But the people could not be deceived.

"Will the pope die this time?" was the earnest inquiry of many a broken-hearted being, whose relatives were then groaning in dark humid dungeons.

The very idea of his death sent a thrill of joy to many hearts — it opened the door of hope to the afflicted mothers, wives and sisters of the victims he held in the dungeons and prisons of the "Holy Inquisition," as each pope has the privilege of turning out the victims of the preceding pope, to make room for his own.

The pope died on the 1st June, 1846, without the viàticum and extreme unction, which he believed essential to salvation! This was in consequence of the intrigue of several of the aspiring cardinals, for the throne; and the dean, upon whom the duty devolved, was suspected of being a candidate for the succession! He could not therefore, be trusted by the premier with the dying pope! Fifteen hundred bells, attached to the five hundred and six churches of Rome, were tolled for "the benefit of the holy father."

"The greatest confusion," says Gajani, "prevailed at the Vatican. The pope's 'family,' consisting of servants, priests, waiters, and prelates, have a right when he dies to ransack the apartments completely." "The corpse was laid on a large marble table, and a noble guard attended in an adjoining room. The officer whose business it was to open the door, associated with fifty others, said no one could tell when the pope died, as the physician found him a cold corpse when he came in the morning. He died allone, being literally abandoned as soon as his death was certain, without the consolation of the sacraments."

"Yesterday morning, at nine o'clock," said the officer, "I ventured, on hearing a violent ringing of the bell, to enter the pope's room—I was moved at the sight. Alone in that hot and mephetic room, feeble and fainting for food, he was tormented by thirst and flies. He almost supplicated me to remain. He was no longer the haughty and frowning sovereign: bitter disappointments had broken down his spirits and his hopes. I was there almost three hours, and was very glad when he dismissed me, as I was afraid of being discovered, and the air of the room was insupportable."

"Gregory XVI. having now departed this life, and his body having been duly and solemnly deprived first of political power, and then of religious authority, the surgeons of the papal court came in and took the corpse, in order to have it dissected and embalmed immediately; for the hot weather, and the condition of the body, would have made the operation impossible if delayed any longer. The stomach, the heart, etc., were put in a vase, and taken in procession to the church of 'S. Anastasio,' near the fountain of Trevi."

"In the mean time, the embalmed limbs were clad in rich pontifical dress, and exposed to the public in the *cappella ardente*, a chapel, with numberless burning wax candles. I went to see it, and thought that, after so many desecrating ceremonies, and the profane operation of the surgeons, the corpse would have lost all its holiness; but I was mistaken. I was informed that the *feet*, being, perhaps, the most holy part of the papal body (*santissimi piedi*), would retain something of their former virtue for three days more. They had, therefore, been left naked, in order that any one might kiss them, and gain the indulgence of a discount of seven years from their future condemnation to purgatory!

During three days the honors of the court were paid to that embalmed corpse, and three times a day the great dignitaries and officers belonging to the kitchen went to ask for its orders concerning meals, and all these occurrences were registered by the notaries of the reverend Apostolic Chamber. This treatment, which is customary on the occasion of the death of every pope, had then the appearance of a cruel satire, for it was well known that Gregory XVI. had been left to starve during the last days of his life."

"The three days of the exhibition being over, the body was put into a coffin and placed upon the summit of a *catafalco*, or bier, erected in the main nave of St. Peter's Church. The funeral rites were performed around that lofty *catafalco* during nine days, with the usual pomp: a great many masses were said by well-paid priests, excellent music was constantly performed during this time, and a thousand large wax candles were burning day and night. All this was done for the benefit of the soul of the pope, and cost the state a hundred and fifty thousand dollars. At length the costly remains were shut up in a marble tomb, on which Pasquino sat to judge the acts of the deceased."

Pasquino, a poor tailor, was a great poet, and dreaded

for his sarcastic wit. Having satirized the popes, he was caught by one of them, but released from punishment on a full confession and promise to write no more. His life was spared, but his tongue and hands were cut off. One morning this tongueless being, with handless arms, was seen sitting upon the ruined statue, the only one left in Rome in the days of Cola de Rienzi, the "last of the tribunes." Pasquino became the representative of satirical humor of the Roman people. But to trace the authors of the pasquinades could not be done. Pope Gregory's cruelties were fresh with blood, and the prisons groaned with victims when he died. His private life in all respects was abominable.

After the death of Gregory XVI., the Roman Catholic Church was two years without a pope! The despotic authority was now in the cardinals, and the system, with all its oppressive regulations, remained unchanged. All the former agents and executioners were retained in office as before.

But the cardinals knew they were hated by the people, and they feared their threatened fury. At this period all Europe was convulsed, and they knew not when the outbreak might engulf them; yet they were concerned chiefly in enriching themselves. Then arose a voice of independence, patriotism, and courage, from the men of Italy, who dared to deny the authority of the papal yoke.

The municipal authorities in most of the cities of the Roman States, addressed the cardinals with protests against the late diabolical administration.

The city of Rome had no municipal authority since Pope Sixtus V., who abolished it; but in a more earnest and significant way the people cried out, "We will have no pope!" "Down with the Papacy!" This was the salutation made to the cardinals, as they were on their way to elect a new pope. There was one general expression of exasperation on that day. This fear of a massacre caused the old pope, in his sickness, to make a bull, (found unfinished among his papers,) giving any number of cardinals, however small, the right to elect a new pope, who would be as lawfully his successor as though elected by a full college of cardinals.

On the 13th of June, 1846, the cardinals assembled in conclave at Rome to elect a new pope. They drove in their gala carriages to the church of S. Silestro on Fueiual hill, attended by their numerous servants, &c. Here they dismissed all, except the few persons a cardinal is allowed to take with him to the conclave; who are a secretary, a train-bearer, a chief waiter and a common servant. They sang in private their usual hymn, "Veni Creator Spiritus." Then, coming out in procession, proceeded to the palace of Quirinale, which is one belonging to the pope. Here every comfort and luxury was prepared for their reception. The six deacon cardinals, who led the procession, have the same authority as the others; but they can be taken from laymen without ever having been priests. Sometimes the pope confers the cardinalship upon a layman of a princely house, or on a great scholar, who is willing to dress in purple and live without a wife. The whole number of cardinals is seventy. There were fifty-one present on this occasion. There never can be of this college more than ten who are not natives of Italy. These foreign cardinals, if present, can vote in an election for pope, but cannot be voted for, as the pope must be born in Italy. There was a grand reception of dignitaries, who called on the cardinals before they shut themselves in conclave, expressing compliments, good wishes, etc. It was a great time in the kitchens, each cardinal having his own cook, and each trying to excel the other in the number of dainty dishes he could present his royal master. Two old cardinals headed two powerful parties, both candidates for pope. There was, beside, another party, who determined to vote for no one who was a friar. This was the Jesuit party, which other religious orders of Rome opposed, and who were suppressed by Clement XIV., himself a friar.

The same day the conclave met, the cardinal "grand penitentiary" was approached by a mysterious person, who requested to be confessed. Secrecy having thus been secured, the statement was made at the confessional of a conspiracy in existence to blow up all the cardinals, and that the mine and gunpowder were in readiness.

Architects were set to work, and twice searched the building in vain to find the mine. The cardinals, however, were in terror, while intrigue, personal ambition and interest were at work. They, pretending that the election of pope was made by them, under the influence of the Holy Ghost, and yet, having France, Austria, Spain and Portugal interfering through their ambassadors, who every year receive large sums of money as "protectors" of the cardinals!

Mark it, reader!—the pope is head of the Roman Catholic Church throughout the world, but no country but Italy can furnish a pope; while it is a notorious fact, that the prelacy of Rome is more corrupt in Italy than in any other papal country upon earth. But the reason why the impostors invented the theory of electing the pope by the Holy Ghost, was, that when not confined to Italy, France also elected a pope, and Germany did so likewise, and these several popes warred on each other! The French pope moved the Holy See to Avignon, in France, and was near ruining the character of the Roman chair, when Catharine, from Siena, carried it back to Rome, and for which she was made a saint! After Adriano VI., the cardinals passed a law that none but an Italian should be pope. But to the election. It was mortal fear that hurried on the cardinals and restrained their ambition. Waiting for the foreign cardinals, it was usual to cast votes on some iron-head. The iron-head chosen was Cardinal Mastai Ferretti, whom no one believed could get one genuine vote! This was the person agreed upon by the confusion and fright of the cardinals, neither party being aware that he was selected by the other. The result was, he got thirty-six votes, and became by that mistake the living head of the Universal Roman Catholic Church! The cardinals saw their error, but the pope was elected! Those thrones on which the seventy cardinals sit, (all are equal sovereigns while the Holy See is vacant) are so arranged, that by pulling a rope, at any time, the canopy or upper part disappears; so, as soon as the election was made, the ropes were all pulled to lower the canopies of the thrones, and each cardinal went by turns to kneel before the throne of the newly elected pope, and worshipped him humbly as the *Holy of Holies!*

Next morning, 16th June, 1846, the solemn announcment of the pope's election was made. Cardinal Camerlengo took the golden hammer, with which he struck the dead pope's head, to ascertain the fact, and struck the door which led into the interior of the palace, which was walled up during the conclave. He then advanced, and announced the pope's election in these words: "I announce to you a great joy: we have as pontiff John Maria

Mastai Ferretti, from Sinigallia, who has assumed the name of Pius IX." He then presented the pope in his pontifical robes, who, coming forward, stretched his right hand, and with his two first fingers extended, made the sign of the cross upon the people; and successively turning to the north, west and south, imparted in the same manner his blessing to all the earth!

Pius IX. had been for eighteen years a bishop, acting as a secret police, a duty bishops generally perform very thoroughly. In this way he knew better than the cardinals that the people were against him. He very soon took care to say to the foreign ambassadors that he was desirous to give an amnesty to political opponents, and wished the people to wait for these peaceful changes. It had been usual for other popes to liberate prisoners confined in the dungeons on the second day after their election, as they visited St. Peter's Church. But Pius IX. did no such thing. When he saw, however, ladies in mourning waving their little white banners, with the word "Amnestia" upon it, and the crowd which thronged the streets crying out that one word, (amnesty,) he told the officer of his guard to "let the people know he was preparing for it."

In the meanwhile, he retained in office every agent of past tyranny, and enforced those inhuman and oppressive laws that it was not believed possible then to have done. He enrolled all the corrupt servants and courtiers of Gregory XVI., even to the famous Gaetanino!

Popes have the power to absolve themselves, from a solemn promise; and when a month elapsed, and no amnesty was made, it began to be surmised that Pius did not mean to grant a single pardon. But on the 16th of July, 1846, an edict did appear from the pope, written in Italian, granting a conditional pardon to those classes of political offenders who would beg for it, acknowledge their crimes, and promise to behave better in future! There were so many exceptions, that few could expect, under this to be benefited. All political offenders who belonged to the clergy, or were guilty of any offence against the established religion, were excluded. This embraced by far the largest number of prisoners, who were mostly influential persons opposed to papal oppression, consequently, of the liberal party. Then all who had been employed in public institutions were excluded. All who had before enjoyed an amnesty were likewise debarred the hope of pardon; and, finally, that class who were charged with some common crime, as well as political offence, were excepted. So that, in fact, it was a sham affair—the very essence of Jesuitism. But it was as much as was expected from a pope, and the people who cared not for him, determined to make the most of it. They were for having their friends come out of the dungeons at once, instead of waiting for any investigation. A "great demonstration" was therefore agreed upon, and had been agitated several days before the edict issued. Every class of citizens united in it, to show the feelings of the whole people. They illuminated Rome, formed into a procession, and shouted vehemently, "Long live Pius the Ninth!" This cry was simultaneously made, by previous arrangement, throughout Italy, and against the will of the pope; and in disregard of the laws and regulations then in force, the prisoners were set free! Pius IX. was afraid of his life, and dared not resist the popular clamor. So little did he confide in the good will of the people, that, when the procession halted at his palace, and cried out, "Viva Pio Nono!" he could scarcely be prevailed on to appear on the balcony; He knew that the same voice of the people which cried "Long life," would have cried "Death!" the next moment, had he attempted to keep down the bars of the prisons. "Now the greatest attraction was the liberated prisoners," says Gajani, "and deep interest in them was felt by every one. When taken from their cells and brought to light among the large crowd of their friends and relatives, they looked astonished and bewildered, as if suspecting that their triumph was but a dream! Many of them were entirely disabled and worn out by ill treatment, and some were brought, blindfolded, upon chairs, because the slightest movement, and the light would have injured them. I saw among them in Rome a venerable old gentleman carried by four of his sons, all full-grown men, formerly his fellow-prisoners. A ray of joy animated his dying face, and his heart was overwhelmed with happiness at the imposing sight of the Roman people once more free, and evidently determined to maintain their freedom. Excess of joy terminated in a few days his already worn-out life. His last words were, 'Never trust a pope.'

"I did not see my brother when he came out from prison, for he was in Rimini. My mother had been waiting there for the amnesty ever since she had heard of the election of the new pope. 'They brought him to my arms,' she wrote to me, 'because he could not walk at all, or even change his sitting position. The dampness of his dungeon deprived him of the use of his limbs, and want of air and light made him look pale as death. His sparkling black eyes were shut, because he could not bear the light. I need not say what I felt at this sight. But he was in excellent spirits, and bade me be of good cheer, as he would recover in a few days. So thinks, too, our friend, Dr. Michele. But I feel that I am not able to hope for the best, for I have a sad presentiment. I have seen the amnesties of five popes during my life, and know how much to rely upon them."

The family of Pius IX. had such an opinion of Mastai Ferritti, that his own brother, Joseph, exclaimed, "We shall have a bad pope!" and refused to live in Rome, or take office under him. Another member, a nephew, said the pope was a selfish man, "a true priest." To show his hatred to the liberals, Pius IX. had his nephew imprisoned.

Properly speaking, there is no nobility in Italy, no true aristocracy, having distinct privileges. In the time of the middle ages the political party were the nobility, but equal oppression made it a common party. Now, any family of fortune, and living in style, may be enrolled among the nobility.

Grazioli, now a baron and a nobleman, was thirty years ago, a poor baker! Sometimes the title of prince, marquis, knight or count is conferred by the pope on some influential name. In this way the family of Mastai Ferritti was made noble.

The pope was the youngest of four sons. His father was in the highest degree opposed to entering his younger boys in monasteries or making priests of them. He was an intelligent liberal, and in favor of having his sons educated in a way to be useful to themselves and their country.

But John Maria was so exceedingly stupid, and had such an aversion to study, that his father found him not only obstinate but unable to receive an education. The Latin language, which is the key to the university and to every scientific profession, was the especial object of his dislike, for he could not grasp its meaning. His parents concluded to make him a soldier to the pope, and put him under the dominion of the priesthood of Rome. This is regarded as the severest punishment for dissipated young men, who can do nothing better than wear a mean livery, as a "pope's soldier." It signifies in Europe a coward, fit for nothing but papal parades. John Maria held the post of light horseman, on account of his noble family, and his duty was to escort the pope's carriage. He obtained admittance into good society in Rome, and improved in manners and mode of expression, but grew worse in morals. He was enamored with a beautiful and accomplished girl, though not a legitimate daughter, but she was virtuous and declined the advances of such a low, debased fellow. He then sought to recover from the disappointment by going to Naples, and deserted his place of pope's soldier to follow a famous actress, Madame Morandi. In Naples he ruined his health for life, was again disappointed, and lost all his little property. He went back to Rome, and found Clara Colonna married to one worthy of her, and the pope's troop of horse disbanded, as the pope wanted a "noble guard," in place of the cavalleggeri. John Maria applied for admission to Prince Barberini, who had the right to enrol the noble guard; but he was refused, as his sickness would not allow him to ride on horseback, as well as from his former want of discipline. Here, denied employment, disappointed in love, ruined in reputation, broken in fortune, and lost in character, he ventured to approach Pius the Seventh, then an old man, who, seeing his miserable condition, in mind and body, said to him, "Repent of your sins, and make yourself a priest, and God will bless you."

From that time, John Maria became, in external acts of devotion, a bigoted fanatic. Abbot Graziosi, a learned and liberal priest, gave him some lessons in theology, and without any distinct ideas of the matter, he was ordained a priest, at the age of twenty-three. But, even then, he despised study, and devoted himself to an institution for vagrant and abandoned children, called Tata Giovanni.

Abbot Mastai Ferritti desired then to go abroad as a missionary, and he was sent with Abbot Pecci to Chili, in South America. Though unacquainted with the language of the country (Spanish), he was successful among the Creoles, who liked his earnest manner and gesture, and perhaps respected him the more from not comprehending *his* language. When Ferritti returned to Rome, he was made a canon of the church of Santa Maria, in Via Lata, and Pope Leo the Twelfth after that made him bishop of Spoleto, an old city, eighty miles from Rome.

An instance occurred in 1831 which marked the treachery of Mastai Ferritti, now Pius IX. The revolutionists of Italy were being pursued by the Austrians, and resolved to reach Rome in advance of them, and prepare to go into battle. When they got as far as Spoleto, they found the Austrians fifty miles behind. The bishop of Spoleto, Monsignor Mastai Ferritti, and his cousin Joseph, bishop of Rieti, had just received a large sum of money from the pope, to be used in retarding the march of the revolutionists. The bishop of Rieti proposed to join with the Sanfidesti, and make battle on them; but the Bishop of Spoleto, Mastai Ferritti, more cunning, corrupted the leader of the revolutionists, and this traitor deceived them and fled. This same bishop of

Spoleto, the present pope, after bribing the man and making him a traitor, came in the meek Christian character, and told them, that they had no chance to reach Rome before the Austrians, and that they had better lay down their arms and accept the pope's pardon. They relied upon him, surrendered arms, and every man of them was punished with long imprisonment.

For this exploit, he was promoted to the bishopric of Imola, which is very lucrative and generally given to a cardinal, or a prelate aspiring to that office. A few years later, both he and his cousin, bishop of Rieti, were created cardinals!

This man, now Pope Pius IX., was detested in Spoleto by all the inhabitants. In Imola, his election of pope caused great excitement, so much was he despised, and it was the same case in Sinigallia, his native town.

. Pius IX., was aged fifty years, when he was elected pope; and is consequently now in his sixty-seventh year. It was not expected, at the time he came to the throne, that he could have lived half so long. His health was then, comparatively gone, and he was subject to epileptic fits. His family have never been on familiar terms with him, at any period of his life. His profligate character, in early life, and the sickness which followed after, is supposed to have made him the coward he has now become. To his moral isolation, is attributed his moroseness; and when elected pope, he was without a friend.

Except supreme selfishness, he is less profligate than most of the popish priesthood at present; but the change in his mode of life, is ascribed to the loss of his health. He thinks Divine Providence has separated him from all other men, and manifested it, in saving him, when a child, from being drowned; in arresting his life of dissipation, and in making his colleagues cast their unwilling votes on him, and thus made him pope, in order to do some great deed, to subserve the interests of popery.

It was his most extraordinary bigotry, which led to so much persecution when a mere bishop, both in Spoleto and Imola. A few days after he was made pope, he went to the church *del Gesu*, the Jesuit head-quarters, to say mass, and there declared the Jesuits to be "the strong and experienced oarsmen who kept from shipwreck the bark of St. Peter." The press was, and is still under the censorship of the Holy Inquisitors; and never a word or act, which shews the pope in his true character, is seen in any part of the world.

But, the people were not satisfied at this; they wanted liberty of the press, recognized by law; they wanted the Jesuits expelled from Rome, and a national guard for their own protection. It was impossible to trust the solemn oath of the pope, and what was done, had only been the result of his cowardice; the moment he could restore despotism and put down the people, he would do it!

A conspiracy was at once arranged by the Sanfidesti, by which the leaders of the liberal party of Rome, who instigated these reforms, were to be put to death. The 16th of July, 1846, was the day fixed for the accomplishment of the deed of darkness.

One, two or three assassins were hired, according to the importance of the person's life. Among the leaders, at least three of the Sanfidesti, were employed, to compass the death of each man. These emissaries of Papal despotism, were to have their poniards aimed at a short distance from their victims, and strike only when there was a tumult raised. The occasion was to be a great procession, which furnished a fine opportunity for the work.

The man who discovered this Jesuitical conspiracy and whose life was particularly sought, was a carman, by the name of Angelo Brunetti, called Cicernacchio. He got the information from one of the three assassins, who had been appointed to kill him. The assassin could not understand the general plan; for it is not a part of the organization of the Sanfidesti, to know any thing more of a plot, than the part they are ordered to play in its execution. Their oath binds them to do whatever the superior authority commands. The plan, however, was discovered by searching the house of a former infamous spy, named Minardi, who fled from Rome on its discovery. A letter was found in that house from a certain Virginio Alpi, which set forth the whole matter.

A large band of these ruffians were arrested; and on each was found a poniard, and their purses filled with gold. When interrogated as to where and how they procured these weapons and money, all were silent, except two; who, overcome by fear of death, acknowledged that a prelate and a cardinal had given them the poniards, after having blessed the deadly weapons! The prelate was Monsignor Grassellini, the governor of Rome. The moment he heard the plot was revealed, he fled to Naples. The cardinal on whom suspicion at once rested, was Lambruschini, the premier of the last pope; and the only doubt of this, was caused by the confession of the two ruffians, who insisted, the one they saw, was a young man.

The pope, on being informed of what had passed, ordered his Swiss guard to close up and watch his palace gates.

He appointed Monsignor Morandi Governor of Rome, an honest lawyer, who immediately issued orders for the arrest of the soldiers, and stated to the people that the whole plot was discovered, and important documents in hand, etc., which would lead to a full arrest of all the culprits. "I am preparing for the trial," said this honest man, "and justice will be done quickly."

Freddi, colonel of the gend'armes, Nardoni, chief spy of the late pope, and other conspirators, were brought back to Rome. The pope wrote, himself, for the arrest of the late governor of Rome, who had fled to Florence, and peace ensued, while the people waited for the trial. The pope was so very amicable, that he no longer opposed the establishment of a national guard.

Austria knew all about that conspiracy, and her troops had crossed the Po, into the Roman country on their way to the city, when they met Virginio Alpi, flying for his life; and they recrossed the river and took him along with them. This Alpi, was the man who had enrolled the Sanfidesti band, who were to act in concert with the Austrian troops, to slaughter the Roman people! In the official correspondence concerning Italy, which was published by order of the English cabinet, we find that the English ambassador, writing to Lord Palmerston, a few days before, uses this significant language: "Prince Metternich has made a verbal communication to me of a probable intervention of the Austrian troops in Rome, in order to deliver the pope from the popular anarchy. He did not say that the pope applied for this intervention, but I have no doubt of it."

What does all this mean? We shall see. Fifteen days after, the pope appointed Monsignor Morandi governor of Rome, and whose integrity would have insured a trial of all who were implicated in the conspiracy, he removed him to another office, and put in his place Monsignor Savelli, the most notoriously depraved of all the prelates then in Rome, and who was believed to have been a member of the Sanfidesti society. What followed? Why the trial of the Sanfidesti conspirators was never mentioned again. So far from that, the pope, when restored to Rome in 1849 by Frenchmen, rewarded all those who were concerned in that diabolical plot to assassinate the friends of liberty. To Monsignor Grassellini, the prelate, who blessed the poniards of the Sanfidesti, and then put them in their hands, he gave the rich bishopric of Palermo. Monsignor Savelli, who was made governor of Rome to prevent the trial of the conspirators, received a cardinalate. Colonel Freddi, the chief spy of Gregory XVI., who fled on being detected and was brought back to Rome, he gave a generalship. The base spy, Nardoni, also, was made a general. Minardi, in whose house the letter revealing the plot was found, became a general director of police; and Alpi, who enrolled the assassin band of Sanfidesti, was rewarded by being appointed the general director of the Custom House, etc., etc.

The cardinal who blessed the poniards with Grassellini, was afterwards believed to be Antonelli, the present premier of the pope. The father of Antonelli was sent to the galleys for life, under the government of Napoleon, in 1813, but when the pope was told that the only reason he was condemned was, that he belonged to that *holy* order, the Sanfidesti, he set him free and rewarded him.

After the pope agreed to have a national guard, which was about the time the plot of assassination was detected, the Jesuits applied for its aid to protect their convents from the mob. The people were infuriated against the monks, and the cry every night around the convents was, "Death to the Jesuits," etc. The pope ordered the national guard to attend each convent; but finally there was a positive and general refusal on the part of the guard to do so. The cunning Jesuits saw the storm and began to pack up. The people were openly discussing their expulsion, an old shepherd remarked, "To drive the fox from its hole, the best way is to set fire to it."

At that moment of excitement, the convents were suddenly deserted, and a large and chosen cargo of these enemies to human rights, were sent by the pope as a gift to these United States, here to erect their convents and monasteries, and by all means to increase and defend the power of the papacy.

The day following that stormy night, the official newspaper of the pope announced the withdrawing of the Jesuits, and said: "His holiness, who has ever looked with favor on these servants of the church, as unwearied fellow-laborers in the vineyard of the Lord, is bitterly grieved at this unhappy event. Considering, however, the growing excitement, and the numerous parties which threaten serious trouble, the pope has been forced to look at these dangers: he has, therefore, made known to the father-general of the company, his sentiments, as well as the concern he feels on account of the difficulty of the times and the prospect of serious disturbance." Upon this announcement the father-general resolved to yield to the force of circumstances.

The papers merely announced that the Pope had expelled the Jesuits. The French papers eulogized him, and even blind Protestant nations called him a religious reformer!

It should be stated, that Angelo Brunetti, who first discovered the plot of the Jesuits to assassinate the people, very mysteriously disappeared with his son, who undoubtedly were seized by the holy Inquisition. This man was possessed of great influence among the people on account of his virtues and his intellect. The pope tried to win him by favors, but the man was above flattery or papal honors. He fought at the siege of Rome for liberty, and lost one son in the battle. For this crime he was taken off!

In September, 1848, Cardinal Antonelli, announced that he had prevailed upon the pope to appoint Rossi prime minister. This was very startling intelligence. Rossi was a Calvinist, and as such was exiled by Pope Pius VII. He had lived in Geneva a long while, and there married the daughter of the distinguished French author, Guizot, himself a Huguenot.

Rossi went to France after the revolution of 1830, and enlisted under the party, of which Guizot was leader. He was made professor of political economy, the most distinguished chair in the University of France, and after that, was created to the dignity of a peer of France. But two foreigners have been so honored by the French: those were Rossi and Bixio, both Italians. In 1845, the Jesuits and the French Universities had an embittered contest, and Louis Phillippe decided to expel the hated intriguers.

Rossi was designated as the Ambassador to the pope to obtain his consent. But Gregory XVI., was enraged at the idea of sending a Protestant to him, and refused to receive Rossi as the representative of a nation styled "very Christian," (Christianissimo). But Rossi went to Rome in view of all this, and at the end of two months accomplished his mission, and the Jesuits were ordered by the pope to leave France!

It was said, Rossi effected this through the favorite servant of the pope, Gaetanino, who being bribed kept the old pope continually drunk! When Louis Phillippe went into exile, Rossi refused office under the French republic, and returned to Bologna in Italy, where he was elected to the constitutional council of Rome. He was in favor of separating the spiritual and temporal power of the pope, and the last man on earth, for this reason, to be at the head of this ministry. But he went into office like a man, and began the work of reform among the clergy; which was very distasteful to them.

On the 15th of November (1848), was the second great opening of the deliberate bodies of the State.

Rossi drove up to the palace in his magnificent carriage, with two of his friends and attended by his three servants in gala livery. An unknown man touched his arm, as he mounted the steps, and as he turned his head, another plunged his knife into his neck, and then calmly withdrew among the crowd, and pressed forward to see what had attracted it! No one thought of the assassin, but all of Rossi, who was dead in a few minutes. A trial was ordered, but all the information obtained, was, that a man had boasted the previous night, that he could earn a thousand dollars next day!

Yes, Rossi was murdered by a hired assassin, and one who was experienced in his profession. It was for the sole purpose of sacrificing him, that Cardinal Antonelli and the pope put him in that position. The perfidious pope, immediately after, appointed Antonelli to the premiership, who, to this moment, exercises absolute sway over the pope in this capacity. He is the head of the Sanfidesti, or Society of Holy Faith; and coming to Rome when it was in the hands of Frenchmen who were about to cause a trial, to discover the murderer of Rossi; he requested to have all the evidence that had been collected put in his hands, and then sought to destroy every trace of the event!

The sudden death of Rossi, was believed, by the people, to be the signal of a revolution by the Sanfidesti and Austrians, similar to the plot eighteen months before. The pope shut up himself, and would admit no one, but Cardinal Antonelli, and the foreign ambassadors. The next day the constitutional deliberative bodies of the State were in session, and sent a deputation to the pope, requesting a new and responsible ministry. The pope refused the deputation and the message. The crowd of the common people now began to gather around the palace, and while making no seditious cry, and totally unarmed, the Swiss body-guards of the pope, armed with guns inside of the palace, fired on the crowd, killing two and wounding many. This was done by order of Antonelli, who, anxious to shed blood, collected before the piazzi of the palace all the pope's hired soldiers, good and bad, amounting to about one thousand.

This aroused the Roman people, who marched to the palace and through the thousand unresisting soldiers on the piazzi, met and overpowered the Swiss guards, whom they then, generously forgave. The national guards garrisoned the palace, levelled a cannon against the private apartment of the pope, and sent the same deputation, whom he had refused to see. The pope saw them then, gladly, and agreed to their request to appoint a new ministry, which he promptly did.

The people, then, had the government in their own

hands. The pope knew he had not a friend in Rome, and he was eight days devising the means to fly from the city. He might never have been able to do so, but for the aid of a beautiful Roman lady, who encouraged him. She was the wife of the secret Chargé d'affaires in Austria. She was a shrewd and courageous woman, and the foreign diplomatists in Rome had engaged her to influence the pope, and so far overcome his peculiar cowardice, as to persuade him there was no danger, if he would accompany her.

This lady was somewhat famous for political intrigues, and as Teresina Girand, neice of the writer of popular comedies, she had had many admirers.

On the 24th of November, 1848, the papal ministry announced to the Roman people that the pope had run away! The people were perfectly delighted, but made no particular demonstration. The first act which looked like an exercise of liberty, was taking all the confessionals out of the churches and piling them together, to burn them. The papal police insisted on their restoration, and at the instance of Angelo Brunetti, the most powerful tribune, they were restored. "I formerly thought," said he, "it would be good and right to burn these instruments of corruption to our wives and daughters; but now we are free, no one will go to the confessional."

The people then brought out the "guillotine" and all the instruments of torture used by the late pope, and burned them, and threw the ashes into the Tiber. It may be added here, that when the pope got back to Rome, he was very much distressed to find his instruments of death destroyed. He could find no one in that city to make another for him. But the Bishop of Marseilles hearing his trouble, kindly sent him two new guillotines, with all the modern improvements. So grateful was the pope for the service, that he determined to make the bishop a cardinal, when a vacancy afforded the opportunity.

When the pope heard there was no anarchy in Rome, and that the people, instead of concerning themselves about him, were attending to their own business, and exercising the right of universal suffrage, he sent forth his bull of "major excommunication" against all his ministers who aided in preserving order, or who took part in the new government of the Republic.

Cardinal Antonelli sent this bull to all the bishops in the Italian States, to be published at the elections. The effect was, to increase the vote, so that in a population of two millions and a half, three hundred and fifty thousand voters attended the polls, and thus manifested their contempt for the papal edict. The election furnished a noble example of republican dignity and decorum. The next day, the Roman people held a large public meeting, to consider the propriety of excommunicating the pope, who had been "an object of scandal to the Christian world and deserved to be cut off from their Christian communion." In the address, to be sent to him, were these significant words: "When you, sir pope, left the city by one gate, the Bible entered it by the opposite gate, and now there is no longer room for you."

The 5th of February, 1849, the representatives elected by the universal suffrage of the Roman people, assembled at the capitol. Among these two hundred men, there was scarcely one, who had not suffered by the persecutions of papal tyranny. Some were yet lame from the heavy chains worn so long in the dungeons, and others still suffering from the effects of the various tortures and torments there inflicted. But, in the midst of it all, it was glorious to behold the spirit of forgiveness, and who but the omniscient God could have inspired it?

All these representatives were liberally educated men, chiefly lawyers and land-holders. There were among them two Jews, two Romish priests, and a prelate. The question of deposing the pope was brought forward, as soon as the preliminary proceedings were concluded. It elicited an animated discussion, from ten o'clock in the morning until after midnight; but not one voice was raised in favor of the papacy. The only difference of sentiment was, as to the expediency of delay. European diplomacy, was not only intriguing to prevent the deposition of the pope, but had threatened to reinstate him. In that case, death for "high treason" would be the sentence on every member of the assembly. But, like our fathers, in 1776, these men felt the responsibility with which they were entrusted, and resolved to discharge it; fearless of all personal consequences. The vote was accordingly taken, and the pope deposed. The proposition was then made to establish a republic for Italy, and was immediately carried. The most intense interest was evinced, by the people, pending the deliberations of the assembly; and when it was proclaimed that the pope was deposed and Italy was a republic, the joy was tumultuous. The decree, deposing the pope and the enactment of the republic, was carried in a procession, embracing almost every soul, through the city, and afterwards to the capitol, as a triumph of moral principle over the institution of popery. The decree was published the 9th of February, 1849: "In the name of God and of the people." The colors of the new government were white, green and red, and the motto on their flag was, "God and the people." This passage from papal power to republican liberty, did not cost a "drop of blood nor a tear."

For six months this republic maintained absolute liberty for the people: that is, the people governed themselves. There was no standing army, no confiscation of property, for political opinion, and so entire a freedom of the press, that a newspaper, called "Constituzionale," openly advocated the restoration of the pope without being molested.

The pope taxes his subjects over ten millions of dollars annually, beside a larger sum which they have to pay for the public works and salaries of the various government offices. Leo XIIth was the first pope to create a public debt.

In 1828, when the Catholic emancipation bill was before the English parliament, the pope sent two millions of dollars to England to corrupt the public journals and the orators. From that time, the public debt continued to increase, and when Pius IXth fled from Rome it amounted to forty-two millions! This ruined financial condition, in which the pope left the people, was a serious impediment to their progress; nevertheless, the free possession of political and religious liberty, personal freedom and private property, a free press, gratuitous public instruction, etc., soon made the condition of the republic a prosperous one.

While things were looking so happily for Italy, under the auspices of as wise, virtuous and dignified statesmen, as ever adorned any country, the pope was preparing to involve her in war. Austria, France and Spain entered into an alliance, in April, 1849, to put down the Italians and restore the pope.

Louis Napoleon pledged himself to reinstate his holiness, in order to gain the Jesuitical party, by whom he was intrigued to the throne of France. When the

Italians found that the French were sold to the pope, the republic sent an ambassador to England to entreat her government to oppose the league. At that moment, England held the destinies of Europe in her hands. It was a glorious opportunity for that Protestant power to have secured a liberal policy, throughout Europe! But, how did England act? She sided with the pope and the despots! Her own aristocracy were at the head of the government, and the triumph of liberal principles were inimical to their interests!

Lord Palmerston absolutely refused to see the Roman ambassador, except, in a very private manner, and ended the matter by saying, "papacy must be restored in Rome, because it is expedient in order to maintain the equilibrium and the peace of Europe."

Not only did France, Spain and Austria, conspire with the pope and the king of Naples; but England, Russia and Prussia favored him. Rome, stood alone then, with all Europe against her; but still determined upon resistance. With this disadvantage, the Romans met a French soldiery, inured to war in Africa, and repulsed them. They fled from the city to a hill, called Castle Guido, and sent an officer to Rome to implore an armistice. Numbers of their men were killed and six hundred were wounded—beside in their camp, numbers lay wounded, with no means of relief; as the French never imagined the possibility of defeat! The Romans generously granted the armistice and sent provisions and surgeons, to the French quarters. The next morning, after treating their prisoners to breakfast, sent them back, also free.

The joy of the Romans was boundless, at the result of that battle, as it was fought almost exclusively by the citizens. There were not in Rome at the time, either foreigners, or Italians, from other parts of Italy.

The French, Jesuit-like, were deceitful and peaceful, until they landed more troops at Civita Vecchia, and then broke the armistice and treacherously renewed the war. The French began throwing their bombs into the city and then entered it, by a subterranean way, which they learned by a Prussian officer who was in Rome. The fight was now a nocturnal one, short arms were used and the result was bloody. The Romans fought until their men and provisions were both nearly exhausted. They stopped at length the progress of the French, and no further effort was possible. In the meantime, Austria had conquered all the northern cities. The king of Naples had taken the eastern provinces and a Spanish army was in possession of the kingdom of Naples.

On the 3d of July, 1849, Sunday, the streets of Rome were silent and the city was covered in gloom. The sun of liberty had set, and the oppression of popery was again the doom of that fated people.

The French entered quietly and took possession of Rome, on that day. They proceeded to the capitol where the representatives of the people were sitting, and pointing their bayonets at their breasts, commanded them to leave. The Romans protested; but the French having all power, insisted. By orders of Louis Napoleon, the French allowed twenty-four hours for the Romans to escape, before the papal government was restored. The vengeance of the pope was boundless, and when he found the principal agents of the revolution had fled, he wreaked his cruelties upon those who had acted with them.

"A papal priest," says Richelieu, "never pardons."

So we find from the statistics, that Pius IX. had 230 persons executed in the two first years after his restoration; beside those who died in the prisons, which contained over 8,000 victims! 6,000 lives were destroyed by the war; and more than 20,000 were exiled from their native land, including those who fled, from fear of persecution. These statistics were published in 1851, by a Conservative Newspaper at Florence, under the censorship of the Austrian government. Such is the history of the persecution and cruelties of the restored pope Pius IX. the present head of the Roman Catholic Church in these United States! While the four Catholic armies were bayoneting the Roman Republicans, to replace the pope, he was receiving the homage of gentlemen of the Court, and giving his hand to be kissed by the ladies. He went too, on a pilgrimage to a Madonna, midway between Gaeta and the fortress, and vowed that if he got back to Rome, by her intercession, he would make her a magnificent present! He sent Savelli to tell the French to bury the Republicans under the ruins of Rome, if necessary; and Bedini, his particular friend, (afterwards nuncio to the United States,) was dispatched to aid the Austrian army, in its ferocious and merciless war upon the Italians. This Romish prelate issued his ordinance *from the headquarters of the Imperial troops*, and countersigned the bloody orders of Corzkowski; by the authority and in behalf of the pope! Nor should it be forgotten, that afterwards when the French violated their military honor, and treacherously renewed the attack upon the Romans, some persons devoted to the pope and his church, believing he was ignorant, that so much blood was being shed in his name, went to Gaeta to inform him. But to their surprise, they found the court rejoicing, at the news; which was received twice a day from Rome; and the more sad and distressing the condition of the inhabitants became; the greater was the joy of the pope and his courtiers.

The deputation in view of this, determined to see the pope and tell him of the torrents of Catholic blood which were being shed, and to beseech him to stop the immense sacrifice of life. Pius heard the recital without being in the least moved, and calmly replied, "God has doomed them to destruction: the anger of God is terrible; no prayers can disarm Him. They have refused *our* mercy, let them feel *our* justice." The messengers were appalled at the daring impiety of those blasphemous words!!

It was on Sunday, the 3d of July, 1849, that the French renewed the assault upon the Romans, and the inglorious victory of Pius IX. was won. The next day, the 4th, Oudinot, the French commander, repaired to Gaeta, to congratulate the pope and receive his acknowledgments.

He was received as an angel of mercy, for having slaughtered the citizens, to restore the pope's temporal authority; and the valor of himself and his troops, was extolled to the skies. "The vindictive priests rejoiced at the relation of the slaughter, and at the numbers and quality of the victims, who had perished."

The pope, to prove his delight and satisfaction, immediately honored the French general with the title of Duke of St. Pancrase. The pope, the head of the Roman Catholic Church, gives the name of St. Pancrase to the man, whose cannon had battered into ruins, the church of St. Pancrase!

A gold medal was also presented by the pope to General Oudinot, bearing these words: "For having thought of the salvation of the citizens and the fine arts."

These were the memorials which the French soldier received at the hands of the pope, the price of the blood of his massacred subjects! Then the pope ordered a *Te Deum* to be chanted for the French victory.

Nor was this all. At the beginning of the war, the Roman ladies of the highest rank took charge of the hospitals, and attended personally to the wounded. The spiritual direction of them was confided to thirty or forty priests, headed by Gavazzi, who devoted themselves to that duty. Instead of the pope praising the Christian action of these ladies, he denounced them in his Encyclica, excommunicating the ladies and imprisoning the priests.

These ladies were the wives and daughters of liberals, and the patients were patriots. But they had soothed and consoled their fellow creatures, whom Pius had declared accursed, and they were expelled from Christian communion!

It is impossible to describe briefly the proofs of heroism which were given by the Roman people in their struggle against the pope; the ardor and intrepid action of the men, the devotion and charity, the self-sacrifice of the women. The old and the young; master and servant; friend and foe, were all united in defence of the city.

The women were indefatigable in conveying food to their sons and husbands, to save them from dying from exhaustion; and many in their self-denying mission, perished from the showers of shot and shells which fell from the French invaders.

The wife of an officer who had not left the ramparts for several days and nights, prevailed upon her husband to leave for a few minutes and partake of the food she had brought to him. As they sat down on the ground, she placed herself between him and the enemy, saying: "If a bullet comes this way, I will defend thee from it." And so she did; for as she sat wiping his brow, arranging his hair, and encouraging his valor by her gentle sympathy, a bomb struck her fatally. The brave soldier could not restrain his tears and lamentations, but the dying woman faltered: "Go, dearest! weep not for me. Go, rather, and avenge me! Farewell!"

Another case, peculiarly touching, was that of an aged father whose son and brother were in the battle. His little daughter of eleven years, was kneeling at her bed side praying God to bless them and save her country from popery, when a bomb crushed the roof and killed both.

The wife of Garibaldi, the bravest of the brave, is eminently characteristic of the ancient Roman women. After the pope's army had put down the Romans, she fled with her husband by secret by-paths to Piedmont. But they were tracked like wild beasts, and were often without food or shelter; finally, the lady, soon to become a mother, sank under the fatigue, and could proceed no farther. She thought not of herself; but solicitous only for her husband's safety, begged him to leave her to her fate, and seek refuge for himself. Garibaldi, not less affectionate than brave, of course remained with her, who after lingering a short time, died in his arms. He contemplated for some time the pale corpse of his most faithful wife, the mother of his children, the partner of his dangers; then, digging a place with his sword, he laid her sorrowfully beneath the earth, and swearing to avenge her, he alone and unguarded, reached Piedmont, and afterwards came to America!

From the 6th of August, 1848, to the 22d of that month, *nine hundred and sixty-one capital sentences* were pronounced against the Lombardo-Venetians; for the most trifling offences—such as having a knife, a fowling-piece, or a percussion cap, in their pockets. How many more perished in secret, without the semblance of trial, there is no means of ever knowing, in this world.

When the victim was not old enough to be shot, they used the bastinado. A boy, too young to be shot with his father and brother, had sixty blows inflicted, and died under the torture!

At Milan, October 7th, a fruiterer was found with a bayonet under his matrass, for which he was sentenced and shot.

Three married men, with seventeen children to support, were shot for "having sought to induce imperial soldiers to enlist in other service."

In Mantua, two priests were shot as they descended the pulpit, for preaching rather too liberally for the pope's taste. At Camo, about the same time, Antoine Cresceri, and Joseph Maztiazzi, were shot, for giving a glass of brandy to two soldiers, who called out, "*Vive l'Italie! Vive l'Hongrie!*"

Ernesti Galli, of Cremona, and Maria Conti, of Florence, young women, received thirty blows, after being grossly insulted.

Dumas, in his Journal *Le Mais*, says: "This is not a page from the old Chronicles of the Inquisition; this was not dark torture imposed upon traitors to God and man. No; it all passed in the open air, under God's heaven, in the sight of all nations, in the year of grace, 1849, and of the French republic, the second."

The Austrian marshal ordered the city of Milan to pay

the Courtezan Olivari, 30,000 livres for carrying the flag on that occasion.

March 18, 1851, Don Dominique Bolzani omitted to recite the prayer for the Emperor of Austria's prosperity, on his Majesty's birth-day; for which he was sentenced for high treason and imprisoned for two years. In 1851, October 11th, Louis Daltesio, a native of Como, was hung in Venice, for having had a prospectus of a historical work he had written, found on his person. The work was a liberal one and published in Switzerland. The names of the judges never appeared, nobody defended the poor victims—nobody was present at the trial, or read their papers. The sentences were simply countersigned by the commandant.

In 1854, Count Montanari, and five of his friends, all of noble family, were arrested for conspiring with Mazzini for Italian liberty; they were doomed to die. The mothers and wives o the poor victims went to Verona to implore Marshal Radetski to mitigate the sentence. He refused amidst their tears and groans, to give them an audience. Radetski's chief staff officer, General Benedek, famous for cruelty, pretended to be interested in these ladies, and said to them: "Listen, I will make another application to the marshal in your behalf." In a few moments he returned, very cheerful, and said: "Return to your homes, ladies, and be comforted; his excellency commands me to say to you, that no blood will be spilled." These ladies, overcome with joy at the thought, that life at least was spared to their friends, and hope might be indulged for the future, went home to Mantua. They were sentenced to be shot; but by "special favor they were hanged," and "no blood was spilled!"

In the chronicles of despotism in Italy, in 1849, immediately after Pope Pius IX. was restored, we find enough to sicken the most obdurate heart. In Gubbio, the sentence for heresy, was to stand in the church with their lips sewed up, and liable to be burned to death. In Parma, two men were shot, because a hangman could not be found. Everywhere, the finding of arms on or near a person, had to be atoned by death.

In Naples, more than 30,000 were in prison for political offences.

In Venice, a lady was bastinadoed to death, for reproaching an Austrian soldier, who had insulted her.

The Roman Republican Government desirous to have a legal recognition by the United States, in 1849 sent Signor E. Felice Foresti, as an ambassador to this country. He had, in 1820, conspired for the freedom of Italy from popish despotism, and for this offence, was sentenced to death; but it was afterwards commuted to twenty years of severe imprisonment at Spielberg. When he had served fifteen years, he was banished to America, with nine other distinguished Italian citizens. His sisters, without his knowledge applied to Pope Gregory XVI., who sent back their petition in silence. Then, after that, to Pius IX., who, in 1848 allowed him to return, but without civil or political rights. His sufferings were excruciating—in the darkest dungeon for full fifteen years!

Citizens of New York, undoubtedly remember the mild and unpretending manners of Foresti, seemingly unconscious, as he walked the streets, of the severe suffering he had undergone.

NOTE.—To G. B. Nicolin, of Rome, Deputy of the Constitutional Assembly, and officer of the General Staff of the Roman Army, and to Guglielmo Gajani, Professor of Civil and Canon Law, and representative of the people in the Roman Constituert Assembly of 1849, the author is indebted for the foregoing facts.

SUPPLEMENTAL CHAPTER.

Cases of torture cited in the present and past centuries—An *Auto da fe*—Elizabeth Vasconcellas tortured because she would not abjure her Protestant faith—A Jew —Galileo—Bower—Coustos tortured for being a *Freemason*—Llorente—Montara the Jew—Roman Catholic Nurses baptized—Protestant Infants clandestinely baptized by Romish priests in the United States. The Church claims all such and will secure them.

THE proceedings of the Inquisition begin by a *denunciation.* This soon is changed to a *declaration.* It is related that Blanco White's mother did not, for days, speak to her son, lest he should use some unguarded expression, which would oblige her to denounce him to the Inquisition. The accused is asked, in general terms, if he or she has ever heard anything which was, or appeared to be, contrary to the Catholic faith, or the rights of the Inquisition. If suspected of heresy, the accuser had to state whether it was slight, grave, or violent. *Ludovicus a Paramo* derives the example of confiscating the property of heretics from God himself; "For," says he, "God, as the first inquisitor, teaches other inquisitors, his delegates, how heretics, should be dealt with!" The tortures used upon the victim were "the pulley;" "the fire or chafing-dish;" "the rack," and the trough, in which the prisoner was bound and corded. To illustrate these different processes, we give the reader some of the numerous facts which are recorded in Llorente, Limberch, Geddes, Gavin, Dellon, Bower, Blanco White, Coustos, and other accredited authorities at hand.

We have before us a letter, written by Mr. Wilcox, (afterwards Bishop of Rochester,) minister to the English factory, at Lisbon, to Gilbert Burnet, the historian of the reformation, dated June 15, 1706. "I saw," says he, "the whole process of an *auto da fe.* Of the five condemned, four were burnt. Heytor Dias and Maria Pinteyra were burnt alive, and the other two were strangled. The woman was half an hour alive in the flames—the man about an hour. They were fastened to a pole, six feet higher than the fagots. The wind being a little fresh, the man's back was perfectly wasted, and as he turned himself, his ribs opened before he left speaking, the fire being recruited as he roasted, to keep him just in the same heat; but all his entreaties would not procure him a larger allowance of wood to shorten his misery and dispatch him."

In the eighteenth century, Elizabeth Vasconcellas, the daughter of John Chaffer, of Devon, England, a *Protestant*, was taken to Madeira upon a family misfortune, and under the auspices of the English residents, continued to live in her own faith, eight years. In 1704, while her husband was in Brazil, on business, she was taken seriously ill, and while in an unconscious state, she was visited by a Romish priest, who administered the sacraments, and on her recovering was desired to attach herself to that faith. She absolutely refused, for which she was imprisoned by the bishop of the island seven months, for holding heretical sentiments. She was then removed to the Inquisition at Lisbon, in December, 1705. An inventory of all her effects was then taken in the prison of the holy office, and her person searched. She was made to swear this was all she was worth, and then was taken to her cell, where she was kept for nine months and fifteen days. The first nine days she was allowed only bread and water and a wet straw bed. On the ninth day she was questioned on her religious faith, and she declared herself a Protestant. They told her she must conform to the Romish faith, or be burnt. In a month's time she was again summoned before the fathers and questioned, but without inducing her to recant. The officials stripped her back, and after lashing her with knotted cords, told her to kneel down and thank the court for their mercy, which she refused to do. In fifteen days she was again brought forward, and a crucifix set before her, which she was commanded to bow down and adore; and refusing to do this, she was told she must expect to be burnt with the Jews at the next *auto da fe*. At the expiration of thirty days, she was again called before the judges. Her breast was laid bare by the executioner, who with one end of a hot iron rod, burnt her to the bone in three different places on her right side, and she was sent back to her cell without any application to heal her sores. At a subsequent audience, she was asked whether she would profess the Romish faith, or burn. She replied she was a Protestant and a subject of the queen of England. To this, the inquisitor told her, that being an English subject signified nothing in the king of Portugal's dominions; that the English in Lisbon were heretics and would certainly be damned. The executioner was then ordered to seat her in a chair, and to bind her arms and legs, so as to prevent, even motion. A physician was at hand to decide how far she could be tortured without hazard of life. Her left foot was put into an iron slipper, made red hot, and fastened there, until the flesh was burned to the bone. She fainted under this torture, and the physician advised the slipper to be taken off, and she was sent to her dungeon. After some time elapsed, she was again cruelly whipped, and her back torn all over, and was threatened with greater severity if she did not embrace the Romish faith. On the other hand, liberty was promised, if she would change her *religion.* She finally consented, and wrote her name to a paper, though she knew not what it contained. And then, without returning to her her goods and money, they dismissed her, destitute, upon the charities of the people of Lisbon."

The trial of Galileo, for holding and publishing the opinion that the earth *revolves* around the sun, is familiar to the general reader. He was ordered to Rome in 1615, to be reprimanded for this offence; but, when he wrote upon it, eighteen years later, 1632 and '33, he was cited a second time to appear before the holy tribunal at Rome. He was then seventy years old and in infirm health, which made it dangerous to travel, but he was obliged to leave Florence and appear before his judges. He was subjected to a rigorous examination, and this torture is supposed to have been the reason why he signed the paper abjuring his opinions; as in addition to his previous disease, he became after that afflicted with *hernia*, caused, it was said, by the torture of the cord. He was sentenced to imprisonment during the pleasure of the judges, and to repeat seven of the penitential psalms once a week for three years. Limberch gives an account of Isaac Orobio de Castro, who had been denounced as a Jew, to the inquisition at Madrid. The inquisitor had him put into a linen garment, and almost squeezed to death. When near dying from the pressure, he was suddenly released, which caused as much anguish as the pressure. He then had small cords tied around his thumbs, and so swelled the extremities as to cause blood to spirt from his nails. As he still refused to confess the crime of which he was accused, he was put on a bench against the wall, in which were fastened iron pulleys with ropes. The ropes were fastened to his arms, legs, and around his body, and then drawn to cause exquisite pain. The bench was then knocked from under him to cause the weight of his body to draw the knots closer and increase the agony. He was then tortured on his shins, by instruments made of two upright pieces of wood, and five cross-bars sharpened, somewhat like a ladder. The executioner, by a particular motion, struck his shins with these instruments five blows each way. He fainted, but recovering, the executioner tied two ropes round Orobio's wrists, and put ropes over his back, and then placed his feet against the wall and fell backwards, so that the ropes penetrated the prisoner's bones. This was done three times. After the second, the physician was consulted as to whether the victim could bear another; he decided that he could, and it was again inflicted. He was sent to his cell, and his wounds were not healed in seventy days. He did not confess under the torture, and was condemned to wear the *san-benito* for two years, and then to perpetual banishment. He died before his penance expired, in Amsterdam, 1707.

The escape of Archibald Bower from the Inquisition of Macerata, (of which he was councillor,) 1726, is deserving of attention. All trials took place in the night, and in full court. After it was decided to proceed against a party, he was arrested in the dead hour of the night and locked up, and the key returned to the inquisitor-general. Besides the pulley, just described in the case of the Jew, Bower says: "There was an anvil fixed in the middle of the floor, with a spike, not very sharp, projecting upwards. The accused was hoisted up and lowered by ropes at the four corners of the room, until his back-bone rested on a spike. The weight of his body tended to fracture his spine. This torture lasted eleven hours, unless the prisoner confessed. Matches of tow and pitch were wrapped around the hands of women, and then fired until their hands were consumed; or cords were tied so tightly around the thumbs as to cause the blood to flow from the nails." Bower was appointed one of the *inquisitors* of the Inquisition, and a manuscript giving the directions, was put in his hands to read. It was so barbarous and inhuman that it was not in print, but each member possesses a copy, which is handed back to the inquisitor-general upon the death or serious indisposition of a councillor, with the seal of the Inquisition on it; after which it was death to any one to open or retain it. Bower fainted once on witnessing the torture of prisoners, and was severely reproved. He extenuated himself by ascribing it to nature. "Nature," said the inquisitor; "you must conquer nature by grace!!" To conquer nature, the inquisitor-general ordered him to arrest an intimate friend, who was a nobleman. Bower could devise no means to save his friend, and had to proceed with the guards to his house. He knocked, the maid-servant inquired who was there? "The holy Inquisition; come down and open the door without any noise, on pain of excommunication." The girl came instantly, and showed the way to her master's room. The lady awoke first and shrieked, when one of the ruffians gave her a blow on her head, which caused the blood to flow. The nobleman was astonished to find himself arrested by his best friend, but made no reproach. Bower, next morning, announced the arrest to the inquisitor-general, thus: "This is done like one who is desirous to conquer the weakness of nature." The nobleman underwent the tortures of the pulleys and died in three days. His estate was confiscated to the holy office, a small pension being all given his widow.

John Coustos was imprisoned, in 1743, for the crime of free-masonry: he was a Protestant. He was thrice examined before the inquisitors, and made to swear he would not divulge the secrets of the holy office. He was required to divulge the secrets of free-masonry, which he refused on account of his oath; but the judges said they would *absolve* him from all such oaths. He was doomed to the torture for not discovering the secret of free-masonry. He was laid on his back on a scaffold, his neck fastened to it by means of an iron collar; two rings were attached to his feet, and his limbs stretched with all their strength. They then wound two ropes under each arm and leg, and made them pass under through the holes made for the purpose. On a signal given, they were all drawn tight and cut through the flesh to the bone, making the blood gush. Coustos still refusing to divulge more than he had done, this torture was *four times repeated;* the surgeon being present, time was allowed for him to recover himself between the inflictions. While undergoing this, he was told by the judges it was from his obstinacy, and if he died he would be guilty of *self-murder!* Six weeks after he was again taken from his dungeon and tortured. His arms were stretched until the palms of his hands were turned outward; his wrists were fastened by a cord behind him, and a machine gradually drew the backs of them until they touched. When over, he was taken to his dungeon, and the bones were set by a surgeon, under agonizing pain. Two months after he was again brought out, and his executioners passed a thick iron chain twice around his body, which crossed his stomach and terminated in rings attached to his wrists. He was then placed against a thick partition, at each end was a pulley; ropes were run through these and attached to the rings on his wrists. As the ropes were gradually made tighter, the chains bruised his stomach, and the shoulders and wrists were put out of joint. They were reset by the surgeon, and the same torture was inflicted with a similar result. He was then conveyed to his prison to wait the *auto da fe*, unable for weeks to lift his hands to his mouth, having lost the use of them. He was made to walk in procession at the *auto da fe*, and sentenced as a galley-slave for four years. In four days he was set to work, but became sick and was sent to the infirmary. He was now visited by Irish friars, and his release offered, *if he would forsake the Protestant and adopt the Roman Catholic religion*, which he indignantly refused. By means of the British minister at Lisbon, he was demanded as a British subject, and the inquisitor commuted his sentence to banishment. He was ordered not to leave for England without giving the holy office information of the vessel in which he sailed; but he ventured to go without doing so, and for three weeks he was obliged to lie concealed in the ship at Lisbon before sailing. Coustos arrived in England in December, 1744, and published his narrative a year or so after that period.

The first bull against free-masonry was issued by the pope in 1738. Clement XIIth excommunicated all free-masons. Philip, in 1740, published a royal ordinance against them. In 1739, the punishment of death was decreed against them by the Cardinal Vicar of Rome, in the name of the high priest of the God of peace and mercy!

Llorente states, that when the Inquisition was opened in Spain, in 1820, *twenty prisoners were found who did not know the name of the city in which they were;* not one knew, perfectly, the nature of the crime of which he was accused. One of these prisoners had been doomed to suffer death the following day. His execution was to have been by the "pendulum." The condemned, by this process, is fastened on his back, in a groove, to a table; suspended above him is a pendulum, with a sharp edge, and so constructed as to become sharper every movement. The victim saw this coming nearer and nearer every moment; at length it *cut the skin of his nose*, and gradually cut on, until life was extinct. This was the invention of the inquisitors to dispose of their victims at a time when they were afraid to celebrate their *auto da fe.* This mode of putting to death may be used wherever the Romish church has dungeons. Who will say this or similar modes of torture are not now practised in the subterranean vaults of the Roman Catholic churches in the United States to-day?

Mendonca was imprisoned in Lisbon, 1820, for the crime of free-masonry; the most prominent questions to him were the *amount of treasure* belonging to the order, and *where it was deposited.* He was four years a prisoner for not being able or willing to disclose it.

The papal *Journal de Bruselles* stated, in the autumn of 1858, that a Jew, named Montara, residing in Bologna, had a child baptized a papist, by the nurse. Five years after, the ex-nurse communicated this fact to the Roman Catholic Church, when the boy was declared *de facto* and *de jure* a Christian. He was torn from his infidel parents, by the Church, in spite of their remonstrances, and sent to Rome, to be educated by popish priests, in her faith. They consented that the father might see his child, and that they would even release him, if the Jew would promise to educate him a Romanist. This he refused to do, and appealed to the Emperor Napoleon. The Jew declared that the evidence by which the Romish Church justifies itself is insufficient, —first, because the uncorroborated story would not be strong enough to deprive him of an *old* garment, much less of his son; and, secondly, that the child was in no danger of dying, and, therefore, by the papal creed, this lay baptism would have no virtue.

Here is a *principle* worthy of consideration in the United States, when parents' rights and feelings can be outraged whenever a papist chambermaid chooses to sprinkle their infant in the face, and invoke the blessing of the Roman Catholic Church upon it!

From Mr. Hogan, the Roman priest, and former pastor of St. Mary's Church, in Philadelphia, we have the most undoubted confirmation of this fact. He states that every morning on his return from the church in Philadelphia, he found Roman Catholics waiting in his house with *the infants of Protestants, which he baptized*, and further says, that this is the *universal practice* in all the cities of the United States where *Catholic nurses* have the opportunity. "I would not be surprised," says he, "*if one half of the children of Boston* are not now baptized Roman Catholics." If so, parents, tremble, for if ever an opportunity occurs to claim them, they will be claimed as subjects of the Romish Church, and treated accordingly!!

"Every day each individual belonging to the 'Company of Jesus' is obliged to communicate to the spiritual father or the superior of the college where he lives, *everything he sees*, *hears*, or *thinks*. These fathers make extracts and communicate them to the father of the province, (who is archbishop or bishop of the diocese) who, in his turn, makes a selection, and lays them before the pope in a particular audience every Thursday evening. The father-general of the Jesuits holds in his hands by means of consciences all the reins of Catholic society everywhere. If he believes, for instance, that the greater glory of God demands the creation of a revolution in any place, the general sends the order to his assistants, who give notice to all the associates, and these obeying as machines, speak and act as *commanded* in the *confessional* and the pulpit, so that, if the father-general is not afraid of unveiling his intrigues, he might often predict an event many months, or even years, before its occurrence! This is the reason *why Jesuits are protected* by sovereigns and *governments*. If any power is opposed to them, it must sooner or later *fall*. In those places where Jesuits have no legal existence, the influence of the father-general is still greater, for there (as in the United States) the Jesuits exist as missionaries, or under some other name. The father-general sends to these countries the *most artful* men, who propagate their opinions *secretly*, and many who would not dare to avow themselves Jesuits, connect themselves with the company under some other name without being aware of it. In spite of all persecutions, the Jesuits *never* abandoned England. There are more Jesuits *there* than in Italy: they are to be found in all classes of society, in Parliament, *among the Protestant clergy*, among its bishops, and among the aristocracy!

"I did not comprehend how a Jesuit could become a Protestant minister, or a Protestant minister a Jesuit; but my confessor soon taught me by saying, "Omnia Munda Mundis," that St. Paul became a Jew to save Jews; so that there was nothing astonishing that a Jesuit should *turn Protestant among Protestants*, to *convert* Protestants. Protestant countries, (as the United States) especially, furnish revenues to Jesuits. They educate in Rome a certain number of young men from *foreign* countries, and this furnishes them with a pretext for making secret collections in those countries for the support and education of Rome in their missionaries. Each class of men and women have their appropriate corresponding confessor."—*De Sanctis, Qualificator of the Inquisition, etc.*

CONCLUDING REMARKS.

DANGER, like a vast rock on a railway, lies before this people, and we are bound to swing the lantern of warning before their eyes, that they may see their impending ruin! But that the friends and apologists of Romanism may not charge us with exaggeration or misrepresentation, we have met them in this work upon the statements and arguments of the highest Romish authorities. We have thereby proved that the system of popery has nothing whatever to do with the Word of God. That the confessional is destructive to the liberties of the nation, and incompatible with the morals of the people—that the consecration of nuns, is a polluting marriage ceremony with the bishop, and while these victims "cannot possibly escape," they are often doomed to a life of gross licentiousness or the severest inflictions of bodily torture. That Romish bishops in the United States are *Inquisitors*, in correspondence with the pope of Rome, and sworn to watch every opportunity for advancing the interests of the Inquisition in our land; that each bishop makes his own form of confession to suit our country and *penetrate the secrets of families, individuals and the nation*, which are regularly reported to the pope. We have exposed the mode of denouncing and torturing victims of the Inquisition in the eighteenth and nineteenth centuries, for the crimes of Protestantism, Free Masonry, *Ju-*

daism, etc.; and that it is as potentially in existence *to-day* as it was in the middle ages. Furthermore, that the pope sent his nuncio to establish the Spiritual Court of the Inquisition upon American soil. We have unveiled the "Constitutions" of the "Society of Jesus" that this people may at once realize the imminent danger which imperils their liberties—while the entire Roman Catholic Church is controlled by this fearful order, and that the prelates and priests are either members of it, or bound by their oath to the pope to support it. The Jesuit swears that his superior, *be he who he may*, *holds the place of God*, and is *to him in the place of Christ*." We learn how they interfere with, and seek to control the politics of, this country, and support for office such Protestants as they can use as their own instruments, for the advancement of the interests of the Roman hierarchy. The various secret associations or societies to which we have referred, are but the legitimate offspring of this "Society of Jesus."

The time has come when the people of the United States must defend their civil and religious liberties against the aggression of this deadly foe. The morals, the manners, the homes, the institutions and laws of our country are endangered, while we have a foreign hierarchy in our midst, corrupting and enslaving the people.

Shall the education of our young men and women be longer surrendered to popish priests, whose Bible is the breviary and whose God is the pope? Shall the crusade upon our Protestant Bible, begun anew through the "Circle of Jesus," bear sway upon the common school system, founded upon God's Holy Word—the pillar upon which this republican government rests? Who will stand idle while this is being undermined? The system of Romanism, as revealed in this volume, accords to the pope, power to be a tyrant, and to betray the liberties and independence of this free country. Shall it say to the tide of human civilization "Go back?"

Will not the press unite in enlightening the people of our land, who have believed long enough in the delusion that allegiance to the pope is purely spiritual? The very assumption of infallibility makes the papal church intolerant. Its arrogant claim to supremacy over all governments and nations in things spiritual, must make it so. The crimes it punishes against the State is heresy, and its punishment extends even to taking the lives of heretics, "whose blood," as their Romish Testament asserts, "is no more than the blood of thieves, mankillers, and other malefactors; *for the shedding of which, by order of justice, no commonwealth shall suffer.*" The fact is undeniable, that wherever popery has had the the power of enforcing her sanguinary laws, (Protestants) have been put to death. They who boldly deny that papists are not bound to obey the pope in temporal things, must also deny that they are not bound to obey him at all! Because the spiritual authority of popery is all-pervading, since it compels a man to renounce Protestantism.

Influenced solely by a spirit, patriotic and christian, we seek to excite public attention immediately to this subject, feeling assured that every American heart will thrill when they once perceive the hand of popery, secretly moving, misdirecting or holding in check the rights of the people. The Jesuits and their allies have several times changed their policy towards their own presses and those of Protestants, and are still dissatisfied with their position in regard to it; they have successively multiplied their own presses, and then curtailed their number; made great efforts to extend their circulation, and then condemned them as injurious. They cannot suppress the extension of knowledge among their people here, for newspapers are and will be read. Their policy now is, that while the Romish journals in the United States publish a few hundred sheets, the American newspapers, which send out daily, millions, are to be propitiated *to guide* and influence public sentiment *in their behalf*, either by open praise or studied silence upon their practices or proceedings in our country.

One of the Irish Journals, edited by a papist of New York, says: "For every musket given into the State armory, let three be purchased forthwith; let independent companies be formed thrice as numerous as the disbanded corps—there are no arms acts here yet—and let every "foreigner" be drilled and trained, and have his arms always ready. Be careful not to truckle in the smallest thing to American prejudices. Do not, by any means, suffer Gardner's Bible (the Protestant Bible) to be thrust down your throats. There must be peace or a *war of extermination*. We are here on American ground, *either* as *citizens or as enemies*."

Will not our editors, as good and true men, seriously contemplate this momentous subject, and express their sentiments fearlessly thereon? Will they not suggest decided and suitable measures for the protection of our civil and religious rights? Will they not look to the future tendency of Romish influence in the United States? To the pulpit and the press, in a great degree are entrusted the dissemination of light against darkness; of American civilization against Romish barbarity, of Christianity against priestcraft, which is raging in the land of your fathers and of your children! Will not editors be true to the cause of liberty, and openly confront the enemy who is laboring to fasten tyranny upon men's consciences in this land of liberty, where every good thing, with God's blessing, prospers and comes to maturity? Papal Rome looks upon the United States as pagan Rome did on her Punic rival. While the warriors of Africa, after the first struggle, were standing idle within a few miles of Rome, she sent her legions to the very walls of Carthage. Remember we have to renew now the struggle of the Reformation, and we must resist even to the very walls of the Vatican. Let the press be warned before the baneful influence of popery has taken deeper root in our soil. When once it has possession of this republic, farewell to liberty, to virtue, and to happiness!

NOTE.—In Connecticut in the winter of 1857, application was made for the appropriation of public funds to relieve all mortgages and incumbrances upon Roman Catholic church-property in that State! In other words, they simply proposed that the State should give the Roman Catholic churches money enough to *pay their debts.* This was done not under the expectation of success, but to incur favor with the Jesuits, and make capital with their Roman Catholic retainers. A proposition to repeal the church property law and give the bishops exclusive right to ownership, also passed the House but was defeated in the Senate. In Ohio they have repealed the law. The press was to a large extent responsible for these acts.

NOTE.—There is in Ireland a society for the protection of Roman Catholic priests who are converted to Protestantism. "The following document has been issued from these Protestant converts, in Dublin, addressed to Cardinal Wiseman:

Irishmen! We offered to return to the modern Church of Rome, if Cardinal Wiseman would prove in the presence of twelve honest, rational men, from St. Paul's Epistle to the Romans, that any one or all of the following articles in his church of the popes existed in the ancient primitive church of Christ, in that city, namely: Invocation of saints—Worship of images—Infallibility of the Church—Celibacy of the clergy—Transubstantiation—Auricular confession—Supremacy of the pope—Sale of indulgences—Services in Latin—Withholding the cup from the laity—Purgatory—Marialty, or worship of Virgin Mary—Seven Sacraments—Apochryphal books—Priestly intention—Venial, or mortal sins—Sacrifice of the mass for the dead—Monastic institutions—Insufficiency of the Scripture as a Rule of Faith—Prohibiting the reading of the Bible—Interpretation of the Scriptures according to the sense of the Church—Extreme unction—Works of supererogation—New creed of Pius IX—The Inquisition.

And, lastly, the immaculate conception.

Irishmen! We staked our present and future existence on this offer, and what has he (Cardinal Wiseman) done? Why, he found it impossible to bring those articles to the test of God's word, and he has run away, and you all know what a man is who does this. We must, therefore, continue to hold fast the old faith we have embraced—the faith of the early Irish Church—the faith of the primitive Church of Rome—the faith of the holy Catholic Church, &c.

Irishmen! As you love truth, honesty and valor, and your own souls, also, follow our example, and join us in our progress to light, liberty, independence, social improvement, national greatness, and a heaven at last."

APPENDIX.

The Breviary was re-compiled by a number of learned men, by order of Pius V., and sanctioned by a bull in February, 1566, for the use of all bishops, orders of monks and monasteries; Clement VIII., in 1602, again revised it, and finally, Urban VIII., in 1631, and this last revision is the one in general use in the Roman Catholic churches.*

The Romish church attaches so much value to this book, that all who are professed in any order, of both sexes—all deacons, sub-deacons, and priests—are commanded to repeat the whole service of the day out of the breviary, under the pain of being guilty of mortal sin. As we have seen the *nuns* are particularly. The whole teachings of the legends are so infamous and polluting, that they cannot be reproduced in these pages; and yet every young nun, in the United States, is compelled every day to read and ponder over them! We shall conclude this subject with an account of the marriage of St. Veronicà. In laying this legend before the American people, we have the advantage of giving the narrative in the

* Brevarium Romanum ex decreto Sacro Sancti Concilii Tridenti restitutum Pii V. Pont. Max. jussu editum et Clementis VIII. primum nunc denno Urbani P. P. VIII. Anctoritate recognitum. Fol. Ant. 1697.

very words of Cardinal Wiseman—the renowned Wiseman, now in Prorestant England. St. Veronicà was only canonized in 1839, by the late Pope Gregory XVIth. This is therefore no old legend. As Cardinal Wiseman and the late pope are good authorities with all Roman Catholics, we give the odious, unmeaning and offensive narrative from Wiseman's book.*

We pass over, as foreign to our immediate purpose, the accounts of her literal compassivity with her Spouse, the story of her being a perfect copy of the Divine passion; and we proceed to that which more immediately concerns our subject—her literal marriage to Christ, according to the forms of earthly marriage.

On this subject Cardinal Wiseman says:

"This spiritual union, with certain devout souls, God has been pleased to make manifest to them, by more sensible signs, *accompanied by formalities like those used in ordinary marriages.* Of such we read in the life of the ecstatic St. Catharine of Sienna. To this exalted dignity God was pleased to exalt Veronicà, as he revealed to her during the crowning of thorns, of which we have already spoken. But he prepared her for it by several visions, of which we will allow herself to speak. She says:

"While I was one morning at mass, suddenly an *application* came upon me. During the course of it I felt certain touches in my heart, which excited me to a strong desire of uniting myself wholly to God. On a sudden, it seems to me, that God took me out of my senses, and,

* Lives of St. Alphonsus Liguori, St. Francis de Girolamo, St. John Joseph of the cross, St. Pacificus of San Severino, and St. Veronicà Giuliani, whose canonization took place on Trinity Sunday, May 26, 1839, edited by N. Wiseman, D.D., Bishop of Melipotamus. London: C. Dolman, New Bond Street, 1846.

by communication, gave me to know, *ab intra*, that he wished to be espoused to me. This news made my heart to leap anew, and I felt it burning within me." She adds, "that in inviting her to his marriage, Jesus frequently appeared in the form of a beautiful infant; and in the feast of the Circumcision, 1694, intimated to her, that her preparation for it was to be by all kinds of sufferings. . . . . . On the 27th of that month," she adds, "our Lord comforted her, by showing her with what delight he looked upon a beautiful jewel, fixed in the wound of his sacred side, and telling her that *it had been formed of all the sufferings she had undergone for his sake.* She offered herself anew to be crucified with him, and he seemed to stoop down and embrace her soul, giving it a kiss of love." . . . . Two day previous, our blessed Lady was pleased to prepare her for her espousals. This was by an intellectual vision, as she calls such in her writings, wherein she beheld the great queen of angels upon a magnificent throne, accompanied by St. Catharine of Sienna, and St. Rose of Lima. To their prayer that she would consent to the espousals of her servant, with her divine son, our Lady sweetly replied, that they should be brought about. Veronica saw in her hands a beautiful ring, intended, she was told, for her. . . . . .

During Lent she practised the most cruel mortifications and austerities. On holy Saturday our Lord appeared to her; and showing her the nuptial ring, invited her to his marriage on the following day. . . . .

As she approached the altar, she heard the angels singing in sweetest melody, *Veni Spousa Christi;* then being rapt out of her senses, she beheld two magnificent thrones, that on the right hand, of gold, decorated with the most splendid jewels, whereupon was seated our blessed Lord, with his wounds shining brighter than the sun; the other formed of alabaster, of purest whiteness, and brilliant with gems, and thereon was seated our blessed Lady, in a white mantle of surpassing richness, who besought her Son to hasten his marriage. Innumerable were the multitudes of the heavenly court, in the midst whereof were the holy virgins St. Catharine and St. Rose; the former of whom intimated to Veronica what she was to do in that most august solemnity. They conducted her slowly to the thrones; and at the foot thereof, put upon her, over her religious habit, various robes, each surpassing the other in splendor. As she approached the throne of Christ, whose garments, she knows not, she says, how to describe, she beheld in each of his wounds a beautiful gem; but from that in his side, which was open, rays more bright than the sun, darted on every side. In it she seemed to perceive the nuptial ring. When he raised up his hand to bless her, he entoned the words *Veni Spousa Christi;* and our lady, with the whole court taking them up, continued, *accipe coronam, quam tibi Dominus præparavit in æternum.* St. Catharine then took off her rich attire, leaving only her religious habit, *to show*, the saint intimates, *its value in the eyes of God, being allowed to appear in that glorious assembly.* After remaining in this dress for a short time, our Lord made a sign to his blessed Mother, to clothe her with the nuptial garment. It was a magnificent mantle, covered with gems, and appeared of different colors. Our Lady gave it to St. Catharine, who put it upon Veronica, and placed her between the two thrones. Then, feeling herself more than ever *pierced with love*, she saw our Lord take the ring out of his side, and give it to his mother. "This ring," she writes, " shone with splendor. It appeared to me to be made of gold, but all wrought in enamel, which formed in the stone a name of the good Jesus. . . . . . From time to time *I gave looks of love* towards my Lord, and seemed to address him, urging him to the espousals." The heavenly queen commanded her to stretch out her hand to St. Catharine, which Jesus took, " and at that moment," she writes, " I felt myself united more closely than ever with him. Together with Mary ever-blessed, he placed the ring upon my finger, and then blessed it." In that instant heaven again resounded with the songs of the angelic choir, after which her divine spouse gave her new rules. . . . . . *He told her he would be* ENTIRELY *hers.*"

Thus ended this mystic ceremony of her espousals . . . She adds, " that nearly at every communion the same marriage was renewed . . . . . and that the ring remained upon her finger. (! ! ! !) . . . . . . Sister *Mary Spacciani* attests that she saw it once distinctly with her own eyes. (! !) . . . . In the *Processes** two other rings are mentioned *as having* been given to her at the espousals, and the renewal of them. . . . . . Likewise another which was enriched with three gems."

Mark all this—Sister Spacciani saw the ring! and Cardinal Wiseman fully believes it. Like St. Francis, St. Catharine, and others, she received the honor of the *stigmata*, or wounds in her hands, and feet, and side, as Cardinal Wiseman relates it.

" Her loving spouse rewarded her constancy and love, by the wound which he made in her heart, in the year

* The formal official acts upon which the Bull of Canonization was made out.

1696." "I seemed to see," she writes, "in the hand of the holy infant, a rod of gold, at the point of which was, as it were, a flame of fire, and at the foot a small piece of iron, like a little lance: and he placed this rod against his own heart, and the point of the lance in my heart; and it seemed that I felt my heart pierced through and through. In an instant I saw nothing in his hand; but full of grace and beauty he invited me to love him, and by way of communication, he made me to understand that he had bound me to himself by a closer tie." . . . Through modesty she abstained from looking at the wound, but she put a linen cloth upon it, which was immediately *covered with blood.* Her confessor ordered her to examine it, and she found it open, and observed that it was large enough to admit the blade of a good-sized knife—*as is attested in the Processes.* (! ! !) On Good Friday she received the rich pledges of love which were vouchsafed to the seraphic St. Francis, St. Catharine, and other saints: for our Lord after having previously foretold these graces, and after displaying his mercies in other ways, to her, was pleased to imprint on her hands and feet the *stigmata* or wounds of his most sacred passion. These wounds were afterwards renewed upon several other occasions. . . . .They were the wounds which her blessed spouse had made.

Those in her hands and feet, as *Florida Ceoli and other sisters attest,* (!!!) were on the upper side, round, and about the size of a farthing, but less on the under side, deep and red when open, and covered with a thin cicatrix or crust when closed. The wound in the left side above the left breast, was between four and five fingers in length, and about one finger broad in the middle, growing thinner towards the two extremities, exactly like the wound of a lance!!

The following work is our high Romish authority for the ceremonies of *espousalship* to Christ:*

* Pontificate Romanum Pars Prima De Benedictione et Consecratione Virginum, Brussels, 1735; Foyes' Romish Rites, Offices and Legends. London, 1839.

NOTE A.

(See Page 86.)

De largitatis tuœ fonte defluxit ut cum honorem nuptiarum nulla interdicta minuissent ac super sanctum con jugium nuptialis benedictio permaneret existirent tamen sublimiores animæ *quœ in viri ac muliebris copula fastidirent connubium** concupiscerent sacramentum, nec imitarentur quod nuptiis agitur, sed diligerent quod nuptiis prænotatur.

* This is said to a girl of sixteen.

www.ingramcontent.com/pod-product-compliance
Lightning Source LLC
LaVergne TN
LVHW010143110826
845151LV00002B/408